The Politics of Jesus

"The Gospel is firmly rooted in a story of that which once happened. The story is familiar. But we should observe that the situation into which Jesus Christ came was genuinely typical (the outcome of much previous history) and too long to tell here. The forces with which he came into contact were such as are permanent factors in history:—government, institutional religion, nationalism, social unrest. . . ."

C. H. Dodd, "The Kingdom of God and the Present Situation," *Christian News-Letter*, May 29, 1940, supplement No. 31.

The
Politics of Jesus

Vicit Agnus Noster

JOHN H. YODER

WILLIAM B. EERDMANS PUBLISHING COMPANY
Grand Rapids, Michigan

Preface

The meaning of this book is not immediately or easily classified. On the least sophisticated, most argumentative level, it is the simple rebound of a Christian pacifist commitment as it responds to the ways in which mainstream Christian theology has set aside the pacifist implications of the New Testament message.

On the deepest level, it represents an exercise in fundamental philosophical hermeneutics, trying to apply in the area of the life of the Christian community the insights with regard to the distinct biblical world view which have previously been promoted under the name of "biblical realism." Since the pioneer statements of Hendrik Kraemer, Otto Piper, Paul Minear, Markus Barth, and Claude Tresmontant, it has become thinkable that there might be about the biblical vision of reality certain dimensions which refuse to be pushed into the mold of any one contemporary world view, but which stand in creative tension with the cultural functions of our age or perhaps of any age. The main thrust of the "biblical realist" movement a generation ago was in the areas of metaphysics and the personality of God. It led to a renewal of concern for ecclesiology and for eschatology without which neither ecumenical developments since then nor Christian thinking about hope since then would have been understandable. What the present volume offers is a late ripening, in the field of ethics, of the same biblical realist revolution, in which precisely ecclesiology and

5

eschatology come to have a new import for the substance of ethics.

Between the argumentative and the philosophical levels, this work testifies to the conviction that, well beyond the questions of formal orientation, there is a bulk of specific and concrete content in Jesus' vision of the divine order, which can speak to our age as it seldom has been free to do so before, if it can be unleashed from the bonds of inappropriate a prioris.

The preparation of this text has been facilitated by the support, here gratefully acknowledged, of the Institute of Mennonite Studies and the Schowalter Foundation, and by the counsel and critique of many friends and colleagues.

Contents

Abbreviations

ASTI Annual of the Swedish Theological Institute in Jerusalem (Leiden)
BJRL Bulletin of the John Rylands Library (Manchester)
BR Biblical Research (Amsterdam; Chicago)
CBQ Catholic Biblical Quarterly (Washington)
CC Christian Century (Chicago)
CR Cahiers de la reconciliation (Paris)
EvT Evangelische Theologie (Munich)
HTR Harvard Theological Review (Cambridge, Mass.)
HzNT Handbuch zum Neuen Testament (Tübingen: Mohr)
JBL Journal of Biblical Literature (U.S.A.)
JES Journal of Ecumenical Studies (Philadelphia)
JJS Journal of Jewish Studies (London)
MQR Mennonite Quarterly Review (Goshen, Ind.)
NovT Novum Testamentum (Leiden)
NTS New Testament Studies (Cambridge)
RHPR Revue d'histoire et de philosophie religieuses (Strasbourg; Paris)
SBT Studies in Biblical Theology (London: SCM; Naperville: Allenson)
SJT Scottish Journal of Theology (Edinburgh)
ST Studia theologica (Lund)
ThEx Theologische Existenz heute (Munich)
ThSt Theologische Studien, ed. K. Barth (Zurich)

TQ	Theologische Quartalschrift (Tübingen; Ravensburg; Stuttgart)
TT	Theology Today (Princeton)
TZ	Theologische Zeitschrift (Basel)
USQR	Union Seminary Quarterly Review (New York)
ZNW	Zeitschrift für die neutestamentliche Wissenschaft (Berlin)
ZTK	Zeitschrift für Theologie und Kirche (Tübingen)

1

The Possibility of a Messianic Ethic

The Problem

One of the sorer spots in the recent intergenerational tension of Western post-Christendom—and one of the inner contradictions of our age's claim to have left Christendom behind—is the peculiar place of Jesus in the mood and mind of many young "rebels." It may be a meaningless coincidence that some young men wear their hair and their feet like the Good Shepherd of the Standard Press Sunday school posters; but there is certainly no randomness to their claim that Jesus was, like themselves, a social critic and an agitator,[1] a drop-out from the social climb, and the spokesman of a counterculture.

---

[1] The bellwether of this trend is probably Stephen Rose's article "Agitating Jesus" in *Renewal* (Oct. 1967), reprinted in his booklet *Alarms and Visions* (New York: Association, 1967), p. 125. Somewhat similar are Jean-Marie Paupert, *The Politics of the Gospel* (New York: Holt, 1969), and John Pairman Brown, *The Liberated Zone* (Richmond: John Knox, 1969). Paupert and Brown are more serious than Rose, but their style is still sufficiently impressionistic that the theological reader is not sure how much of what they say about "Mahatma Jesus" should really be taken seriously as exegesis, and how much is simply the new symbolic dress for something they could say without it.

The equation is so glib and so surrounded by the
not-sure-I-really-mean-it indirection of the age of Mc-
Luhan, that the Christian ethicist can just as glibly pass it
off as not only irreverent but also irrelevant to his real
business. But is it that simple? Or might it be that in this
half-spoofing exaggeration there is breaking into common
awareness a dimension of biblical truth that we—precisely
the reverent and relevant ethicists—had been hiding from
ourselves?

This study makes that claim. It claims not only that
Jesus is, according to the biblical witness, a model of
radical political action, but that this issue is now generally visible throughout New Testament studies, even
though the biblical scholars have not stated it in such a
way that the ethicists across the way have had to notice
it.[2]

This "stating it" is all the present study tries to do; to
let the Jesus story so speak that the person concerned
with social ethics, accustomed as he is to a set of standard
ways to assume Jesus not to be relevant to social issues,
or at least not relevant *immediately,* can hear.

Such an effort at interdisciplinary "translation" has its

Still closer to the concerns of this study, but focusing only on Jesus'
death, and with detailed textual analysis, is William Stringfellow's "Jesus the
Criminal" in *Christianity and Crisis,* 30/8 (June 8, 1970), 119ff.

The most parallel stance of all is that of my Brethren brethren Dale
Brown (*The Christian Revolutionary* [Grand Rapids: Eerdmans, 1971]) and
Art Gish (*The New Left and Christian Radicalism* [Eerdmans, 1970]); they
presuppose a view like that of this book, but without arguing it at length on
New Testament grounds.

[2] "Despite a greater readiness now frankly to face the problems that
inevitably result regarding a historical person as the incarnation of God,
there is still a curious reluctance to consider the possibility that Jesus might
have had political views." S. G. F. Brandon, *Jesus and the Zealots* (Manchester U. P., 1967), p. 24. Brandon is an outsider in the New Testament
guild. It would probably be a more correct description of contemporary New
Testament scholarship if he had said that in particular texts scholars are
quite ready to recognize the political dimension of the ministry of Jesus but
that there is a reluctance to synthesize these observations. Cf. below, p. 60 n.
52, the comment of Etienne Trocmé.

own set of serious perils. To both the parties whom it attempts to bring into hailing range of one another it must seem to be oversimplifying, since it begins by disrespecting the boundaries, and the axioms, of each discipline, and since the "translator" or bridge-builder is always somehow partly an alien, partly a layman blundering beyond his depth. We may plead only that if the experts had built the bridge we need, the layman would not have needed to.

Our study, then, seeks to describe the connection which might relate New Testament studies[3] with contemporary social ethics, especially as this latter discipline is currently preoccupied with the problems of power and revolution.[4] Theologians have long been asking how Jerusalem can relate to Athens; here the claim is that Bethlehem has something to say about Rome—or Masada.

By what right does one dare seek to throw a cable

[3] The kernel of this material was presented to the second "Puidoux" Conference on Church and Peace at Iserlohn (Germany) in July 1957, and expanded in *Nachfolge Christi als Gestalt politischer Verantwortung* (Basel: Agape Verlag, 1964), pp. 37ff. Its present outline (up to p. 114) reflects a paper prepared for presentation April 27, 1968, to the Chicago Society for Biblical Research, as a strictly New Testament study. It has been released for publication in this expanded form by the editors of *Biblical Research*. Its preparation has benefitted from numerous suggestions of William Klassen and John E. Toews.

[4] The wide visibility of the question dealt with in this paper goes back at least to the writings of the brothers Niebuhr in the 1930s; yet it reaches a new height of intensity in the current of ecumenical thought on political ethics, especially strong in Latin America, which found strong expression in the Geneva Conference on Church and Society in July 1966. Here "revolution" becomes the key term (e.g. Richard Shaul, *Containment and Change* [New York: Macmillan, 1967], pp. 215ff). In this context there is often an appeal to Jesus as a revolutionary and political figure; yet this appeal is a slogan-like formal one. It is not linked to a substantial concern for the *kind* of politics Jesus incarnated. It is thus marked by the absence of precisely the concerns to which the present paper is devoted. We referred in note 1 above to other attempts in recent religious journalism to deal with "Jesus as an Agitator" but without posing seriously the questions, either of biblical hermeneutics or of contemporary systematic social ethics, that would enable such a parallelism to stand serious criticism.

across the chasm which usually separates the disciplines of New Testament exegesis and contemporary social ethics? Normally any link between these realms of discourse would have to be extremely long and indirect. First there is an enormous distance between past and present to be covered by way of hermeneutics from exegesis to contemporary theology; then still another long leg must be covered from theology to ethics via secular sociology and Ernst Troeltsch. From the perspective of the historical theologian, normally perched on an island between these two spans and thus an amateur on both banks, I can justify leaping into the problem in such an amateur way on only two grounds. For one thing, it seems that the experts who set out to go the long way around never get there. The Scripture scholars in their hermeneutic meditations develop vast systems of crypto-systematics, and the field of ethics remains as it was; or, if anything new happens there, it is usually fed from some other sources.

The other reason for my boldness, which would be in its own right also a subject for debate in the exegetical guild, is the radical Protestant axiom, which more recently has been revitalized and characterized as "biblical realism," according to which it is safer for the life of the church to have the whole people of God reading the whole body of canonical Scripture than to trust for her enlightenment only to certain of the filtering processes through which the learned men of a given age would insist all the truth must pass.[5]

---

[5] The case for the continued legitimacy of theological recourse to the wholeness of the Gospel texts in their received form has been persuasively restated by Floyd Filson in the paper, "Thinking with the Biblical Writer," *BR*, 11 (1966); and similarly by Theodore Wedel, *The Gospel in a Strange, New World* (Philadelphia: Westminster, 1963), pp. 17ff. Hans Conzelmann, in his *Theology of St. Luke* (London: Faber & Faber, 1960), pp. 9ff, likewise argues that although it is part of the scholar's task to seek to evaluate his documents and reconstruct the events behind them, the *first* interest of the student of any text must be what the author of that text means to say. In

It is thus not unawares, nor irresponsibly, that in the present paper I take the risk of synthesis in proposing to bring the Jesus of the canonical Gospels into juxtaposition with the present. This hazardous venture involves no disrespect for the many kinds of historical questions which might be appropriately asked about the link between Jesus of the canonical Gospels and the other Jesuses whom scholarship can project.

Mainstream Ethics: Jesus Is Not the Norm

The classically naive approach once could assume an immediate connection between the work or the words of Jesus and what it would mean today to be faithful "In His Steps."[6] To this there is an equally classic non-naive answer, which can be played back from every age in the history of Christian thought about society. Thus if we can restate this mainstream answer we will have set the stage for our argument. The first and most substantial affirmation of this classic defense against an ethic of imitation is the observation that Jesus is simply not relevant in any immediate sense to the questions of social ethics. The great variety of ways of grounding this nega-

saying this of Luke, Conzelmann cites a similar argument of M. Dibelius concerning Acts. Yet our concentration for present purposes on the text as we have it by no means concedes that further research into events behind the text would weaken what it says to our point; cf. pp. 24, 49 n. 35, 60 n. 52, 104.

[6] The classic of turn-of-the-century popular Protestantism which Charles Sheldon published under this title is not a serious sample of the vision of discipleship which we are here describing. The values to which the devoted disciple Henry Maxwell is committed are not *materially* related to Jesus. "Do what Jesus would do" means for Sheldon simply, "do the right at all costs"; but *what* is the right thing to do is knowable for Sheldon apart from Jesus. Sheldon is rather an advocate of the mainstream view being characterized here, which finds the substantial norms of ethics elsewhere than in the Gospels. For a serious advocacy of Jesus' exemplarity in social ethics one would need to go back to Franciscan, Czech Brethren, or Anabaptist models. The beginnings of a modern restatement of the claim can be found in G. H. C. MacGregor, *The New Testament Basis of Pacifism* (New York: Fellowship of Reconciliation, 1936). Cf. also C. H. Dodd, below, p. 96 n. 3 and above, p. 2.

tive statement can perhaps not unfairly be summarized in
three theses, the first being the sixfold claim of Jesus'
irrelevance.

1. The ethic of Jesus is an ethic for an "Interim"
which Jesus thought would be very brief. It is possible for
the apocalyptic Sermonizer on the Mount to be uncon-
cerned for the survival of the structures of a solid society
because he thinks the world is passing away soon. His
ethical teachings therefore appropriately pay no attention
to society's need for survival and for the patient construction of permanent institutions. The rejection of violence,
of self-defense, and of accumulating wealth for the sake
of security, and the footlooseness of the prophet of the
kingdom are not permanent and generalizable attitudes
toward social values, but make sense only if it be assumed
that those values are coming to an imminent end. Thus at
any point where social ethics must deal with problems of
duration, Jesus quite clearly can be of no help. If the
impermanence of the social order is an axiom underlying
the ethic of Jesus, then obviously the survival of this
order for centuries has already invalidated the axiom.
Thereby the survival of society, as a value in itself, takes
on a weight which Jesus did not give it.[7]

2. Jesus was, as his Franciscan and Tolstoyan imita-
tors have said, a simple rural figure. He talked about the
sparrows and the lilies to fishermen and peasants, lepers
and outcasts. His radical personalization of all ethical
problems is only possible in a village sociology where
knowing everyone and having time to treat everyone as a
person is culturally an available possibility. The rustic
"face-to-face model of social relations" is the only one he
cared about. There is thus in the ethic of Jesus no
intention to speak substantially to the problems of com-

[7] The classic American statement of the dependence of Jesus' ethic upon
his expectation of an early end to history was Reinhold Niebuhr's *Interpretation of Christian Ethics* (New York: Harper, 1935); it is followed by Paul
Ramsey and many others (below, pp. 17ff).

plex organization, of institutions and offices, cliques and power and crowds.

3. Jesus and his early followers lived in a world over which they had no control. It was therefore quite fitting that they could not conceive of the exercise of social responsibility in any form other than that of simply *being* a faithful witnessing minority. Now, however, that Christianity has made great progress in history, represented symbolically by the conversion of Constantine and practically by the "Judeo-Christian" assumptions underlying our entire Western culture, the Christian is obligated to answer questions which Jesus did not face. The individual Christian, or all Christians together, must accept responsibilities that were inconceivable in Jesus' situation.[8]

4. The nature of Jesus' message was ahistorical by definition. He dealt with spiritual and not social matters, with the existential and not the concrete. What he proclaimed was not a social change but a new self-understanding, not obedience but atonement. Whatever he said and did of a social and ethical character must be understood not for its own sake but as the symbolic or mythical clothing of his spiritual message.[9] If the Gospel texts

[8] "Jesus deals only with the simplest moral situation . . . the case of one person in relation to but one other. He does not undertake to say how men, who themselves ought not to resist at all . . . when they themselves alone receive the blows, ought to act in more complex cases. . . ." Paul Ramsey, *Basic Christian Ethics* (New York: Scribner, 1950), pp. 167ff. A representative of the tendency to dehistoricize Jesus' teaching even when intending to take it seriously is Ernest C. Colwell, *Jesus and the Gospel* (New York: Oxford, 1963). Although the thrust of Colwell's book is a reaffirmation of the basic historical reliability of the Gospel reports, he says this must not be so read as to include social concreteness. The temptation legend (p. 47) is a dramatic parable of humility, not a temptation. The frequency of economic topics in parables and ethical teaching should not be taken to indicate an attitude to wealth or labor (p. 60). What is wrong with greed is not that one takes bread from the brother but that it is spiritually seductive.

[9] A standard statement of this stance is that of Roger Mehl, "The Basis of Christian Social Ethics" in John C. Bennett, ed., *Christian Social Ethics in a Changing World* (New York: Association, 1966), pp. 44ff. According to Mehl, Jesus' concern was centered exclusively on the individual. He was

were not sufficiently clear on this point, at least we are
brought to a definitive clarity by the later apostolic
writings. Especially Paul moves us away from the last
trace of the danger of a social misunderstanding of Jesus
and toward the inwardness of faith.

5. Or to say it just a little differently, Jesus was a
radical monotheist. He pointed men away from the local
and finite values to which they had been giving their
attention and proclaimed the sovereignty of the only One
worthy of being worshipped. The impact of this radical
discontinuity between God and men, between the world
of God and human values, is to relativize all human
values. The will of God cannot be identified with any one
ethical answer, or any given human value, since these are
all finite. But the practical import of that relativizing, for
the substance of ethics, is that these values have become
autonomous. For all that now stands above them is the
infinite.[10]

6. Or the reason may be more "dogmatic" in tone.
Jesus came, after all, to give his life for the sins of men.
The work of atonement or the gift of justification, where-
by God enables men to be restored to his fellowship, is a

indifferent to social and political issues, and far from the Zealots' preoccupations. It is thus an innovation (according to Mehl, a salutary one) when
Christian ethics, only in modern times and in response to socialism's challenge, comes to deal with matters of social structure.

It could be shown at greater length how this pattern of thought may
often persist even under the cover of language that would seem to mean
quite the opposite. When, for instance, Jesus is spoken of as "unveiling true
humanity," or when incarnation is spoken of as revelation, this could well
mean that we could or should go to the man Jesus in all his contingent
humanity to see what kind of man God wants. Yet in the actual practice of
contemporary "incarnational theology" this language generally serves as the
preamble to or as validation for a definition of essential or common humanity derived from quite other sources, which incarnation is held to have
ratified.

[10] This is the central thrust of H. Richard Niebuhr already in his *Christ
and Culture* (New York: Harper, 1951), esp. pp. 234ff, and further in his
Radical Monotheism and Western Culture (Harper, 1960), and *The Responsible Self* (Harper, 1963).

forensic act, a gracious gift. For Roman Catholics this act of justification may be found to be in correlation with the sacraments, and for Protestants with one's self-understanding, in response to the proclaimed Word; but never shall it be correlated with ethics. Just as guilt is not a matter of having committed particular sinful acts, so is justification not a matter of proper behavior. How the death of Jesus works our justification is a divine miracle and mystery; how he died, or the kind of life which led to the kind of death he died, is therefore ethically immaterial.

It results from this consideration of the type of thinking and teaching Jesus was doing, that it cannot have been his intention—or at least we cannot take it to have been his achievement—to provide any precise guidance in the field of ethics. His apocalypticism and his radical monotheism may teach us to be modest; his personalism may teach us to cherish the values of face-to-face relationships, but as to the stuff of our decision-making we shall have to have other sources of help.

What Other Norm Is There?

The second substantial affirmation of the mainstream ethical consensus follows from the first. Since, as we have seen, Jesus himself (either his teachings or his behavior) is not finally normative for ethics, there must be some kind of bridge or transition into another realm or into another mode of thought when we begin to think about ethics. This is not simply a bridge from the first century to the present, but from theology to ethics or from the existential to the institutional. A certain very moderate amount of freight can be carried across this bridge: perhaps a concept of absolute love or humility or faith or freedom. But the substance of ethics must be reconstructed on our side of the bridge.

Thirdly, therefore, the reconstruction of a social ethic

on this side of the transition will derive its guidance from
common sense and the nature of things. We will measure
what is "fitting" and what is "adequate"; what is "relevant" and what is "effective." We shall be "realistic" and
"responsible." All these slogans point to an epistemology
for which the classic label is the *theology of the natural:*
the nature of things is held to be adequately perceived in
their bare givenness; the Right is that which respects or
tends toward the realization of the essentially given.
Whether this ethic of natural law be encountered in the
reformation form, where it is called an ethic of "vocation" or of the "station," or in the currently popular
form of the "ethic of the situation," or in the older
catholic forms where "nature" is known in other ways,
the structure of the argument is the same: it is by
studying the realities around us, not by hearing a proclamation from God, that we discern the right.[11]

Once these assumptions about the sources of a relevant social ethic and about the spirituality of Jesus' own
message have been made, we may then observe a kind of
negative feedback into the interpretation of the New
Testament itself. We now know, the argument runs, that
Jesus could not have been practicing or teaching a relevant social ethic. Then the Jews, who thought he was
doing just that and condemned him for it, must have
misunderstood very seriously what he was about. This is
an evidence of the hardness of their hearts. Matthew as
well, who organized and interpreted the teachings of
Jesus so as to make of them a simple kind of ethical

---

[11] That this source of ethical substance is "other than Jesus" of course
need not signify that it is unrelated to revelation. It may well be spoken of in
terms of the order created by God the Father, or as an imperative discerned
in the situation by the work of the Holy Spirit, or as the "Cosmic Christ" or
"God at work in history." All such popular phrasings, as they currently
function in ethical thought, point away from the concreteness of Jesus to
some other source of norms. More examples of the stand that relativizes
Jesus in the name of "revelation" are noted below, pp. 135ff.

catechism, misunderstood Jesus: from his misunderstanding arises that regrettable phenomenon which Protestant historians call Early Catholicism.

Fortunately before long, the explanation continues, things were put into place by the Apostle Paul. He corrected the tendency to neo-Judaism or to early catholicism by an emphasis upon the priority of grace and the secondary significance of works, so that ethical matters could never be taken too seriously.

> Let those who have wives live as though they had
>   none,
> And those who mourn as though they were not
>   mourning,
> Those who rejoice as though they were not re-
>   joicing,
> And those who buy as though they had no goods,
> And those who deal with the world as though they
>   had no dealings with it. (I Cor. 7:29ff)

The second Pauline correction was that the apparent social radicality of Jesus himself (not only the Judaizing misinterpretation of Jesus) was clarified and put in its place.[12] Positive respect for the institutions of society, even the subordination of woman and slavery; acceptance of the divinely sanctioned legitimacy of the Roman government, the borrowing of Stoic conceptions of ethics conformed to nature, were some of the elements of Paul's adjustment, so that the church was ready to construct an ethic to which the person and character and especially the career—of Jesus made no unique or determining contribution.

Looking back over this hastily sketched pattern of prevalent structures of ethical thought, systematic and historical theology will need to ask some careful questions. There is the question of the authority of these

[12] Cf. our fuller description of this view below, pp. 163ff.

hermeneutic assumptions.[13] If the meaning of Jesus is this different from what he was understood by his Palestinian disciples and adversaries to mean, and if those ordinary meanings need to be filtered through a hermeneutic transposition and replaced by an ethic of social survival and responsibility, what then has come of the concept of revelation? Is there such a thing as a *Christian* ethic at all? If there be no specifically Christian ethic but only natural human ethics as held to by Christians among others, does this thoroughgoing abandon of particular substance apply to ethical truth only? Why not to all other truth as well?

A second kind of question we will need to ask is what becomes of the meaning of incarnation if Jesus is not normative man? If he is a man but not normative, is this not the ancient ebionitic heresy? If he be somehow authoritative but not in his humanness, is this not a new gnosticism?

There could be problems of inner consistency as well. Why should it be important for Christians to exercise social responsibility within the power structures, if what they do there is to be guided by the same standards which non-Christians apply?

But this would not be biblical study if we were to pursue those questions now from the systematic and historical end. What I propose here is rather that, once we are sensitized by those questions, we might begin at the front again by seeking to read one portion of the New Testament without making the usual prior negative assumptions about its relevance. Or let me say it more sharply: I propose to read the Gospel narrative with the constantly present question, "Is there here a social

[13] Graydon F. Snyder, *The Continuity of Early Christianity,* unpublished Ph.D. dissertation, Princeton Theological Seminary, 1961, pp. 18ff, makes clear that much of this analysis was dictated by the prior philosophical commitment (to Hegel) of the students of the Tübingen School.

ethic?" I shall, in other words, be testing the hypothesis that runs counter to the prevalent assumptions: the hypothesis that the ministry and the claims of Jesus are best understood as presenting to men not the avoidance of political options, but one particular social-political-ethical option.

This study is then addressed to two quite discrete tasks. In substance and procedure the two will be distinct, calling for different kinds of methods and demonstration.

1. I will attempt to sketch an understanding of Jesus and his ministry of which it might be said that such a Jesus would be of direct significance for social ethics. This is a task of New Testament research immediately within the concerns of biblical scholarship.

2. I will secondly state the case for considering Jesus, when thus understood, to be not only relevant but also normative for a contemporary Christian social ethic.

Let us be fully aware that the endeavor will have any meaning at all only if both of the answers turn out to be affirmative. If for general reasons of systematic and philosophical theology such as have been widely dominant in theological ethics for a long time, Jesus, whoever he was, is no model for ethics, it then becomes immaterial in the detail just who he was and what he did.

If, on the other hand, Jesus was not like other men a political being, or if he demonstrated no originality or no interest in responding to the questions which his sociopolitical environment put to him, it would be pointless to ask about the meaning of his stance for today.

To simplify the question and bring it within workable dimensions, I propose to concentrate largely on one document, on the canonical text of the Gospel according to Luke. Luke's story line provides us with a simple outline, and his editorial stance is often taken to have been a concern to deny that the Christian movement was any threat to Mediterranean society or Roman rule. This centering upon Luke for our scattered soundings is not meant to slant the reading; any other Gospel text could equally well have been used, and we shall occasionally observe the parallels and contrasts in the other Gospels.

Nor is our simply beginning with the canonical text meant to convey any lack of respect for the significance of the critical and historical problems which lie behind the canonical text. But the distance between the canonical text and the "historical Jesus" as he "actually was" is not the subject of my present study. The bridge from the canon to the present is already long enough.[14]

---

[14] This simplification of the present task by setting aside the critical questions is not done with the intent of avoiding contrary evidence. Critical studies tend to confirm this study's thesis; cf. below, p. 49 n. 35.

It should not be thought that by failing to deal at length with such historical-critical problems the present paper makes any neo-fundamentalist assumptions about the composition of the Gospel text, or about diversities within the development of the early churches and during the formation of the canonical texts. Neither are any particular "old quest" or "new quest" assumptions being made about how to reach behind the Gospel texts in their received form to an understanding of the "historical Jesus." Further debate or the construction of hypotheses about these matters is here set aside not because it is felt unimportant, and not because the writer has settled in his own mind just what they would have to produce, but only because a careful reading of the canonical text suffices to make our present point. It would, of course, be a count against our reading of the Jesus story if the historical questers were to come up with solid demonstrations that the "real Jesus" they find is quite incompatible with what we find in the canonical account. We shall need to meet that challenge when it arises, but thus far neither the old questers nor the new questers nor the nonquesters have done so. Thus far, the more skeptically the critics root around behind the documents for what they can recognize as "hard fact," under the assumption that the Gospel writers were less concerned for such data, and the more confidently the critics project their new vision of how it must really have been instead, the less likely it will become that interpretations can result that will support the traditional dogmatic picture of the apolitical Jesus, and the more likely will be the confirmation of the believability of those elements of the picture with which we are here dealing.

The traditional dogmatic rejection of the relevance of Jesus' social example for ethics was not based upon an alternative critical reconstruction of "what really happened," and therefore a challenge to that tradition need not await new agreed critical results.

Yet after having stated my serious openness to the critical task, it may be

The case I am seeking to make has to do not narrowly with the New Testament text but with the modern ethicists who have assumed that the only way to get from the gospel story to ethics, from Bethlehem to Rome or to Washington or Saigon, was to leave the story behind. I shall be looking more at the events than at the teachings, more at the outlines than at the substance. The next pages present soundings rather than a thorough survey.

Nor is it the intention of this paper to be exegetically original. At no point do I mean to be hazarding unheard-of textual explanations. All that I add is the focusing effect of a consistent, persistent question. It is because I claim no originality at this point that I may dispense with some of the pedantic paraphernalia which would be helpful or needful if I were making claims never heard before.

in order to testify to some skepticism about the degree of clarity that can be promised by the techniques currently used in that field of research. Anyone comparing the present effort to be honest with the canonical text with the highly confident and creative reconstructions of Carmichael or Schonfield, Brandon or Hamilton, would hardly conclude that the latter are self-critically hesitant to risk questionable hypotheses.

2

The Kingdom Coming

The Annunciation: Luke 1:46ff, 68ff; cf. 3:7ff

We are not used to thinking of the maiden Myriam as a Maccabean. Yet if it were not for the history of vain repetition in the liturgical use of the *Magnificat*, we should all have been impressed that that is precisely what she sounds like:

> *"He has shown strength with his arm,*
> *He has scattered the proud in the imagination of*
> *   their hearts,*
> *He has put down the mighty from their thrones,*
> *And exalted those of low degree;*
> *He has filled the hungry with good things,*
> *And the rich he has sent away empty."*

It is not important for our present purposes what kind of literary source Luke is drawing upon, nor what kind of liturgical source Mary might have been drawing upon.[1] In

---

[1] Nor does it make a deep difference if, as some radical critics suggest, the earlier sources of this narrative may have had these words in the mouth of Elizabeth; cf. Paul Winter, "Magnificat and Benedictus—Maccabean Psalms?" *BJRL*, 37 (1954-55), 328ff.

The Jewish contemporary would likely have heard in this song the echoes

the present testimony of the gospel we are being told that
the one whose birth is now being announced is to be an
agent of radical social change. The preoccupations of
those who await the "consolation of Israel," with which
he comes to deal, are not cultic nor doctrinal, and thus in
the narrow sense they are not "religious" preoccupations;
he comes to break the bondage of his people.

A few verses later Zechariah, as soon as his lips are
loosened, proclaims as the meaning of the birth of John,

> *"That we should be saved from our enemies,*
> *And from the hand of all who hate us;*
> *. . . to grant us that we,*
> *Being delivered from the hand of our enemies,*
> *Might serve him without fear."*

This expectation is all the more clear when John
himself spells it out:

> *"Even now the ax is laid to the root of the trees;*
> *Every tree that does not bear good fruit is cut*
> *   down and thrown into the fire. . . .*
> *His winnowing fork is in his hand,*
> *To clear his threshing floor,*
> *To gather the wheat into his granary,*
> *But the chaff he will burn with unquenchable*
> *   fire."*

This is the language with which John "preached good
news to the people." Too hastily we have passed all of

of the song of Hanna (I Sam. 2), whose imagery is not only revolutionary
("Those who were full have hired themselves out for bread, but those who
were hungry have ceased to hunger") but also military: "the bows of the
mighty are broken . . . the adversaries of Jahweh shall be broken to
pieces. . . ." Winter holds that this was a Maccabean battle song, embedded
in an earlier document circulating among the disciples of John the Baptist,
which Luke took over. To posit such a borrowing would make Luke's
assumption of political meaning in the text all the more conscious.

this language of annunciation through the filter of the
assumption that, of course, it is all to be taken "spiritually."[2] Of course, John was wrong in what he was
expecting, was he not?

We shall see later in what sense the fulfillment which
Jesus brought differed from the expectations of John;
but certainly the difference was not that John's hopes
were socio-political and the fulfillment Jesus brought was
"spiritual." If the difference had been of that character,
Luke would have had to begin his story differently. There
would have had to be some hint in these first three
chapters to warn us of the impropriety of the hopes of
Mary and Zechariah as well as of John. Failing such a
warning flag, we can only conclude that even at that late
date when Luke compiled his story for Theophilus, presumably with some apologetic concern to avoid giving the
impression that Christians were insurrectionists, he still
had no choice but to report that the pious hopes which
awaited Jesus were those in which the suffering of Israel
was discerned in all its social and political reality, and the
work of the Awaited One was to be of the same stuff.

For the sake of brevity we shall skip over the birth
narrative, with the prominence there given to Caesar's
census, with all its meaning for a subject people:
registration, taxation, policing identities. We need not
dwell on the evident political significance of Bethlehem's
being identified by Luke as the city of David; on the
angels' proclamation of "peace on earth," or the expectations of Simeon and Anna, or Matthew's reporting
Herod's fear and the massacre of the infants; it will have

[2] The current epithet, especially in the writings of those who interpret
the social teachings of the councils of churches, for this kind of dehistoricizing interpretation is "pietistic." We renounce the use of this simpler label
because of the injustice it does to the historical movement known by that
name, which was creative and critical in social ethics. Cf. my paragraph on
"The Bogey of Pietism" in *Christian Witness to the State* (Newton: Faith
and Life, 1964), p. 84; and Dale Brown's article by the same title in the
Covenant Quarterly, 25 (Feb. 1967), 12ff.

to suffice to pick up the threads again where the account becomes public.

We could also have followed further than we do the theme of Jesus' relation to John the Baptist, as being of evident political import. John's ministry had a pronounced political character, and to some extent Jesus took up his succession (note the time linkage in Matt. 3:12). The instruction John gave his hearers called for an immediate community of consumption (Luke 3:11); the only categories of listeners indicated by Luke in addition to the "multitudes" (Matthew names Pharisees and Sadducees) are the socio politically slanted publicans (3:12) and soldiers (3:14). According to Josephus, John's imprisonment was connected with Herod Antipas' fear that he might foment an insurrection.[3] Luke's account of John's offense speaks not only of "Herodias, his brother's wife," but also of "all the evil things Herod had done," which might well involve some substantial political critique. Herod's putting away his first wife and taking in her place Herodias was itself a public political issue, as it brought on a war with the first wife's father, Aretas IV of Nabatea. Even if John's judgment upon the remarriage was motivated first by his rejection of divorce and adultery, his imprisonment had a political symbolic meaning, as did perhaps the choice of Machaerus, the fortress on the Nabatean border, as the place of John's imprisonment and execution. Jesus' answer to the emissaries of John (7:22) is directly reminiscent of his first Nazareth sermon (4:18). The report of his ministry leads Herod to see him as a possible successor to John (9:7ff). He sets in juxtaposition his fate and that of John (16:16 and par.).

This scanty summary must suffice to show that in whichever direction we might have turned, fuller study of

---

[3] *Antiquities* xviii.5.2. Cf. Carl H. Kraeling, *John the Baptist* (New York: Scribner, 1951), pp. 85ff.

the tributaries would constitute further reinforcement of what we find in the mainstream of the story.

The Commissioning and Testing: Luke 3:21-4:14

"Thou art my beloved Son;
With Thee I am well pleased."

We need not speculate about how explicitly in the mind of Jesus—or of John, or of Luke—these words from heaven were understood as an allusion to Psalm 2:7 or to Isaiah 42:1b. If the double allusion is clearly intended, this is then an explicit merging of the themes of enthronement (Ps. 2) and suffering servanthood (Isa. 42). Be that as it may, with or without *explicit* messianic cross-reference, we certainly have to do here with the conferring of a mission in history. "Thou art my Son" is not the definition or accreditation of a metaphysically defined status of sonship; it is the summons to a task. Jesus is commissioned to be, in history, in Palestine, the messianic son and servant, the bearer of the goodwill and the promise of God. This mission is then further defined by the testing into which Jesus moves immediately.

The tempter's hypothetical syllogism "If you are the Son of God, then. . ." is reasoning not from a concept of metaphysical sonship but from kingship. "Son of God" cannot very well in Aramaic have pointed to the ontological coessentiality of the Son with the Father, so that it would then be appropriate for the tempter, as the first Chalcedonian, to contemplate how, sharing the divine attributes, Jesus is by definition omnipotent and subject to the temptation to put his omnipotence to improper use. The "Son of God" in Psalm 2:7 is the King; all the options laid before Jesus by the tempter are ways of being king.[4]

---

[4] Rudolf Schnackenburg, "Der Sinn der Versuchung Jesu bei den Synoptikern," *TQ*, 132 (1952), 297ff, agrees that the title is meant messianically and not metaphysically (p. 317 n. 37).

Luke's report of the testing begins with the economic option. The spiritual filter through which we are now used to reading has dealt with the attraction of this temptation as a purely personal and carnal one. Jesus was hungry: would he by miracle abuse his omnipotence selfishly to feed himself? But one does not break a fast of forty days with crusty bread, certainly not with a whole field of boulder-sized loaves. The option here, suggested or reinforced by Jesus' own renewed sensitivity to the pangs of hunger, was that his messianity would be expressed by his providing a banquet for his followers. That this is no idle imagination, the later story was to demonstrate. Feed the crowds and you shall be king.[5]

The same is true in other Synoptic usages: e.g. Luke 22:76-23:3 (substantially the same in the parallels) equates "Messiah" and "Son of God" (in a Jewish context) with "King of the Jews" (before Pilate). All three titles referred in standard usage not to incarnate deity but to a divinely mandated royal man; cf. R. H. Strachan, in *The Interpreter's Bible*, VII, 15; and W. J. Foxell, *The Temptation of Jesus* (London: S.P.C.K., 1920), p. 81.

Following suggestions of Dupont and Grant, R. W. Stegner posits both a contemporary cultural rootage of the vision of "testing in the desert" within the Qumran tradition, and a scriptural model for it in the story of Israel's testing in the desert. ("Wilderness and Testing in the Scrolls and in Matt. 4:1-11," *BR*, 12 [1967], 18ff.) Neither of these dimensions stands in the way of discerning as well a dimension of political choice, unless it be argued that the temptation narratives were *fabricated* out of the scriptural and cultural models.

Erich Fascher surveyed the opinions of historical-critical scholarship in his *Jesus und der Satan: Eine Studie zur Auslegung der Versuchungsgeschichte* (Halle, 1949). The themes he surveys are numerous: whether the story goes back to Jesus himself or was composed by later preachers; whether it is reported as having been a vision, a poetic meditation, or a more literal (and therefore less believable) physical translation of Jesus by the tempter from desert to temple to mountaintop; where this concept of Satan's authority came from. Yet it does not occur to Fascher to ask whether the account has real social meaning. The theme of Jesus' clash with diabolical forces (which Fascher then pursues beyond the temptation accounts) is located for Fascher in Jesus' inner spiritual experience.

Birger Gerhardsson, *The Testing of God's Son, Conjectanea Biblica* (Lund, 1966), illuminates the temptation with a wealth of parallels to the testing of Israel in the desert, but avoids any social concreteness in Jesus' own situation.

5 Cf. below the "fulfillment" in Luke 9 (p. 42), " . . . surely it was not his own hunger alone that was in Jesus' thoughts in these desert days. There

The second temptation according to the sequence of
Luke is the one most widely recognized as socio-political
in character.[6] The voice from heaven (3:22) had quoted
Psalm 2:7; now the tempter simply goes on to the
promise of 2:8. Here there is no ambiguity about the
political nature of the promised reward, "All the kingdoms of the world; . . . all this authority and their glory";
the question is rather what it would have meant to "Bow
the knee before me." Are we to imagine some sort of
Satan cult? Or does it not yield a much more concrete
meaning if we conceive of Jesus as discerning in such
terms the idolatrous character of political power hunger
and nationalism?

Then Jesus was taken to the "pinnacle of the temple."
Niels Hyldahl[7] ingeniously combines the Mishna's prescriptions for the execution of the death penalty with
some ancient accounts of the martyrdom of James, and
concludes that being thrown down from a tower in the
temple wall (which might well be called *pterygion*, the

was the hunger of the great multitudes of the world's poor. . . . It was a
question of the regular method to be adopted for his whole public
career. . . . First the early paradise, then the heavenly paradise—was that not
the right order?" James Stuart Stewart, *The Life and Teaching of Jesus
Christ* (London: SCM, 1933), pp. 39ff. Schnackenburg, *op. cit.,* p. 315, is
one of the commentators who accentuate the parallel to Deut. 8:3.

6 "Certainly the story means that secular power is not to be acquired at
the price of worship of Satan; but do we grasp the import of the story fully
if we think the only thing wrong with the offer is that it came from
Satan. . . ? The offer is not rejected because Satan is unable to deliver what
he promises; it is rejected because secular power is altogether inept for the
mission of Jesus, indeed because the use of secular power is hostile to his
mission." John L. MacKenzie, S.J., *Authority in the Church* (New York:
Sheed and Ward, 1966), pp. 28f.

Robert Morgenthaler, by a careful analysis of the difference between
Matthew and Luke, concludes that the sequence and vocabulary of Luke's
account of the temptation are intended especially to point up the political
nature of the temptation in its relevance for Luke's contemporaries. "Roma-
Sedes Satanae," *TZ,* 12 (May 1956), 289ff.

7 *ST,* 15 (1961), 113ff. H. A. Kelly, "The Devil in the Desert," *CBQ,* 26
(1964), 213, suggests an alternative reading of the pinnacle symbolism; it is
equally messianic-political in character.

term usually translated "pinnacle") into the Kidron
valley, followed by stoning, if necessary, to bring death,
was the prescribed penalty for blasphemy. The testing
would then mean that Jesus was tempted to see himself
as taking on himself the penalty for his claims to divine
authority, yet being miraculously saved from the consequences.[8] Hyldahl does not decide whether the accent
should lie on Jesus' contemplating the punishment and
counting on the escape, or on his throwing himself down
at his own initiative, as a kind of ordeal. In either case, it
is the quasi-blasphemous claim to divine kingship which
underlies the testing.

If, instead of following Hyldahl's suggestion of a fall
outside the temple wall, we stay with the more traditional picture of an apparition suddenly from above *within* the temple court, we must in any case agree with
Hyldahl that the concern is not with a mere acrobatic
marvel as accreditation for Jesus' status as a worker of
wonders. This would have been the kind of "sign" which
Jesus consistently refused to give to the curious and the
dubious. If we seek at all to reconstruct what might have
been conceived of as a concrete human possibility, in
Jesus' testing of the meaning of his mission, would not an
unexpected apparition from above have been the most
self-evident way for the messenger of the covenant, in the
words of Malachi (3:14), to come "suddenly to his
temple to purify the sons of Levi"? Then (even more
clearly in Matthew's account, where this temptation is
not the culminating one, but rather leads to the offer of
world supremacy) we see Jesus contemplating the role of
religious reformer, heavenly messenger, appearing un-
heralded from above to set things right.

---

[8] Hyldahl discerns here a recurrent motif: "escape-from-the-conse-
quences-of-your-claims," which he sees as well in the other invitations to
Jesus to avoid prospective suffering:
—Peter's plea which Jesus explicitly attributes to Satan (Mark 8:31ff);
—the possible angelic deliverance in Gethsemane (Matt. 26:53);
—the mocking call to come down from the cross (Luke 23:35 and par.).

"Would such a descent from such a symbolic place mark the signal for a religio-political freedom fight, making Jesus ultimately the Triumphator, in the way sought after by those pseudo-messianic pretenders, of whom the New Testament and Josephus report examples enough in this period?"[9]

The Platform: Luke 4:14ff

Luke does not begin with a capsule statement of what Jesus "began to preach." Matthew and Mark do. Then both report that Jesus' initial message was in the same words as were used before by John the Baptist (and were to be used later by the disciples): "The kingdom of God is at hand; repent and believe in the good news." The language, "kingdom," "evangel," is chosen from the political realm. This peculiar selectivity of vocabulary would be most out of place if Jesus' whole point had been that over against the expectations of John, he was not interested in this realm. It hardly needs to be argued that "kingdom" is a political term; the common Bible reader is less aware that "gospel" as well means not just any old welcome report but the kind of publicly important proclamation that is worth sending with a runner and holding a celebration when it is received.

Luke also speaks of proclaiming "the evangel of the kingdom" (4:13), yet he does not use just these phrases at the very beginning of the ministry; for Theophilus they would not have had the same density of technical meaning as for Mark's readers. Luke instead unfolds the same claim in a fuller statement in the synagogue at Nazareth.

Here the passage from Isaiah 61 which Jesus turns upon himself[10] is not only a most explicitly messianic

9 Schnackenburg, *loc. cit.*

10 We cannot answer the question whether Jesus chose his own text or followed a set cycle of readings. The presence or absence of a fixed lectionary tradition in Jesus' time has become a subject of intense and

one: it is one which states the messianic expectation in
the most expressly social terms.

> *"He has anointed me to preach good news to the*
>   *poor;*
> *He has sent me to proclaim release to the*
>   *captives;*
> *And recovering of sight to the blind;*
> *To set at liberty those who are oppressed,*
> *To proclaim the acceptable year of Jahweh."*[11]

complex scholarly debate for reasons quite apart from our concern. One
school of Gospel critics, working quite independently from the mainstream
of commentary writers, claims that the contents of the Gospel narrative are
treated in a sequence dictated by the synagogue lectionaries, in such a
correlation that the contemporary reader would gather a wealth of between-
the-lines meaning from the connection between the Old Testament readings
and a given episode from the life of Jesus (A. Guilding for John, P. P.
Levertoff for Matthew, R. G. Finch for most of the New Testament).
Suggestive as this hypothesis seems to the inventive scholar, it would be very
hard to support with any degree of certainty. Cf. Leon Morris, *The New
Testament and the Jewish Lectionaries* (London: Tyndale, 1964). The fruit
of this debate for our concern seems to be that it points away from the
likelihood that the choice of Isa. 61 was dictated by a lectionary. According
to Paul Billerbeck (*ZNW*, 55 [1964], 143ff) there was at that time no
regularly prescribed reading of the prophets. That this passage is not included in the (known, but later) lectionaries would tend to indicate Jesus'
choosing the passage for his own purposes, rather than his seizing the
occasion of the text's having been chosen for him. This then points to a very
self-conscious preparation for the claim with which he caps the reading.
    Much of the effort to link Jesus' reading in the synagogue with the
existence of a fixed lectionary tradition has been dominated by the desire of
scholars to prove that such a lectionary tradition existed in synagogue
Judaism at the time. Others are arguing for the hypothesis that dependence
upon the Jewish lectionary determined the form of the Gospel redaction,
and therefore constitutes a key to Gospel interpretation. These two theses
are dependent upon one another in a petitionary way. Neither has been
followed far enough that we could conclude either that the passage was
chosen for Jesus by the calendar, or that the choice of the passage permits
dating the Nazareth event. To understand the claim Jesus makes, the distinction is immaterial; though, of course, its dramatic effect and the immediate
sense of eschatological fulfillment would have been greater if it were the case
that the text was chosen for him. Cf. L. Crockett, "Luke iv. 16-30 and the
Jewish Lectionary Cycle: A Word of Caution," in *JJS*, 17/1f (1966), 13ff.
    [11] As this quotation now stands, it breaks off in mid-verse, omitting
61:2b, "the year of the Lord's vengeance." One might surmise that to

It may well be that "the acceptable year of Jahweh" in the book of the prophet referred to some particular event either at the end of the age or in the immediate future of the Babylonian captives (or both); but for rabbinic Judaism and thus for the listeners of Jesus it most likely meant neither of these but rather the jubilee year, the time when the inequities accumulated through the years are to be crossed off and all God's people will begin again at the same point. The expectation is thus not that Jesus is going to take Palestine off the end of the scale of temporal sequence but rather that there is to come into Palestine the equalizing impact of the sabbath year.

In a most ingenious booklet,[12] André Trocmé has gathered the evidence that Jesus' concept of the coming kingdom was borrowed extensively from the prophetic understanding of the jubilee year. This hypothesis throws light on many allusions and on some of the difficult parables. In the consistency with which Trocmé uses his hypothesis as a key, he may be found too original and imaginative. But it is not the case, as the silence with

listeners familiar with the text this omission would have been striking. J. Jeremias, *Jesus' Promise to the Nations* (Naperville: Allenson, 1958), pp. 44ff, builds upon this surmise the suggestion that the omission, rejecting thereby Jewish concepts of vengeance and opening the covenant to the nations, was the whole point of the narrative. This would then see in the abrupt end of the quotation the same issue as is spoken to later in the same chapter, namely Jesus' open attitude to Gentiles. But the talmudic practice of introducing a citation by the first phrases, leaving the reader to fill in the rest of the chapter, probably forbids reading this much meaning into the absence of a phrase. The openness to Gentiles remains, however, as an offense in its own right, in the next episode. (There may be a new narrative beginning v. 22 or 23, or at least some omission between 21 and 22 or between 22 and 23. The pleased surprise of v. 22 is not quite the same as the disbelief of v. 23.)

12 *Jésus-Christ et la révolution non-violente* (Geneva: Labor et Fides, 1961). A section of Trocmé's text is included below, ch. 3. An earlier book on a similar theme was E. Stanley Jones, *Christ's Alternative to Communism* (New York: Abingdon, 1953), a sermonic elaboration of themes from Jesus' Nazareth declaration, written after Jones' visit to the Soviet Union.

which continental New Testament specialists have responded to Trocmé's book might indicate, that it is a brand new or unthinkable idea. Such standard commentaries as LaGrange and Plummer had already given the same interpretation of this particular passage.[13] The difference lies rather in the degree of readiness to take seriously the light this passage might throw on the rest of Jesus' ministry and on his self-understanding.

It is not our purpose here to discuss the origins of the sabbatical year and the jubilee, which apparently arose out of some kind of bankruptcy and mortgage arrangement in ancient Israel.[14] Nor need we discuss whether or to what extent the provisions of Leviticus 25 were ever literally observed,[15] either in the form of a fifty-year term on particular obligations or as a sweeping economic realignment redistributing all property at once. Our interest is in the prophetic use of the jubilee vision. The place of Leviticus 25 in the Bible kept alive the vision of

[13] Rabbi Stephen Schwarzschild indicates (in personal correspondence) that according to the (perhaps later) talmudic lectionaries, particular prophetic readings were correlated with Torah texts, and in such a way as to link Isa. 61 indirectly with Lev. 25 (the jubilee provisions). Hugh Anderson in a recent survey of the status of criticism on this passage ("Broadening Horizons. The Rejection at Nazareth Pericope of Luke 4:16-30 in Light of Recent Critical Trends," *Interpretation,* 18 [1964], 259ff) deals with the tension between acceptance and rejection by the audience, and with underlying questions about the pre-Lucan background of the narrative and about Luke's redactional intention; there is, however, no analysis of whether what Jesus is reported as saying had any social meanings. David Hill, "The Rejection of Jesus at Nazareth," *NovT,* 13 (July 1971), 161ff, pursues Anderson's questions. He holds that the linking of the two segments is a construction dictated by Luke's missionary theology.

[14] Robert North, S.J., *Sociology of the Biblical Jubilee* (Rome: Pontifical Biblical Institute, 1954).

[15] "There is not a single Hebrew who does not, even now, obey his sabbath year legislation just as if Moses were present to punish him for infractions; and this even in cases where violation would pass unnoticed" (Josephus *Antiquities* iii.15.3). North, who cites this claim from Josephus, is inconclusive as to whether the procedure was ever carried out; in any case it was hardly done regularly. Note however the emergency revival of it by Zedekiah.

an age when economic life would start over from scratch; and the testimony of Isaiah 61 demonstrates its fruitfulness as a vision of the coming renewal.

At least once in Israel's experience it came to life as a concrete experience of national revival. Jeremiah (ch. 34) carries the report of a covenant of renewal in besieged Jerusalem, where King Zedekiah again put into effect the ancient law, proclaiming liberty to all Hebrew slaves. The slaveowners, however, turned around and took back the male and female slaves they had set free, and brought them again into subjection.[16] In immediate response, the prophetic words proclaimed by Jeremiah in the name of Jahweh, God of Israel, were a reminder of the place of manumission in the Sinai covenant and the express statement that it was because of this failure to live up to the renewed covenant that Jerusalem would fall to Nebuchadnezzar. "You have not obeyed me by proclaiming liberty, everyone to his brother and to his neighbor; behold, I proclaim to you liberty [i.e. I deliver you] to the sword, to pestilence, and to famine, says the Lord" (v. 17). That the renewal of God's people, both the concrete renewal which is possible and has happened occasionally in past history, and the renewal after the end of the age, will have the form of the jubilee, is thus integral to the prophetical vision. The same vision is evident in Isaiah 58:6-12. Thus Jesus' use of Isaiah is in no way arbitrary.[17]

---

[16] The text does not indicate whether we should consider this return to slavery as having been the result of force or of economic difficulties. If the public proclamation of liberation had been clear, it is hardly thinkable that the former slaveowners would simply have gone out and physically seized their former slaves. The point must rather be that the slaves, having no means to make their own way economically, again rapidly fell into debt. Thus the owners are reprimanded not simply for not releasing the slaves but also for not providing them with the wherewithal to function economically and independently.

[17] The continuing fecundity of the image is demonstrated as well in creative twentieth-century theology: "Jubilee is exodus spelled out in terms of social salvation. . . ." Johannes Hoekendijk, "Mission—A Celebration of Freedom," *USQR*, 21 (Jan. 1966), 141.

We must conclude that in the ordinary sense of his words Jesus, like Mary and like John, was announcing the imminent *entrée en vigueur* of a new regime whose marks would be that rich would give to the poor, the captives would be freed, and men would have a new mentality (*metanoia*), if they believed this news.

We cannot assume that we know *exactly* what was meant by Jesus' statement that "this word is fulfilled." In what sense was Jesus claiming that something was beginning to happen right then in his person? Did anything really happen at all? Was he announcing an event the realization of which was dependent upon the faith of his listeners, so that it could not come to pass after all because of their unbelief? Or was he announcing what actually then did happen, namely nothing very visible for a while?

This is a serious question. But let us recognize that it is a question of systematic hermeneutics which is read into the Lucan text by readers who were not there. It has to do with the sense in which the fulfillment Jesus promised was a historical reality. It does not, however, have anything to do with the clear affirmation that the subject of the text is a social event. We may have great difficulty in knowing in what sense this event came to pass or could have come to pass; but what the event was supposed to be is clear: it is a visible socio-political, economic restructuring of relations among the people of God, achieved by his intervention in the person of Jesus as the one Anointed and endued with the Spirit.

The second theme of the encounter in the synagogue provides Jesus' first direct offense to his hearers; appealing to prophetic precedent, he proclaims the opening of the New Age to Gentiles. This second thrust does not seem to be derived from the jubilee proclamation; it grows rather out of Jesus' response to the disbelief bred in his hearers by their familiarity with his family. There is rather a negative correlation between the two themes; the undercutting of racial egoism by the second thrust pre-

vented the former from being taken in a nationalistic
sense. The prophet's reference to the captive and oppressed can thus not refer to Israel or Judaism at large as
collectively oppressed; the liberation is too wide for that.
The New Age is for all men, and the hesitance of the
Nazarenes to believe will only hasten its wider proclamation.

The Platform Reaffirmed: Luke 6:12ff

From the move to Capernaum (4:31) Luke reports a
rising tide of effectiveness among the multitudes, the
sick, and the tax-gatherers. Soon the backlash of the
religious establishment begins, with objections to Jesus'
authority to forgive (5:21) and his disreputable associates
(5:30). Almost immediately the opposition mounts to
the point of angry scheming (6:11). Luke emphasizes
that it was "in these days" that Jesus, after a night-long
vigil, named twelve key men, firstfruits of a restored
Israel. To organized opposition he responds with the
formal founding of a new social reality. New teachings
are no threat, as long as the teacher stands alone; a
movement, extending his personality in both time and
space, presenting an alternative to the structures that
were there before, challenges the system as no mere
words ever could.[18]

Cognate as the *functioning* of this inner circle may
have been to the way any other rabbi would live with his
favored disciples, there is more to its *formation* than that.
Their number, the night of prayer,[19] and the following
ceremonial proclamation of woes and blessings all serve

[18] In connection with the preaching tour of the seventy Jesus sees
"Satan fall like lightning from heaven" (10:18). The mission of the church in
the world is the destruction of Satan's dominion, as the acceptance of the
tempter's shortcut would have been his triumph.

[19] Luke 6:12. Reference to Jesus' prayer is one way Luke indicates
major landmarks in his story; cf. 3:21; 5:16; 9:18.

to dramatize a new stage of publicness. The opening
beyond Judaism which was predicted in the synagogue at
Nazareth is now beginning; the "seacoast of Tyre and
Sidon" is represented on this great plain. Despite the
extensive parallels with the Sermon on the Mount, the
emphasis in Luke's report is different. The blessings are
balanced with woes, after the fashion of ancient Israel's
covenant ceremonies. The blessing is for the poor, not
only the poor in spirit; for the hungry, not only those
who hunger for justice. The examples drawn from the
sexual realm (Matt. 5:27-32) are missing; only personal
and economic conflict are chosen as specimens of the
New Way, in which seized property is not reclaimed and
the delinquent loan is forgiven. As in the jubilee, and as
in the Lord's Prayer, *debt* is seen as the paradigmatic
social evil. In short, the announcement of the synagogue
is being repeated and spelled out in detail, this time with
a structured social base (both the believing multitude and
the defined nucleus)[20] and in plain view of the crowds
("in the hearing of all the people," 7:1). An ethic which
is to be guided by the twin foci of imitating the bound-
less love of God for his rebellious children (6:35f) and
being strikingly different from the ordinary "natural law"
behavior of others ("what credit is that to you? Even
sinners . . . ," 6:32-34), is conceivable only if a new age
has begun, and if that age's novelty is at the point of
economic realism.

---

[20] "The physical movement—of the preacher towards the people, of the
disciple following the teacher—involves a social and professional uproot-
ing. . . . Thus the decision for the Gospel claimed by preaching is expressed
concretely, first of all, in an immediate decision to depart and to follow the
teaching." Michel Philibert, *Christ's Preaching—and Ours* (Richmond: John
Knox, 1963-64), theses 3 and 7. The realism of Jesus' proclamation included
its power to create its own sociological base; without this he would have
been no threat.

This awareness is the valid kernel of insight in the otherwise exaggerated
article "The Power Tactics of Jesus Christ," in the book of the same name
by Jay Haley (New York: Grossman, 1969), pp. 17ff.

The Bread in the Desert: Luke 9:1-22

The link that binds together the sending of the twelve
(9:1-10), the feeding of the multitude (9:11-17), and the
first confession of Peter (9:18-22) is worked out much
more fully in the account of John 6, which Maurice
Goguel has justifiably taken to have serious historical
value. This crowd of thousands was not the hard core of
tested disciples but the first wave of inquirers coming to
see if this kingdom which the twelve had been announcing was for real. As the devil had said it would, the
distribution of bread moved the crowd to acclaim Jesus
as the New Moses, the provider, the Welfare King whom
they had been waiting for. His withdrawal from their
acclamation is the occasion for his first statement (in all
of the Gospels) that his ministry was to be one of
suffering and that his disciples would needs be ready to
bear with him that cross. This is the moment when he
elicits and then silences Peter's confession, followed immediately by Peter's first sign of unwillingness to conceive of the Christ as suffering. This is the moment when
other disciples draw away from his "hard saying" (John
6:60, 66). This is the moment when he "sets his face to go
to Jerusalem." However meager may be the possibility of
constructing a continuous narrative biography out of the
Gospel records, this episode of the bread in the desert is
certainly one of the hinges of whatever did happen.[21] It

21 Goguel was hardly the type of scholar to be over-optimistic about the
chances for writing a biography of Jesus. Nevertheless, he deals with what he
calls the "Galilean crisis" as the crucial turning in Jesus' ministry outside of
Jerusalem.

In a slightly different way William Manson also makes the wilderness
meal the hinge between the Galilean ministry and the later less public
ministry. He further suggests that the gathering in the wilderness was
precipitated by the public impact of the first sending of the twelve, and by
Herod's growing concern about Jesus (with a conjectural dating of Luke
13:31-33 to the time of ch. 9 to coincide with the Tell Galilee movement).
Manson takes as historically reliable Mark's report (8:29ff) that it was from
now on that Jesus discourages the use of messianic vocabulary and begins to

marks the culmination of the popular Galilean ministry
and the transition both to a ministry centered more on
the disciples and to the approach to Jerusalem. "Going to
Jerusalem" (9:51) is the superscription of the second
third of Luke's book.

This first reference to the cross is already most clearly
in its context behind the reference to the crown. Not
only when Jesus says so, as an element of moral instruction to the disciples (cf. below, p. 45), but also in his own
vision of his ministry and in his response to the beckon-
ing acclamation, the cross and the crown are alternatives.
He begins to be estranged not only from the Jewish
leaders, but also from the crowds, because the messianity
he proposes to them is not to their tastes; yet what he
proposes is not withdrawal into the desert or into mysti-
cism; it is a renewed messianic claim, a mountaintop
consultation with Moses and Elijah, and a march to
Jerusalem. The cross is beginning to loom not as a ritually
prescribed instrument of propitiation but as the political
alternative to both insurrection and quietism.

The Cost of Discipleship: Luke 12:49-13:9; 14:25-36

The shadow never lifts from the band on the road to
Jerusalem. The fire Jesus is impatient to kindle (12:49f)
already is flaming up; his message has begun to sow
division even within the family (vv. 51-53). An atrocity,
the massacre of a crowd of Galileans by Pilate, is the kind
of provocation one would report to a political figure on
the brink of a holy revolution.[22] The falling masonry at

teach explicitly about the sufferings of the Son of Man and the disciples'
cross. W. Manson, *The Way of the Cross* (Richmond: John Knox, 1958),
54ff.

[22] "Pilate mingled the Galileans' blood with that of their sacrifices" gives
the superficial impression of a massacre in the temple; but Oscar Cullmann
argues that the meaning may well rather be "with that of their victims" and
may describe a Zealot uprising. *The State in the New Testament* (New York:
Scribner, 1956), p. 14.

the tower of Siloam[23] may well have been relevant
because the aqueduct there had been financed by funds
Pilate had seized from the temple treasury.[24] Jerusalem's
rejection is prefigured in the parable of the fig tree
(13:6-9)[25] and predicted literally soon after (vv. 33-35).
The reason Jesus is intrepid in the knowledge of Herod's
threat (vv. 31f) is that his fate awaits him at Jerusalem;
such a linkage is meaningful only in the perspective of a
Jerusalem ministry analogous to the crowd-gathering,
order-threatening activity which had disquieted Herod.
Herod cannot be seeking to kill Jesus for heresy or
prophecy; sedition would be the only possible charge.

But no longer is this crucifixion perspective reserved
to Jesus himself. The brief warning "not peace but a
sword" is straightway expanded into an extended passage
(14:25ff).[26] It is just when "great multitudes were ac-
companying him" that Jesus speaks his first severe public
word of warning:

Josef Blinzler, "Die Niedermetzelung von Galiläern durch Pilatus," *NovT*,
2 (1958), 24ff, rejects on linguistic grounds Cullmann's interpretation of
"their sacrifices" as the Zealots' (human) *victims,* but he agrees, filling out
with still greater detail, that the massacred Galileans were political enthusi-
asts in whom Pilate saw the menace of rebellion. Ethelbert Stauffer, *Jesus
and His Story* (New York: Knopf, 1959), p. 84, agrees. Blinzler further
believes that this slaughter must have taken place at the Passover, just one
year before Jesus' passion.

[23] This conjecture by Ewald has been widely echoed in the commentaries, but remains pure conjecture. Nonetheless, it looks for meaning in the
right direction; the question put to Jesus in this context ("at that very
time," 13:1) was not about the mysteries of Providence, which lets some
innocent people be killed, but about the stance of faith in the face of the
adversity Jesus had just predicted (12:57-59).

[24] A mass slaughter by Pilate of Jews protesting his seizure of temple
funds to build an aqueduct is reported by Josephus (*Antiquities* xviii.3.2);
cf. below, p. 92.

[25] According to Zahn and Grundmann, the unfruitful fig tree is Jerusalem, the owner impatient to cut it down is John (cf. 3:9), and the
vinedresser pleading for one more chance is Jesus.

[26] This passage has parallels in all the Gospels. In Mark it is linked with
"Thou art the Christ," in Matthew with the sending of the twelve.

> *"If anyone does not hate father and mother and*
> *wife and children and brothers and sisters,*
> *Yea, and even his own life,*
> *He cannot be my disciple."*

Modern psychologizing interpretation of Jesus has been bothered largely with whether the word *hate* here should be taken seriously or not. This is certainly to miss the point of the passage. The point is rather that in a society characterized by very stable, religiously under-girded family ties, Jesus is here calling into being a community of *voluntary* commitment, willing for the sake of its calling to take upon itself the hostility of the given society. The seriousness of the alternative posed before the would-be disciple is underlined by the parables of the builder and the king who too hastily committed themselves to enterprises for the cost of which they were not prepared.[27] Again we could modernize the text and be surprised, and perhaps usefully instructed, by the fact that whereas modern churchmanship tries to make membership attractive to the great number, Jesus was here moving away from the crowd. But again the point is not the tactical question, whether Jesus wanted many disciples or a few. What matters is the quality of the life to which the disciple is called. The answer is that to be a disciple is to share in that style of life of which the cross is the culmination.[28]

---

[27] The standard commentaries support the conjecture that Jesus' hearers clearly heard here the allusion to Herod, who had recently given striking examples of both rash warfare and ambitious unfinished building plans. Thus to allude to the king's foolishness is itself political preaching. Any listener would have caught the mockery in the allusion. In addition to such passages, where the very speaking of the parable implies a political judgment, there are other parables drawn from the political realm. Joachim Jeremias, *The Parables of Jesus* (London: SCM, 2nd ed. 1963), p. 59, suggests that the parable of the nobleman who goes on a journey to claim a kingdom was a reference to Archelaus, who went to Rome to obtain his appointment (Josephus *Wars* ii.80; *Antiquities* xvii.9).

[28] If we read the text alone, assuming that the word "cross" can only

The same warning is still more clear in the reprimand to the disciples in their concern about privilege in the coming kingdom, which Luke incorporates in the Last Supper account.

> *"The kings of this earth lord it over their subjects;*
> *But it shall not be so among you.* . . .
> *For I am among you as one who serves."*
> (22:25ff)[29]

In none of the accounts where this word is reported does Jesus reprimand his disciples for expecting him to establish some new social order, as he would have had to do if the thesis of the only-spiritual kingdom were to prevail. He rather reprimands them for having misunderstood the character of that new social order which he does intend to set up. The novelty of its character is not that it is not social, or not visible, but that it is marked by an alternative to accepted patterns of leadership. The alternative to how the kings of the earth rule is not "spirituality" but servanthood.

There are thus about the community of disciples those sociological traits most characteristic of those who set about to change society: a visible structured fellowship, a

derive its meaning from the later death of Jesus, then its appearance in this text must be an anachronism read back into the story after the crucifixion. This conclusion becomes unnecessary if (Hengel, *op. cit.,* p. 266; Brandon, *Jesus and the Zealots,* p. 57, following A. Schlatter) the cross, being the standard punishment for insurrection or for the refusal to confess Caesar's lordship, already had a very clear definition in the listener's awareness. "Take up the cross" may even have been a standard phrase of Zealot recruiting. The disciple's cross is not a metaphor for self-mortification or even generally for innocent suffering; "if you follow me, your fate will be like mine, the fate of a revolutionary. You cannot follow me without facing that fate."

[29] Luke puts Jesus' reference to himself in the context of the Supper; thereby "I am among you as a servant" becomes a parallel to the washing of the disciples' feet in John 13. Matthew brings the same words into the context of Jesus' going to Jerusalem to be crucified (20:17ff).

sober decision guaranteeing that the costs of commitment to the fellowship have been consciously accepted, and a clearly defined life style distinct from that of the crowd. This life style is different, not because of arbitrary rules separating the believer's behavior from that of "normal people," but because of the exceptionally normal quality of humanness to which the community is committed. The distinctness is not a cultic or ritual separation, but rather a nonconformed quality of ("secular") involvement in the life of the world. It thereby constitutes an unavoidable challenge to the powers that be and the beginning of a new set of social alternatives.

The political import of the formation of a group of disciples is heightened if we take seriously Oscar Cullmann's suggestion that perhaps as many as half of the twelve were recruited from among the ranks of the Zealots.[30] The formation of an inner-team comprising both former Zealots and former publicans, the symbolic number twelve, and the first mission of the twelve which is reported to have been the source of Herod's first perplexity about Jesus, are all supporting evidence of this social relevance of the minority.

The Epiphany in the Temple: Luke 19:36-46

The central section of Luke's Gospel beginning with 9:51, "He set his face to go to Jerusalem," reaches a first level of culmination with the event we celebrate on Palm Sunday. "Blessed be the king who comes in the name of the Lord!" This is the first public use of messianic lan-

---

[30] O. Cullmann, op. cit., pp. 8ff. Martin Hengel, Die Zeloten, provides throughout a host of analogues to Jesus' ministries. S. G. F. Brandon, op. cit., while illuminating at many points, is too conjectural and too interested in proving a thesis to be convincing. Thanks to Hengel's sober objectivity, touching on Jesus only most marginally, the similarity of issues and patterns (withdrawal to the desert, purification of the temple, paying taxes to Caesar, etc.) is all the more striking. Especially the figures Hengel calls "prophets" are like Jesus in some of their behavior.

guage in Luke's account. Quite without the incorporation
of additional reference to a particular text from Zechariah, which Matthew adds at this point in 21:5, the
political meaning of the Lucan account is already sufficiently clear. This language is made all the more striking
when the report tells us that the multitude of disciples
was rejoicing and "praising God with a loud voice for all
the mighty works that they had seen."[31] What were
these "mighty works"? The phrase hardly seems to be
adequately supported by the preceding chapters of the
Gospel; there must be further dimensions of imminent
victory in their minds.[32]

The narrative of Matthew moves immediately to the
cleansing of the temple.[33] Here we have a kind of fulfill-

[31] After the revolt of A.D. 70 had already been begun by the temple
captain Eleazer, son of Ananias, the Zealot leader Menahem entered the city
"like a king" in a processional and took over the control of the rebellion
(Hengel, op. cit., p. 369). William Klassen (Jesus and the Zealot Option,
unpublished lecture) and W. R. Farmer, Maccabees, Zealots, and Josephus
(New York: Columbia U. P., 1956), pp. viff and 198ff, see in the triumphant
procession a recurrent symbolic pattern of Zealot political activity.

Ethelbert Stauffer suggests another juxtaposition: "Pilate had just
entered Jerusalem at the head of his Roman troops, and Jesus at the head of
the pilgrim procession." Christ and the Caesars (Philadelphia: Westminster,
1955), p. 120.

A. T. Olmstead, Jesus in the Light of History (New York: Scribner,
1942), pp. 210f, pictures Jesus as preoccupied with not giving a disorderly
impression, and all the messianic language of the crowds as a misunderstanding due to the teaching of John the Baptist.

[32] The following adjoining events, the "triumphal entry" and the
"cleansing of the temple," have caught the imagination of many contemporary advocates of "non-violent direct action." The parallelism is par-
tially valid. Some of the differences become visible when one asks whether
Jesus' "demonstration" was a "success."

[33] The most imaginative interpretation of the cleansing of the temple is
Ernest F. Scott, The Crisis in the Life of Jesus (New York: Scribner, 1952).
Like other interpreters from his generation, Scott overdoes the disjunction
between the religious and the social dimensions of Jesus' work.

Following Matthew and Luke, our description here underlines the unity
of the procession and the temple cleansing. Scott, op. cit., pp. 21f, argues for
the greater authenticity of Mark's report, according to which by the time the
procession had reached the temple it was already late, so that Jesus simply

ment of the prediction of Malachi; the sudden appearance in the temple of "the Lord whom you seek," coming to "purify the sons of Levi." It is not sufficient to see here a simple expression of prophetic indignation toward the economic exploitation of the temple clientele. Linked as it is in the next sentence with Jesus' initiation of a daily teaching presence, this is a symbolic takeover of the temple precinct by One who claims jurisdiction there. [34] That the "chief priests and the scribes and the principal men of the people sought to destroy him" is linked to the messianic claim acted out in the nonviolent seizure of the holy place, and not simply to the offense against order which might have been involved in his driving out the bulls.[35] In fact, had the cleansing of the temple been in

"looked round at everything" and withdrew to Bethany. While decreasing the dramatic immediacy of the seizure of the temple, such an interpretation accentuates the deliberateness of the act.

[34] "This is the Lord coming to inspect and take possession of what belongs to Him. . . . He consecrates anew as it were, giving sight to the blind and making the lame to walk—the unmistakable sign of the breaking in of the eschaton." Ernest Lohmeyer, *Lord of the Temple* (Richmond: John Knox, 1962), p. 34.

Scott, *op. cit.*, accents the very last words of Jesus' quotation from Isa. 56 (which Matthew and Luke omit) . . . "for all nations." Thus whereas in Matthew and Luke "my house is to be a house of prayer" is directed against the profanation of the temple, according to Mark it is against the exclusion of the Gentiles which is implied when the "court of the Gentiles" is made a marketplace instead of being considered part of the sanctuary. Here as in Luke 4 (above, p. 35 n. 11) it is risky to make much of the phrases omitted in a citation.

[35] All four Gospels connect the cleansing of the temple with a debate on the nature of Jesus' authority. Picking up from a whimsical appreciation of the sensationalistic reconstruction of Joel Carmichael, *The Death of Jesus* (New York: Macmillan, 1962), Etienne Trocmé suggests that there is substantial evidence for ascribing to the episode in the temple a larger, more crucial significance (and perhaps an earlier dating) within the unfolding of Jesus' ministry than the received text makes clear. *RHPR* (1964), pp. 245ff.

This example may stand as another confirmation of the general observation that, if we did seek (as this survey does not) to reach behind the canonical Gospels to "the real historical Jesus," such an effort would surely increase rather than decrease the socio-political dimensions of our picture of his work.

Victor Eppstein seeks to illuminate the temple-cleansing episode by any way disorderly or illegal, this would have provided a clear legal pretext for action against him, which, however, we are told the adversaries could not find.[36]

Ever since the early Christian centuries, the whip in the temple has been considered the one act in the life of Jesus which could be appealed to as precedent for the

placing it within the context of a struggle between priest and rabbi, temple and Sanhedrin. "The Historicity of the Gospel Account of the Cleansing of the Temple," *ZNW*, 55 (Oct. 1964), 44. The priesthood had just expelled the Sanhedrin from the temple grounds; it settled across the Kidron at Hanuth where the vendors of sacred offerings were. The vendors in the temple yard were not a long-standing institution but an innovation, brought in by Caiaphas to compete with the Hanuth merchants and thereby indirectly to undercut the Sanhedrin. Jesus sides with the Sanhedrin, i.e. with the rabbinic class against the priestly class. Eppstein's conjectures may be too ingenious to be convincing; but they have at least the virtue of seeking to read the story with social-historical realism.

The economic dimension of the event is especially emphasized by Neill Q. Hamilton, "Temple Cleansing and Temple Bank," *JBL*, 83 (Dec. 1964), 365ff.

[36] S. G. F. Brandon (*op. cit.*) hinges the entire argument of his book on the likelihood that the temple cleansing report is one of the few remaining indices of an original (historically authentic) memory of a violent Jesus, modified later by all the Gospel writers. We agree with Brandon that any historical reconstruction must find a Jesus who was executed for sedition, and who was socially close to the Zealots. We may agree as well that the depoliticizing of the memory of Jesus in early Christianity (though far less of this than he thinks can have taken place within the New Testament canon) was apologetically motivated. But by no means does it follow from this that the revolutionary initiative for which Jesus was executed must have been violent. At this precise point (esp. pp. 311ff) Brandon's surmising has no critical grounds. The fault we find with Brandon is not that he interprets Jesus as politically relevant, but that he assumes violence is the only model for such relevance.

In his *Jesus and the Politics of Violence* (New York: Harper, 1972), George R. Edwards has brought together the overwhelming scholarly case against Brandon on historical and literary-critical grounds. Edwards (being willing to meet Brandon on that common ground of vocabulary) prefers to use the word "political" in a modern lay sense as including nationalistic violence, and therefore to describe the pacific Jesus as not political.

I have preferred to contest the meaning of the term, insisting that nonviolence and non-nationalism are relevant to the *polis*, i.e. to the structuring of relationships among men in groups, and therefore are political in their own proper way. My difference with Edwards is in semantic strategy not in substance.

Christian's violence. The older versions gave room for such an understanding, as if the whip had been used against the merchants: ". . . he drove them all out of the temple, and the sheep, and the oxen. . ." (AV following Vulgate). The reader can take "them all" as referring to the moneychangers and the vendors of animals. Yet, ever since the earliest centuries,[37] careful analysis of the text has excluded this interpretation, and supported the trend of the newer translations: ". . . drove all the animals out of the temple, both the sheep and the cattle" (Today's English Version; also Moffatt, Goodspeed, the Zurich Bible, and commentators McGregor, Temple, Plummer, Strachan). The normal sense of the conjunction *te kai* is to initiate a list, not to continue a series beginning with "them all."[38] The "them all" (*pantas*) may with equal grammatical propriety refer to the preceding "sellers and changers" or to the following "sheep and bullocks." [39] The "cast out" (*exebalen*) posits no violence; elsewhere in the New Testament it means simply "send away."[40]

Jesus is now in control of the course of events. It would be but one more step to consolidate that control,

---

[37] The following anecdote is recounted by Cosmas Indicopleustes (*ca* 530) concerning Theodore of Mopsuestia (d. 428):

"Rabbula previously showed much friendship toward the famous interpreter (Theodore) and studied his works. Yet when, having gone to Constantinople to attend the Council of the Fathers (381) he was accused of striking priests, and he responded that Our Lord had also struck when he entered the temple, the Interpreter arose and reprimanded him saying, 'Our Lord did not do that; he only spoke to the men, saying "take that away," and turned over the tables. But he drove out the bullocks and the sheep with the blows of his whip.' " Wenda Wolska, *La Topographie de Cosmas Indicopleustes* (Paris: Presses Universitaires Françaises, 1962), p. 91. Cited in Lasserre (n. 38 below), p. 7.

[38] Jean Lasserre, "Un Contresens tenace," *CR* (Oct. 1967), pp. 7ff, surveys all the New Testament usages of *te kai*. In 86 cases a rendering comparable to " . . . as well as the sheep and the oxen" would be impossible. In five it would be possible but is not so rendered by the translators. Only in John 2:15 is the particle ever so rendered.

[39] *Ibid.*, pp. 13ff.

[40] Mark 5:40; Matt. 9:38.

riding the crest of the crowd's enthusiasm and profiting
from the confusion as the liberated cattle stampede from
the court and the traffickers scramble across the cobble-
stones after their money. The coup d'etat is two-thirds
won; all that remains is to storm the Roman fortress next
door. But it belongs to the nature of the new order that,
though it condemns and displaces the old, it does not do
so with the arms of the old. Jesus passes up his golden
chance, and withdraws to Bethany. But the city will not
be the same again. Now it is clear that he must be killed
(19:47; 20:19; 22:2).

Between the triumphal entry and the purification of
the temple, Luke (alone among the Evangelists) has inserted a poignant vignette.[41] Here in a kind of prophetic
lament, Jesus at the gate of the city weeps because the
city "did not know its time of visitation." There is about
the very coming of the King a built-in illustration of that
rejection which is already sure. At the point of the city's
most uninhibited welcoming of the Messiah, Luke will
not let the reader forget that his rejection was already
sealed. Despite the joyous crowds, this man on the don-
key is beginning his passion.

Every pericope in the section 19:47-22:2 reflects in
some way the confrontation of two social systems and
Jesus' rejection of the status quo. The trap question
about the denarius (20:20-25) is the most openly political, but differs from the others only in that this meaning
is more transparent.[42] The challenge to Jesus' authority

[41] Scott, *op. cit.*, p. 24 and *passim*, makes much of the strategic importance of this event for the Gospel narration. It forms the hinge between the
teaching ministry and the passion; it is the point of irruption of the
messianic secret, the first outright challenge to the sacerdotal class, and the
detonator of the antagonisms that had been building up against him. Jesus
himself chooses the time and the shape of the final clash, and precipitates it.
"He thereby decided how his enemies would have to proceed against him. He
defined the issue on which they would have to meet him and forced them to
accept it" (p. 124).

[42] Cf. J. Spencer Kennard, Jr., *Render to God: A Study of the Tribute
Passage* (New York: Oxford, 1950); and E. Stauffer, *op. cit.*, p. 112.

(20:1-8), the parable of the unfaithful vineyard-keepers cast out by the owner (20:9-18, with the allusion to Ps. 118, also quoted in the triumphal entry), the Davidic sonship of the Messiah (vv. 41-44, with reference to Ps. 110), the scribes who devour widows' houses (vv. 45-47), rich scribes and poor widows (20:45-21:4), tribulation and triumph (21:5-36); all is cast in the mood of impending clash between two regimes.

It is hard to see how the denarius question could have been thought by those who put it to be a serious trap, unless Jesus' repudiation of the Roman occupation were taken for granted, so that he could be expected to give an answer which would enable them to denounce him. Once again, the "spiritualizer's" picture of a Jesus whose only concern about politics was to clarify that he was not concerned for politics is refuted by the very fact that this question could arise. In the context of his answer "the things that are God's" most normally would not mean "spiritual things"; the attribution "to Caesar Caesar's things and to God God's things" points rather to demands or prerogatives which somehow overlap or compete, needing to be disentangled. What is Caesar's and what is God's are not on different levels, so as never to clash; they are in the same arena.[43]

The Last Renunciation: Luke 22:24-53

These thirty verses bring together in remarkable density four episodes. Following the institution of the Supper, there is first the dispute about who would be the

A special depth of analysis of the denarius passage is offered by Stauffer, "The Story of the Tribute Money," ch. 8 in *Christ and the Caesars*, pp. 112ff; and by Donald D. Kaufman, *What Belongs to Caesar?* (Scottdale: Herald, 1969), pp. 35ff.

[43] Paul's echo of the criterion, "to each what is due to him" (Rom. 13:7), is likewise not a distinction between two realms, nor a listing of what is due to Caesar, but a guide for dissecting competing claims for loyalty. (Cf. below, p. 211.)

greatest, in response to which Jesus calls his disciples to
be servants rather than lords. This text has its parallels in
Mark 10 and Matthew 20, where it comes before the
entry into Jerusalem, in response to an overture from
Madame Zebedee or her sons. Next comes the warning of
Peter's betrayal (where Matthew and Mark predict the
falling away of all the twelve). Then the report, unique in
Luke, of the reversal of the disciples' earlier traveling
orders, instructing them to take a purse and a bag *and a
sword,* in order that the Scripture be fulfilled which
predicted, "He was reckoned with transgressors."[44] Then
comes the prayer for the removal of "this cup" (without
the threefold repetition and without the concentration
on the disciples' drowsiness which are emphasized in
Mark and Matthew), followed immediately by the betrayal and capture.

The creation of a literary unit in which two elements
are inserted by Luke which were not present in Mark
focuses even more clearly the question which most tradi-

----

[44] Traditional proof-texting debate for and against pacifism has always
made much of the "two swords" passage. If Jesus had meant his disciples
never to kill why would he now have told them to arm? Is he not preparing
them for legitimate defense while on their post-Pentecost missionary travels?
But Jesus says he is preparing them for his capture, for the fulfillment of the
prediction that he would be found among compromising company. When
they respond, "We have two swords," his response, "Enough," cannot mean
that two swords would be enough for the legitimate defense of twelve
missionaries. He is (in direct parallel to Deut. 3:26, where Jahweh tells Moses
to change the subject, LXX *hikanon estin*) breaking off the conversation
because they don't understand anyway.

According to Hans Werner Bartsch, *Jesus: Prophet und Messias aus
Galiläa* (Frankfurt: Stimme-Verlag, 1970), p. 56, the reference to Isa. 53:12
cannot be Luke's insertion, for it is not according to the Septuagint. Luke in
any case does not give to the fulfillment of prophecy the recurrent function
it has for Matthew. This makes it all the more striking that just here, as in
Luke 24:26 (dealing also with the suffering of the Messiah), the theme of
fulfillment should be thus accented. In the Matthew account of the sword in
the garden (26:54) the reference to fulfillment is in Jesus' own words (rather
than, as usual in Matthew, the Evangelist's) and likewise centers upon the
sword. Thus the "fulfillment of prophecy" theme has a special link to the
garden capture in both Gospels.

tional interpretation has avoided. What would it have meant for the petition to be answered, "Let this cup pass from me?" What else could possibly have happened then?

Both pious and scholarly commentary on this crucial choice have uniformly seen it in the light of what did happen later. In the reverence which surrounds Christian interpretation of the story of Gethsemane, the reader and even the professional commentator seldom have indulged the historical curiosity which would ask what it could have meant for "this cup to pass." In what way would it have been possible, in the situation Jesus' offensive behavior in the temple had brought upon him, for him to avoid the ultimate clash and destruction? What was the option with which he was struggling? Was it that he might silently slip away to Qumran until the storm was over? Or could he have reconciled himself to the authorities by retracting some of his more extreme statements? Should he have announced a deescalation, renounced his candidacy for the kingship, and gone into teaching?

The only imaginable real option in terms of historical seriousness, and the only one with even a slim basis in the text, is the hypothesis that Jesus was drawn, at this very last moment of temptation, to think *once again* of the messianic violence with which he had been tempted since the beginning. Now is finally the time for holy war. All four Gospels report Peter's use of the sword in legitimate defense. All but Mark interpret it in such a way as to suggest that the episode is symbolic of a deeper struggle. According to John, Jesus' rebuke to Peter uses the very language of his prayer: "Shall I not drink the cup which the Father has given me?"

The narrative of Matthew interprets the episode of the sword by spelling out at greater length what Jesus might have done. "Do you think that I can not appeal to my Father, and he will at once send me more than twelve legions of angels? But how then should the Scriptures be fulfilled that it must be so?" The themes of an appeal to the Father and the notion of the fulfillment of prediction again place the sword episode in the context of the words of the Prayer. I have little qualification for surmising what it would have looked like for twelve legions of angels—a Roman legion is said to have been 6000 soldiers—to come into that garden. But what *I* can imagine is not very much to the point. Matthew's report is clear, and Matthew *could* imagine that this final encounter with Judas and the Jewish and perhaps Roman police would have been just the point at which God would unleash the apocalyptic holy war, where the miraculous power of the angelic hosts, Jesus' disciples as shock troops, and the crowds in Jerusalem with their long-brewing resentment would rise up in one mighty surge of sacred violence and would finally drive the heathen from the land and restore to God's people (as Zechariah had predicted) the possibility to serve Jahweh in freedom and without fear.[45]

In the account of Luke the interpretation of Peter's sword is given not after the event but proleptically, in the cryptic instruction to the disciples to have weapons about them, because the Scripture was to be fulfilled according to which the suffering servant would be counted among transgressors. The Matthean account projects a vision of the apocalyptic battle; the Lucan story soberly portrays the formal guilt of attempted armed insurrection into which Jesus was placed by the presence of weapons and by Peter's defense.

This is the third chance. As the tempter has suggested,

---

[45] The assistance of warrior angels was a regular element of the Zealot hope; Hengel, *op. cit.*, pp. 284ff, and 311 n. 2. The hypothesis is not new that the intention of Judas was not to turn Jesus over to the authorities but rather that by his betrayal he might force Jesus, in order to defend himself, finally at the last minute to precipitate that holy war through which Judas the *sikarios* (Zealot) expected the breakthrough of the kingdom of God to be achieved. Mark 13:26f and Matt. 24:30f also see warrior angels in the entourage of the Son of Man. Cf. also W. R. Farmer, *op. cit.*, pp. 180, 194.

Jesus once could have taken over the kingship by acclamation after the feedings of the multitude. His second chance for a coup d'etat had been at the entry into the temple, with the jubilant crowd at his back, the temple police thrown off guard by the noise and the Roman guards cowed by Jesus' air of moral authority. Both times Jesus had turned away from the challenge to take over.

Here is now the last opportunity. As Satan had come thrice in the desert, so the real option of Zealot-like kingship comes the third time in the public ministry. It is not without both literary and theological justification that commentators have pointed to a parallelism between the testing in the desert and the trial in Gethsemane.[46] Once more, now clearly for the last time, the option of the crusade beckons. Once more Jesus sees this option as a real temptation.[47] Once more he rejects it.

[46] We shall leave to the form critics the question whether Matthew's or Luke's sequence in presenting the three temptations in the desert may have been influenced by the parallel between them and the three political crises of Jesus' later ministry. This allusion opens up a larger question which would perhaps reward the same critics. If it is conceivable on the one hand that either Matthew or Luke modified the sequence of the temptations from the way they stood in the prior common source because of a parallel he perceived between the three temptations and three landmarks of the later ministry, then we must also admit the corollary hypothesis, that the structure of the later narrative may have been seen by the Evangelist as the unfolding of the test already present in "digest" form in the desert. Then the temptation becomes the prologue to the entire public ministry, which is conceived as an unfolding of what was already projected there. This would especially fit in with Luke's concluding report that the devil left Jesus "until the appropriate time" (4:13).

[47] Bob W. Brown, in a very lively Lenten devotional article, "He Could Have Saved Himself," *Eternity* (Apr. 1968), pp. 13ff, comes within a hair of recognizing a genuine dimension of social strategic choice in Jesus' acceptance of the cross. Many strands of the historical concreteness of Jesus' career are here discerned in a realistic way. Yet the closed circle of prior assumptions about the nature of atonement ends with the impression after all that while avoiding the cross would have been a concrete human choice, meaningful in the gamut of available social options, accepting it was not.

Execution and Exaltation: Luke 23-24

Just as the passage from the Lord's Supper to Gethsemane was underlined by Luke with reference to servanthood and to the swords, so now the movement from
Pilate's court to Golgotha is interpreted by Luke in
language reminiscent of the triumphal entry. A great
multitude of lamenting people followed Jesus, who warns
them of the disaster yet to come.[48]

Whereas Mark simply names Barabbas, and Matthew
calls him simply "a notorious prisoner," Luke tells us
twice that he was imprisoned for insurrection and emphasizes the ironic tragedy of the trade: "He released the
man who had been thrown into prison for insurrection
and murder, whom they asked for: but Jesus he delivered
up to their will."[49] The story ends with both the inscription on the cross and the mockery of the soldiers focused
upon his kingship and his not saving himself. Jesus was
thus traded for a Zealot leader and put to death as "King
of the Jews."

This is another of those points where spiritualistic-
apologetic exegesis has always emphasized that the Jews,
or the Romans, or the Zealot-minded disciples, had Jesus
all wrong; he never really meant to bother the established
order. Then the illegality of the proceedings and the
impropriety of the accusation must be demonstrated.
Even then it would need to be explained why a Jesus
whose main concern is to be apolitical would be misunderstood in just this way instead of some other way, and

---

[48] Cf. O. Cullmann, *op. cit.*, p. 48.

[49] Interpreters disagree whether there really existed a settled custom, as
this account infers, of releasing a condemned person in the Passover season,
and whether Pilate's appeal to it should be understood as a sincere effort to
save an innocent man, or else to avoid releasing the more dangerous Barabbas. Paul Winter, *On the Trial of Jesus* (Berlin: De Gruyter, 1961), pp. 91ff,
is the most clear in the claim that such a habit of Pilate (Mark 15:6ff; Matt.
27:39) or such a Jewish custom (John 18:39) never existed.

would not protect everyone against such a radical misperception of his intent. Granted, the trials as recounted are irregular in procedure, and normal due process according to either Jewish or Roman law might have disculpated Jesus by virtue of the lack of *armed* insurgent actions. Still the events in the temple court and the language Jesus used were *not* calculated to avoid any impression of insurrectionary vision. Both Jewish and Roman authorities were defending themselves against a real threat. That the threat was not one of *armed*, violent revolt, and that it nonetheless bothered them to the point of their resorting to illegal procedures to counter it, is a proof of the political relevance of nonviolent tactics, not a proof that Pilate and Caiaphas were exceptionally dull or dishonorable men.

In a sketch of this kind there would be no profit in dealing with the ancient yet constantly recurring discussions of the legality of the condemnation and execution of Jesus by the Romans or by the Jews.[50] Nor need we catalog the incessant efforts, by combining higher-critical, novelistic, and apologetic techniques in ingenious ways, to reconstruct a brand new picture of "how it really happened" which is much fuller, surer, and less complimentary to the Jews or to the Romans or to Jesus (or to the Gospel writers) than the canonical reports.[51] It is perhaps significant—but to seek to prove even this much would divert us—that *any* such serious effort at hypothetical reconstruction does move toward taking more

[50] The most careful book-length study of the trial is that of Paul Winter (*op. cit.*). Another very thorough effort is that of Israeli Supreme Court Justice Haim H. Cohn, "Reflections on the Trial and Death of Jesus," *Israel Law Review*, 2 (1967), 332ff, also expanded in book form, *Jesus alim*, in Hebrew (1968).

[51] Joel Carmichael (n. 35 above) and Hugh Schonfield found a wide readership. S. G. F. Brandon (*op. cit.*) is incommensurably more careful but still marked by some of the same sweeping overconfidence in his ability to second-guess the sources, and by the assumption that Jesus could have constituted a political threat only by being violent.

seriously the economic-political threat Jesus posed to the
Romans than does the traditional ecclesiastical interpretation.[52] But for our purposes the *titulon* on the cross is
sufficient testimony. Whether the legal procedure was
proper or not, whether or not the Jewish authorities
shared a portion of responsibility, all that needs to be
affirmed to make our point is that Jesus' public career
had been such as to make it quite thinkable that he
would pose to the Roman Empire an apparent threat
serious enough to justify his execution.[53]

"We had hoped that he was the one who would
redeem Israel" (24:21) is not just one more testimony to
the disciples' obtuse failure to get Jesus' real point; it is
an eyewitness report of the way Jesus had been heard.
Jesus' rebuke to the unseeing pair on the road to Emmaus

[52] " ... The question of the political dimension of Jesus' ministry... ,
though it remains the object of lively debate, has been public property for a
good two score years, and is only rarely ignored in scholarly works devoted
to the life of Christ." Etienne Trocmé, *loc. cit.*

[53] "There is increasing evidence that the role of Pilate was considerably
greater in the execution of Jesus than the tradition and even the Gospels lead
us to think. The precise role of the Jewish leaders we cannot assess. The
nature of the sources makes it unlikely that we ever will. The crucifixion—a
Roman execution—speaks its clear language, indicating that Jesus must have
appeared sufficiently messianic, not only in a purely spiritual sense, to
constitute a threat to political order according to Roman standards." Krister
Stendahl, "Judaism and Christianity—Then and Now," *New Theology No. 2*,
p. 158 (*Harvard Divinity Bulletin*, Oct. 1963). According to Nils A. Dahl,
Der Gekreuzigte Messias, in H. Ristow and K. Mattiae, eds., *Der historische
Jesus und der kerygmatische Christus* (Berlin: Evangelische Verlagsanstalt,
1962), pp. 149ff, it might even have been the inscription on the cross that
finally determined that Jesus would come later to be called Messiah in the
full, "royal" sense of the title.

This interpretation is supported by J. B. Souček, "Zum Prozess Jesu,"
Communio Viatorum, 6/2 (1963), 201. According to Ferdinand Hahn, *The
Titles of Jesus in Christology* (New York: World, 1969), pp. 160f and esp.
173ff, the outspoken confession of Jesus as Messiah/Christ/King arose in the
church's reflection on the inscription over the cross. Speculative reconstructions of the usages of the very earliest churches must be taken with great
skepticism; yet in any case Hahn's hypothesis underlines the clear meaning
of the inscription, and therefore of the crucifixion as a public event.

was not that they had been looking for a kingdom, and
should not have been. Their fault is that, just like Peter at
Caesarea Philippi, they were failing to see that the suffering of the Messiah *is* the inauguration of the kingdom.
"Was it not necessary that the Messiah should suffer these
things and enter into his glory?" "Glory" here cannot
mean the ascension, which has not been recounted yet,
and in fact is not clearly described in Luke's Gospel at all.
Might it not then mean (as with the concept of "exaltation" in John's Gospel) that the cross itself is seen as
fulfilling the kingdom promise? Here at the cross is the
man who loves his enemies, the man whose righteousness
is greater than that of the Pharisees, who being rich
became poor, who gives his robe to those who took his
cloak, who prays for those who despitefully use him. The
cross is not a detour or a hurdle on the way to the
kingdom, nor is it even the way to the kingdom; it is the
kingdom come.

The preceding account has left major gaps; thoroughness at these points would only have reinforced the
impression already accumulated. We have commented on
the annunciation but passed rapidly over the birth narratives (the significance of the imperial census, Bethlehem
as the city of the King, the angels' cry of "Peace on
Earth"; cf. in Matthew the magi and the slaughter of the
innocent). We have observed the song of Zechariah at the
birth of John, and John's preaching, but given only a
paragraph to his career and fate (the political dimension
of his denunciation of Herod's remarriage, his emissaries'
question and Jesus' answer, Jesus' identification of John's
fate with his own). We have not interpreted in depth
specifically ethical passages like chapter 6. We have not
investigated the special complex of probably politically
oriented narratives in chapter 13 (Pilate's massacre of the
Galileans, the tower of Siloam, the unfruitful fig tree);
nor have we surveyed the extended discussion of the

tribute money (ch. 20). We have not investigated the cases where Jesus was appealed to to take on the role of judge (Luke 13:13f; John 8:1ff).[54]

Without the reinforcement which careful analysis of all this material would have brought, our conclusion is already clear enough to bring the answer to the question with which we began.[55] Jesus was not just a moralist whose teachings had some political implications; he was not primarily a teacher of spirituality whose public ministry unfortunately was seen in a political light; he was not just a sacrificial lamb preparing for his immolation, or a God-Man whose divine status calls us to disregard his humanity. Jesus was, in his divinely mandated (i.e. promised, anointed, messianic) prophethood, priesthood,

---

[54] In John 8, Jesus is challenged to take a stand regarding the condemnation of an adulteress. Often this is understood as a test of his casuistic skill as a rabbi, like Mark 12:13-34 or Luke 10:25ff (cf. 11:53f). Joachim Jeremias ("Zur Geschichtlichkeit des Verhörs Jesu. . .," ZNW, 43 [1950/51], 148) sees in it a challenge to participate in (or interfere with) the judicial process, as a "demagogue from Galilee" might want to.

[55] In retrospect, one may well ask: If the presence and attraction of the Zealot option was as significant as this analysis has made it seem, why is the presence of a Zealot "party" not more visible in the texts? If, as we argue, the fact that Jesus perceived the Zealot alternative, was tempted by it as by no other, and nonetheless rejected it, is of fundamental significance for our understanding of his ministry, why do the Gospels not say so in so many words? The Gospels report frequently that "the Pharisees" or "the Jews" come to Jesus in an identifiable way: why not "the Zealots"? There are good reasons. (a) The Zealot option was present in the disciples' ranks in a stronger way. It was represented in Peter's rejection of suffering (Matt. 16:22) and in the disciples' speculation about who would have the most power in the kingdom (Luke 22:24 and par.). (b) By its nature as a guerrilla movement, the Zealot group would not appear in public identified as such. (c) After the cross, the line between Christians and Zealots was clear, whereas Pharisaism continued to be a factor in Christian/Jewish conversations and even within the church (Acts 15:5). Even after the fall of Jerusalem, the Pharisees remained within the diaspora Judaism with which the church remained in conversation for several generations. Thus, to the extent to which the wording of the Gospel traditions during the period of oral transmission was influenced by the relevance of current concerns, references to Pharisees could be expected to have been retained and reinforced as still relevant, and references to Zealots to have become veiled.

and kingship, the bearer of a new possibility of human, social, and therefore political relationships. His baptism is the inauguration and his cross is the culmination of that new regime in which his disciples are called to share. Men may choose to consider that kingdom as not real, or not relevant, or not possible, or not inviting; but no longer may we come to this choice in the name of systematic theology or honest hermeneutics. *At this one point* there is no difference between the Jesus of *Historie* and the Christ of *Geschichte,* or between Christ as God and Jesus as Man, or between the religion of Jesus and the religion about Jesus (or between the Jesus of the canon and the Jesus of history). No such slicing can avoid his call to an ethic marked by the cross, a cross identified as the punishment of a man who threatens society by creating a new kind of community leading a radically new kind of life.

3

The Implications of the Jubilee

One single discourse, that of Nazareth, is not sufficient to prove that Jesus really proclaimed the inauguration of the year of jubilee. Only a more complete reading of the Gospel texts could support or undermine this thesis. Such a reading would push farther along some of the following lines.[1]

The jubilee year or the sabbath year included four prescriptions: (1) leaving the soil fallow, (2) the remission of debts, (3) the liberation of slaves, (4) the return to each individual of his family's property. The purpose of the present chapter is to examine whether the Gospels contain any other allusions to these four activities.

The Fallow Year

Jesus does not speak directly of leaving the soil fallow. His silence is not at all surprising because, of all the prescriptions for the sabbath year, only this one had become common usage. It would, therefore, have been pointless to exhort the Jews to practice it. But—some-

---

[1] This chapter is adapted freely from André Trocmé, *Jésus-Christ et la révolution non-violente,* ch. 3, pp. 43ff, with permission of the author. Annotation is mine.

what like the case of the fast of the Ramadan, which all Muslims practice but often amid complaint and cheating—it still took great courage for the Jews to leave their fields fallow every seven years, counting on God that they would receive from him what they would need! Many worried. Leviticus (25:20-21), expecting such concern, declared: "If you say: 'what will we eat the seventh year, since we will not sow nor harvest?'—I will give you my blessing on the sixth year and it will produce enough for three years."

Now we find Jesus using practically the same words to his disciples. The proclamation of jubilee in A.D. 26 may have troubled them because they had left their fields untilled and left their boats at the lakeshore to follow Jesus:

> "Do not be anxious, and do not say: 'what shall we eat and what shall we drink, with what shall we be clothed'—for all these things the Gentiles seek to obtain, and your heavenly Father knows that you need them. Seek first of all the kingdom and the righteousness of God and all of these things shall be added to you."[2]

Such an exhortation, often poorly understood because it seems to encourage laziness, is understandable without difficulty as soon as it is placed in the framework of the expectation of the kingdom of God, of which the year of jubilee was one of the precursor signs. Thus, we should interpret the text in this way:

> "If you work six days (or six years) with all your heart, you can count on God to take care of you and yours. So without fear leave your field untilled. As he does for the birds of heaven which do not sow or harvest or collect into granaries, God

2 Luke 12:29-31.

*will take care of your needs. The Gentiles who pay
no attention to the sabbath are not richer than
you."*

Remission of Debts and Liberation of Slaves

In contrast to the above, the second and third provisions of the jubilee order are not marginal but central in the teaching of Jesus. They are even at the center of his theology.

The Lord's Prayer, which summarizes the thought of Jesus concerning prayer, includes the following request: "remit us our debts as we ourselves have also remitted them to our debtors" (the verb is *aphiemi*). Those numerous versions are in error which translate: "Forgive us our offenses as we forgive those who have offended us." Accurately, the word *opheilema* of the Greek text signifies precisely a monetary debt, in the most material sense of the term. In the "Our Father," then, Jesus is not simply recommending vaguely that we might pardon those who have bothered us or made us trouble, but tells us purely and simply to erase the debts of those who owe us money; which is to say, practice the jubilee.[3]

It is remarkable that the verb used by Jesus is *aphiemi,* which means "remit, send away, liberate, forgive a debt," and which is regularly used in connection with the jubilee.[4]

The material meaning of the word "debts" in the Lord's Prayer was so clear that the Evangelist Matthew (or was it Jesus himself?) added a gloss to the "Our Father" in order to explain that the words concerning

[3] Trocmé's interpretation of "forgive us our debts" is strongly supported, independently, by F. Charles Fensham, "The Legal Background of Mt. vi:16," *NovT,* 4 (1960), 1.

[4] *Aphesis,* the noun form of the same verb, is the term regularly used by the Septuagint for the jubilee; Lev. 25:28, 54; Deut. 15:1ff; Isa. 61:2; Jer. 35:8.

debts applied here also to offenses in general: "If you pardon men for their offenses" (here the term is *paraptoma*, "transgression"), your heavenly Father will forgive you as well: but if you do not forgive men, your father will not pardon your offenses (*paraptoma*) either" (Matt. 6:14f).

Thus the "Our Father" is genuinely a jubilary prayer. It means "the time has come for the faithful people to abolish all the debts which tie the poor ones of Israel, for your debts toward God are also wiped away (for that is the gospel, the good news)." Furthermore, this is the way Jesus' listeners understood his prayer. Jesus was establishing a strict equation between the practice of the jubilee and the grace of God. He who was not legalist at any other point, and who was ready without hesitation to pardon prostitutes and disreputable people, was nonetheless extremely strict upon one point: "only he who practices grace can receive grace. The *aphesis* of God toward you becomes vain if you do not practice *aphesis* toward your brethren."

Two parables will help to make more precise Jesus' thinking at this point. The most impressive is certainly the one usually called the parable of the "merciless servant," which states in all its rigor the equation of "Our Father": "no grace for him who is not gracious."[5]

Unfortunately this parable, detached from its sociological background, has too often been considered as a rather pale picture of the forgiveness of sin which is granted by God to those who forgive their brethren.

As a matter of fact, the sad hero of the parable is a real person, a Galilean peasant whose name the disciples of Jesus probably knew. Benefitting, like all those to whom Jesus addressed himself, from the proclamation of the jubilee, he was the object of an act of grace. All his debts had been wiped away: enormous debts, ten thou-

5 Matt. 18:23-35.

sand talents. We should not be surprised at that figure. It expressed the total insolvency of the debtor over against the prince.

S. W. Baron in his history of Israel[6] describes how in the age of Jesus the Galilean peasant who had previously been a free property owner had been reduced to the practical equivalent of slavery by way of progressive indebtedness. Herod the Great was the one responsible for this situation. He had crushed the people with heavy taxes and expropriated the recalcitrant property owners.

To escape such appropriation the peasant would borrow from the usurer, who was often in liaison with the king's representative or the tax collector. His property, which he gave as security, soon fell into the hands of the usurer, and the peasant became his sharecropper or servant. But the problem of the peasant was not thereby resolved. His unpaid debts continued to pile up to astronomic levels. Then, in order to regain his funds, the creditor ordered that the sharecropper should be sold with his wife and children and all his possessions in order to cover the debt.

This is exactly the situation into which the "unmerciful servant" of the parable had come. Jesus describes the relationship between the rising indebtedness of the poor peasant, the loss of his properties, and the loss of his liberty which followed directly.

The jubilee year having been proclaimed, the servant now appears before the king, who forgives his debt. The king, the text says, releases him and "remits" (again the verb *aphiemi*) the debt. If our story stopped here it would be encouraging. But Jesus tells it at a time when the majority of his fellow citizens, even the most humble, had already refused him the jubilee. The rest of the story reflects the bitter disappointment felt in the face of this

---

6 Salo Wittmayer Baron, *A Social and Religious History of the Jews* (New York: Columbia U. P., 2nd ed. 1952), I, 262ff.

refusal. The slave who had been freed by the jubilee, he says, meets one of his fellow slaves, who owed him a modest sum of seventy francs, and refuses him the benefit of the same jubilee forgiveness from which he himself had profited. Instead he seizes him, saying, "Pay me what you owe me."

Denounced by his fellows, the servant was now arrested and led before the king. To this man, without pity and without gratitude, the jubilee is no longer applicable. By order of the king he will be sold for his debts with his wife and children. There is no divine jubilee for those who refuse to apply it on earth.

The frequent remission of debts had a serious inconvenience, already indicated in Deuteronomy 13:7-11: it froze credit. Because of this the rabbis, even the most orthodox like Hillel and Shammai, who had become the champions of the strict application of the law of Moses, hesitated to demand the strict application of the jubilee. The closer the sabbatical year came, the more the wealthy hesitated to lend to the poor for fear of losing their capital. Hereby the economic life of the country was paralyzed. The rabbis sought out a solution to this problem. Adroit commentators of the law, they knew how to make it say the opposite of what it ordered.

It was the most congenial among them, the famous Pharisee Hillel, whom Jesus sometimes quoted, the grandfather of Gamaliel (who was to be in his turn the teacher of Paul), who found a neat solution to the problem.

This solution was called the *prosboul*. This word probably signifies: *pros boulé*, which is Greek for "an action formalized before the tribunal." According to the treatise *Gittin* of the Mishna, Hillel in this way authorized a creditor to transfer to a court the right to recover in his name a debt which the sabbatical year otherwise might have cancelled.

The very existence of the *prosboul* proves that, contrary to the statements of some authors, there was at the

time of Jesus a strong current favoring the strict application of the provision of the jubilee for periodic remission
of debts. Otherwise the institution of this procedure of
prosboul would have been unnecessary. Thanks to such a
subterfuge, lending on interest, which had been forbidden
by the law of Moses (Exod. 22:25) and was always
limited in time by the return of the sabbatical year, again
became possible. The rich, like the Pharisees whom Jesus
accused of "devouring the houses of widows," did not
miss their chance. This is the form of an act of *prosboul,*
the text of which has been preserved in the Mishna:

> I _____ transmit to
> you _____, judges at
> _____ my credit, in
> order to be able to recover whatever sum is due to
> me from _____ what-
> ever might be the date when I express the desire.

This declaration was then signed by the judges and witnesses. Jesus was decidedly an adversary of the *prosboul.*

At this point an important observation can be made.
Generally we are given the picture of Jesus as an adversary of the sabbath laws, whereas in the present case the
contrary applies. As soon as it was a matter of accentu-
ating the humanitarian prescriptions of the law of Moses,
Jesus became more radical than the Pharisees. His constant controversies with them would lose all meaning if
they had had to do with the form religious practices
should take. In reality, the conflict was much more
serious: it had to do with the very nature of the moral
law. "What is the good?" the Pharisees asked, and they
answered by applying the detailed prescriptions in the
midst of which they lost the essential. "What is the
good?" asked Jesus; and neglecting details, he went directly to the essential which he found in Moses without
passing by the detour of the tradition of the scribes.

This radicalism of Jesus was quite different from lati-
tudinarianism. When he said, "God made the sabbath for

man," he meant that God had liberated the Jews by taking them out of Egypt. The sabbatical year, like the day of sabbath, must be practiced. They are both meant to liberate men and not to enslave them. This is why the *prosboul,* like all the other human traditions, which were added to the law in order to attenuate its revolutionary and liberating character, called forth Jesus' indignation.

But how can one avoid the freezing of credit if one rejects the bait of profit? In the Sermon on the Plain Jesus gives the answer. The rich man should be generous, rejecting the fear of not being repaid, because God will take care of him. "If you lend to those from whom you hope to receive, what thank have ye? Sinners also lend to sinners in order to receive the same. But . . . lend without expecting anything or even despairing; and your reward shall be great, and you shall be sons of the most high, because he is good to the ungrateful and the evil. . . . Absolve and you shall be absolved; *give and it will be given to you;* there shall be poured into your lap a good measure, pressed and shaken down and running over."[7]

The honesty of the debtor should correspond to the generosity of the lender. The debtor should not hide himself behind the protection of the law of the sabbath to avoid keeping his commitments. The Sermon on the Mount contains two striking paragraphs where Jesus indicated how the problems over which Hillel and the Pharisees stumbled could be resolved.

Hillel said to the worried creditor: "Transfer your credit to the tribunal, which will collect for you." Jesus says to the negligent debtor: "Don't wait until you fall into the hands of the court to reimburse the debt. If your creditor wants to take you to court by way of the *prosboul* to take away your tunic (which he keeps as security for the debt which you have not been able to pay him), let him (again the verb *aphiemi*) take your

7 Luke 6:33 (my italics).

coat too."[8] Earlier: "Hasten to make your peace with the
adversary as long as you are on the road with him, for
fear that your adversary (using the *prosboul*) might turn
you over to the judge, and the judge to the guard, and
you might be thrown in prison, from which you will not
get out until you have paid the last penny."[9]

Luke, in the parallel to the text quoted, places in the
mouth of Jesus, in the form of the question, a very
interesting thought: "Why do ye not yourself judge what
is right?"[10] thus his disciples are to be free from litiga-
tion. They should not have recourse to the tribunals to
know whether it was just or not to pay their debts.

Now we move on to another parable which also contains a jubilee teaching: that of the unfaithful steward.[11]
Like that of the unmerciful servant, it takes its point of
departure from the situation of the peasant at the time of
Jesus.

We recall what was said above. As a result of the
demands of King Herod and his sons and the Roman
occupant, most of the former rural property owners had
lost their independence. Obliged to mortgage their goods
in order to pay the tax, they were thereby reduced to
half-slavery. The obligations in kind, in oil and wheat,
which they paid to their masters often amounted to half
or more of their harvests.

The peasant situation in Israel was aggravated by still
another plague: the absenteeism of the owners. A hierarchy of intermediate functionaries contracted for the
collecting of debts. They extorted from the sharecroppers
arbitrary sums which widely exceeded the rent and debt
and taxes which were really due. But the poor were
always wrong. They had no recourse because the collec-

8 Matt. 5:40ff.
9 Matt. 5:25.
10 Luke 12:59.
11 Luke 16:1ff.

tors presented fraudulent accounts to their masters, which permitted them to accumulate in very few years what Jesus called "unrighteous wealth." It was by pursuing without cease the possession of this kind of wealth that the collectors lost the real wealth, namely the friendship and respect of their fellow citizens.

Now our parable tells how an owner one day discovered the dishonesty of his steward. Not content to despoil his sharecroppers, this steward was also stealing from his employer to whom he presented falsified records. Now that his cheating was discovered, the steward felt a guilty conscience. He understood that he would never be able to pay back to his employer the amount of his embezzlement. But he decided that at least he would not demand from the sharecroppers the big sums by which he had increased their obligations. He therefore restored to his debtors the unjust excess of the debt which they were supposed to owe him. Jesus pictures him convening his debtors and with a stroke of the pen lowering their debts to the right amount: fifty measures of oil instead of a hundred, eighty measures of wheat instead of a hundred, etc.

Certainly such a decision would only aggravate the insolvency of the steward. It would reduce him to poverty. But in acting this way he acquired genuine wealth, namely the gratitude and the friendship of his former victims. Now poor among the poor, man among men, he shall be received as a brother in their home and this hospitality will continue into eternity. This is what Jesus calls the joy of the kingdom of God. "Make yourselves friends with unrighteous wealth,"[12] he declares in conclusion. "Practice the jubilee which I am announcing. By liberating others from their debts to you, liberate yourself from the bonds which keep you from being ready for the kingdom of God."

[12] Luke 16:9.

What is most remarkable in this parable is the praise which Jesus places in the mouth of the employer who is the representative of God: "Here is an intelligent man," says God, far "more intelligent than the average of those who want to be my disciples."

In the parable of the merciless servant it was God who had taken the initiative. God had first remitted the debt to the man and expected the man to do the same. In the parable of the dishonest steward it is the man who takes the initiative. It is he who first, obeying the messianic appeal, practices the jubilee by remitting the debts of those who are at the same time debtors to God and to him. Consequently God praises that intelligent man who before he was even being touched by grace practices the redistribution of wealth. This man was able to read the signs of the kingdom of God and to understand that the reign of unrighteous mammon is of the past.

The two parables of the merciless servant and the unfaithful steward thus confirm what the Nazareth discourse, the Lord's Prayer, and the Sermon on the Mount had already given us to understand. It is really a jubilee, conformed to the sabbatical instructions of Moses, that Jesus proclaimed in A.D. 26: a jubilee able to resolve the social problem in Israel, by abolishing debts and liberating debtors whose insolvency had reduced them to slavery. The practice of such a jubilee was not optional. It belonged to the precursor signs of the kingdom. Those who would refuse to enter this path could not enter into the kingdom of God.

Fourth Jubilee Prescription: the Redistribution of Capital

Before the invention of the machine, the only wealth of a people was constituted by the soil and the flocks. This is what today would be called capital. Evidently Jesus accepted voluntary poverty for the sake of the kingdom and he ordered his disciples to practice the jubilary redistribution of their capital: "all of these things, it is the Gentiles of the world who seek them. Your Father knows that you need them. Seek rather the kingdom of God and all these things will be added to you. Do not fear, little flock, because your Father has chosen to give you the kingdom; sell all that you have and give it as alms" (Luke 12:30-33). No one doubts that he said this. All that has been debated is whether this redistribution of capital was commanded by Jesus for all Christians in all times and in all places or whether it was just a "counsel of perfection" directed to the saints.

Traditionally the church has chosen the second solution, the easy one. Only he, the church says, who is the object of a very special vocation, for instance the monk, is called upon to abandon all his property. The ordinary believer can be satisfied with "doing charity," i.e. distributing as alms a part of his income.

Such a position would be completely justifiable if Jesus had not been so severe precisely toward those who in his time considered it adequate to practice charity, namely the Pharisees. They did give the tithe of all income and that was not so bad. How few are the people who do as much today!

But Jesus considered the tithe insufficient: "Woe to you, hypocritical scribes and Pharisees, who pay the tithe of mint and anise and cummin (that is, product of the soil) after having neglected the most important points of the law: righteousness, goodness, good faith. This you should have practiced without neglecting that."[13]

Such a word confirms what we were saying about the radicalism of Jesus. He did not wish to abolish tithes. He wished only to go beyond the level of easy fulfillment and easy moral self-satisfaction which could be had by giving the tithe, and to call people to reach the level of "righteousness, goodness, and good faith."

[13] Luke 11:42.

But what was meant by these last three phrases? We have reason to believe that they mean the gratuitous act whereby the disciple, seeking to provide for his own comfort, gives away what he needed for himself, his capital: if your righteousness does not go beyond that of the scribes and Pharisees you will not enter the kingdom of God.

Comparing one day the generosity of the wealthy, who ostentatiously were throwing large offerings in the temple treasury, with that of the poor widow, Jesus exclaimed, "This poor widow has put in more than all of them. They put in from their overflow but she from her poverty has given all that she had to live!"

In modern language we can translate: "The quantity of money that one gives is of little importance. What is important is what one gives. If it is a part of one's income, then this is not righteousness, goodness, and good faith. If it is capital that one gives then everything is in order."

Still it is not our belief that Jesus prescribed Christian communism. If he had done this he would have left to his disciples either monastic rules comparable to those of the Essenes, or some kind of constitution for a Jewish collective state. This he did not do. Collectivism was contrary to the spirit of Moses.

So when Jesus formulated the celebrated commandment, "Sell what you possess and give it as alms" (a better translation would be, "sell what you possess and put in practice compassion"), this was not a "counsel of perfection," but neither was it a constitutional law to found a utopian state of Israel. It was a jubilee ordinance which was to be put into practice here and now, once, in A.D. 26, as a "refreshment," prefiguring the "reestablishment of all things."

Such a redistribution of capital, accomplished every fifty years by faithfulness to the righteous will of God and in the expectation of the kingdom, would today be nothing utopian. Many bloody revolutions would have been avoided if the Christian church had shown herself more respectful than Israel was of the jubilee dispositions contained in the law of Moses.

4

God Will Fight for Us

When modern Christians approach the Old Testament with the question of war in mind, their attitude is a legalistic one and the questions they ask generalize. We ask, "Can a Christian who rejects all war reconcile his position with the Old Testament story?" If the generalization that "war is always contrary to the will of God" can be juxtaposed with the wars in the Old Testament which are reported as having been according to the will of God, the generalization is destroyed.

This approach hides from us the realization that for the believing Israelite the Scriptures would not have been read with this kind of question in mind. Rather than reading with the modern question in mind, whether it confirms certain moral generalizations or not, the Israelite read it as his story, as the account of his own past. A story may include a moral implication, or presuppose moral judgments, but it does not necessarily begin at that point.

One of the traits of the Old Testament story, sometimes linked with bloody battles but also sometimes notably free of violence, is the identification of Jahweh as the God who saves his people without their needing to act. When we seek to test a modern moral statement, we are struck by the parts of the story that do not fit our modern pattern; but the Israelite reading the story was more likely struck by the other cases, where Israel was saved by the mighty deeds of God on her behalf.

We cannot undertake here even a capsule enumeration of the strands of Hebrew history which are taken up and woven into Jesus' story. We are glancing back at the story of ancient Israel, the reader will remember, not for its own sake or for scholarly curiosity, but as a test of modern ethical hermeneutics. We are asking how Jesus and his listeners were likely to conceive of the action of God, against the background of their people's way of telling their history.

The Exodus

"Fear not, stand firm,
And see the salvation of the Lord,
which he will work for you today;
For the Egyptians whom you see today,
you shall never see again.
The Lord will fight for you,
and you have only to be still." (Exod. 14:13)

Every portion of the Exodus account, difficult to interpret at other points, is clear in the report that the Israelites did nothing to bring about the destruction of the Egyptians. The only call to them was to believe and obey. When they did so, the seemingly inevitable menace hanging over them disappeared.

This emphasis of the Exodus story is not reversed by the reporter in chapter 17 of the battle against the Amalekites. It is striking, in comparison to the rest of the narrative in this portion of Exodus, that the decision of Moses and Joshua to undertake a war against Amalek is not reported as having been commanded by Jahweh, even though such commands are quite frequent elsewhere. It is rather the culmination of a period of Moses' being frus-

trated by the people's bitterness and their asking for a
test of the Lord's presence. This time Moses and Joshua
respond in their own way to the Amalekites' attack; they
fight their own battle. Yet the battle goes against them
when Moses' tiring arms lower the symbolic "rod of
God," and they prevail only as the rod is again held aloft.
Thus even when Israel uses the sword, in a most fearful
and destructive way, the victory is credited not to the
prowess of the swordsmen but to the help of Jahweh.[1]
This remains the main point of the accounts throughout
the books of Joshua and the Judges.[2]

It is a general rule of proper textual interpretation
that a text should be read for what its author meant to
say and what its first readers or hearers would have heard
it say. Whether the taking of human life is morally
permissible or forbidden under all circumstances was not
a culturally conceivable question in the age of Abraham
or that of Joshua. It is therefore illegitimate to read the
story of the planned sacrifice of Isaac[3] or of the Joshu-

[1] The name recent scholars have chosen to render as "Jahweh" is the
proper name of the God of Israel, as distinguishable from the generic
appellations "god" or "lord" which applied to other deities as well. The
vocalization is a modern non-Jewish surmise. One of his earliest appellations
is "JHWH of Hosts," i.e. "of the armies"—another index of the place of
these deliverances in Israel's earliest understanding of him.

[2] The institution of "holy war" is only one expression of this providential protection. Its importance as perhaps the most fundamental social
institution of earliest Israel has been pointed up by G. von Rad, *Der heilige
Krieg im alten Israel* (Göttingen: Vandenhoeck & Ruprecht, 1951). The
non-martial deliverances, which for the Israelite were part of the same
picture, have been given less scholarly attention.

[3] The command to Abraham to sacrifice his son has been made a test
case for casuistic ethics by modern Protestant ethical theory, because to the
modern reader it seems so evidently to present the spectacle of God ordering
a man to break his own rules. Such a reading, however, ignores the cultural
context. In the age of Abraham, or even in the age when the account in Gen.
22 was written, the sacrifice of the firstborn was a common cultic custom. It
was no more ethically scandalous or viscerally disturbing than the killing of
the villain in a western film is to most watchers today. It was not conceived
of as coming under the prohibition of murder, for it was a ritual act. The test

anic wars as documents on the issue of the morality of killing. Although the narrative of the conquest of Canaan is full of bloodshed,[4] what the pious reader will have been most struck by in later centuries was the general promise according to which, if Israel would believe and obey, the occupants of the land would be driven out little by little (Exod. 23:29f) by "the angel" (23:23) or the "terror" (v. 27) or the "hornets" (v. 28) of God,[5] or the

for Abraham's faith lay not in the command to sacrifice one he tenderly loved, nor in the command to break the moral law, but rather in that the command put in jeopardy the promise of God that Abraham's posterity should prosper. Even when the sacrificing of human victims later came under the prophets' condemnation, this was at first more because it was idolatrous than because it was murder.

[4] This bloodshed as well must be understood in its cultural context, i.e. cultically. Before a battle the enemy army or city would be "devoted to the lord"; i.e. it was declared to be *herem* or *qadosh*, set apart, holy, tabu; it henceforth belonged to JHWH like the animal on the altar. This is why there was no booty taken; neither slaves, nor cattle, nor gold. The killing was not *instrumental*, contributing in a practical way to a political goal; it was *sacrificial*.

Our purpose here is only to clarify the background for an understanding of what the holy war heritage meant and did not mean in Jesus' time. More study would be needed to exposit its meaning for Christian ethics today. The comments made here are further expanded in my *The Original Revolution* (Scottdale: Herald, 1972), pp. 91ff.

[5] Some interpreters have held that if Israel had been fully faithful, the other peoples in Canaan would have withdrawn without violence in line with this promise. Von Rad (*op. cit.*, pp. 14ff) reconstructs the history on the grounds of his critical understanding and comes to the conclusion that the original pattern of "holy war" was only defensive. In this earliest form an Israelite tribe, already infiltrated among the other Canaanite peoples, was attacked by them and defended itself according to the holy war pattern. Only later was this pattern spread out by the historians the Joshua narratives as if the entire territory had been seized in one aggressive campaign. We are not qualified to evaluate such a critical sifting of the sources and hypothetical historical reconstruction; nonetheless it may be significant that such an effort does not heighten the impression that the holy wars "really" were more aggressive, imperialistic, and self-righteous than the texts indicate.

In any case, it is clear that not *all* the Canaanite centers were destroyed in the age of Joshua; for generations later they were still there.

Yet the thrust of our present argument is not dependent on a reconstruction like von Rad's.

most striking victories of Joshua over Jericho (Josh. 6),
or Gideon's defeat of the Midianites (Judg. 7) after most
of the volunteers had been sent home and the remaining
few armed with torches in order (7:2) not to let Israel
think military strength or numbers had brought the victory: To "believe" meant, most specifically and concretely in the cultural context of Israel's birth as a nation,
to trust God for their survival as a people. This theme
then entered into the theologically oriented view of history which we find most clearly stated in the books of
Chronicles.

The Kingdoms

"O Lord, there is none like thee to help
Between the mighty and the weak.
Help us, O Lord our God, for we rely on thee,
And in thy name we have come against this multi-
tude." (II Chron. 14:11)

This was the prayer with which Asa son of Abijah
went out to meet an Egyptian army four times as strong
as his own. The result was that "the Lord defeated the
Ethiopians before Asa and before Judah, and the Ethiopians fled."
Their flight was not brought about by a simple miracle, and the pursuit by the army of Judah was most
destructive. Yet what was retained in the memory of
Judah was not a record of exceptional prowess in battle
or brutal mopping-up, but rather a victory brought about
by the Lord himself. This is evident in the next story.
II Chronicles 16 recounts the formation of an alliance
between Asa of Judah and Benhadad of Damascus against
the Northern Kingdom. Whether it is the alliance itself or
the attack against the sister kingdom which brought forth
the condemnation of the prophet Hanani one cannot say
for sure. In any case, what the prophet's words condemn

specifically is the reliance upon politico-military resources:

> *"Because you relied on the king of Syria,*
> *And did not rely on the Lord your God,*
> *The army of the king of Syria has escaped you.*
> *Were not the Ethiopians and the Libyans a huge army*
> *With exceedingly many chariots and horsemen?*
> *Yet because you relied on the Lord,*
> *He gave them into your hand.*
> *For the eyes of the Lord run to and fro*
> *Throughout the whole earth,*
> *To show his might in behalf of those*
> *Whose heart is blameless toward him.*
> *You have done foolishly in this;*
> *For from now on you will have wars."*

This vision, for which King Asa was quick to punish the prophet, is one of the leitmotifs of this part of Chronicles. Wars are the outworking of the unwillingness of Israel, especially of the kings, to trust Jahweh.

> *"You will not need to fight in this battle;*
> *Take your position, stand still,*
> *And see the victory of Jahweh on your behalf,*
> *O Judah and Jerusalem.*
> *Fear not, and be not dismayed;*
> *Tomorrow go out against them,*
> *And Jahweh will be with you."* (II Chron. 20:17)

The crowning example of this theme of Chronicles is chapter 20, recording the response of Jehoshaphat to a massive attack from the neighboring tribes to the South. The whole population of Judah, led by the prophet Jahaziel, paraded out to meet the enemy, with the temple singers, the Kohathites and the Korahites, groups of Levitical musicians, leading the total people in songs of praise.[6] As the singing procession advanced they discovered that the enemies had come to blows among themselves and destroyed one another before they even got to Judah.

> And the fear of God came on all the kingdoms of
>   the countries
> When they heard that Jahweh had fought against
>   the enemies of Israel. (20:29)

A second most striking example of this kind of preservation is found in chapter 32, recording the deliverance of Hezekiah and his people from Sennacherib.

> "Do not be afraid or dismayed before the king of Assyria and all the horde that is with him; for there is one greater with us than with him. With him is an arm of flesh; but with us is Jahweh our God, to help us and to fight our battles." (v. 8)

The same story is told at great length in II Kings 18f. The enemy army after all its impressive threats was decimated by "the angel of the Lord" in one night.

In some of these cases there is no way to picture for the modern imagination just what might have happened. In other cases, the Israelite militia[7] or the man of God is actively involved, without making the events any less

---

[6] The cultic form of the event is important. The ceremonial procession is an act of collective worship, just as the sacrificial slaughter of the victim of the holy war had been.

[7] We have already noted that the holy war is more a miracle than a calculating instrument of politics. Still another characteristic that sets it apart from any comparison to modern war was the absence of any professional soldiers. The combatants were a volunteer militia gathered by a trumpet blast from their daily occupations, not professionals paid and drilled for military effectiveness. Once Saul and David had made the transition to an organized state with a standing army, there were no more holy wars of the classic "Joshua" type.

miraculous.[8] Nor is Israel's part, when active, always violent. This is most striking in the story of Elisha's nonviolent misdirection of the Syrians (II Kings 6:11ff). Those with prophetic vision could see that "the mountain was full of horses and chariots of fire about Elisha," but the prophet did not leave it to the horses and chariots to solve the problem; he led the enemy armies together and ordered a banquet of reconciliation.

In the next chapter Elisha's strategy is the opposite; the prophet has to protect himself against his own king, but the enemy army is driven to flight by a noise they hear.

After the Exile

The outworking of this history, as it continued to bear fruit in the minds of pious Israelites, is exemplified in the story of Ezra as he set out from Babylon to return to Jerusalem with the authorization of Artaxerxes.

> Then I proclaimed a fast there, at the river Ahava,
> That we might humble ourselves before our God,
> To seek from him a straight way . . .
> For I was ashamed to ask the king for men,
> Soldiers and horsemen to protect us against the
>   enemy on our way;
> Since we had told the king,
> "The hand of our God is for good upon all that
>   seek him,
> And the power of his wrath is against all that
>   forsake him."
> So we fasted and besought our God for this,
> And he listened to our entreaty. (Ezra 8:21ff)

---

8 By "miraculous" here is meant only what the root meaning of the word accents; that it is cause for wonderment. We are not concerned here for philosophical meditations about the laws of nature, breaking the laws of nature, what miracles prove, or what is meant by miracle stories if they cannot have happened the way it says.

It had thus become a part of the standard devotional ritual of Israel to look over the nation's history as one of miraculous preservation. Sometimes this preservation had included the Israelites' military activity; at other times no weapons at all were used. In both kinds of case, however, the point was the same: confidence in Jahweh is an alternative to the self-determining use of Israel's own military resources in the defense of their existence as God's people.

Our purpose in summarizing this story here is not to seek to reconstruct in just what way whatever happened did happen when Jahweh saved Israel, or whether in each case any of the Israelites used weapons or not. Our present concern is rather with what it meant for Jesus and his contemporaries and his disciples to read this kind of story in their Bible.

We must conclude that the faith of the pious Israelite was nourished by a body of what the cultural anthropologists will call "legend,"[9] the central themes of which were that God himself will take care of his people—

> *"Jahweh will cause your enemies*
> *who rise against you*
> *to be defeated before you;*
> *They shall come out against you one way,*
> *and flee before you seven ways."* (Deut. 28:7)

—and that therefore man's preoccupation with his own power as the instrument of his own surviving or prevailing is misdirected.

---

[9] The term "legend" designates a cultural usage, not a judgment of historicity. The "legend" is that which in a given community is *legendum*, an account to be told over and over, which forms the identity and the values and the self-awareness of that community through the much telling. To identify these stories as Israel's legendarium, as the body of story-telling that made Israel remember what it meant to be Israel, implies no judgment on the historicity of the accounts.

"He will guard the feet of his faithful ones;
For not by might shall a man prevail." (I Sam. 2:9)

The reasonableness of this stance was reinforced by the stories of Abraham's relinquishing the best lands to his greedy nephew (Gen. 13:8ff), of Isaac's relinquishing his pastures and wells to Abimelech and Gerar (26:16ff), of Joseph's and Daniel's rising to prominence by way of exile and prison. What the stories told by example, the prophets made into precept.

"Not by might, nor by power,
but by my Spirit, says Jahweh of Hosts."[10]

Now whatever be the "actual historical shape" of the events lying behind the story, we can be assured that, in the atmosphere of heightened apocalyptic sensitivity into which Jesus came, it was at least *possible* if not *normal* for those who were "waiting for the consolation of Israel" to see in these miraculous deliverances of the Old Testament story a paradigm of the way God would save his people now. When, therefore, Jesus used the language of liberation and revolution, announcing a restoration of "kingdom" community and a new pattern of life, without predicting or authorizing particular violent tech-

---

[10] Zech. 4:6. Millard Lind in several (regrettably mostly unpublished) studies has exposited at length the underlying meanings of this prophetic view of Jahweh's working to save Israel. The prophets remolded the holy war heritage in the use they made of it in recalling Israel to trust in God. Here our concern is much more limited. We are asking not about the prophets' theology but about the Jews' piety, about the sense of reality and the understanding of God's intervention which were common among Jesus' hearers. Gerhard von Rad, *Old Testament Theology* (London: Oliver & Boyd, 1962), I, 347ff, characterizes the history of Chronicles as lacking in theological clarity and unity. Von Rad might consider this theme, "God will take care of his people," as insufficient to meet his criteria of clarity and coherence; nonetheless it is a major theme on the face of the text, and one to which von Rad does not refer explicitly. Cf. Millard Lind, "The Concept of Political Power in Ancient Israel," *ASTI*, 7 (1970), 4ff.

niques for achieving his good ends, he need not have
seemed to his listeners to be a dreamer; he could very
easily have been understood as up-dating the faith of
Jehoshaphat and Hezekiah, a faith whereby a believing
people would be saved despite their weakness, on condition that they "be still and wait to see the salvation of
Jahweh."

To take into account the permeation of pious Jewish
hope with such a body of national legend has serious
implications for the meaning of such "Kingdom Inau-
gural" discourses of Jesus as the Platform statement at
Nazareth or the Sermon on the Plain.

(a) The modern reader is struck by the improbability,
indeed the seeming impossibility, of any such saving
event as a generalized jubilee. Since he assumes Jesus
could hardly have meant what he said, the reader is led to
send his mind down the sidetracks of paradoxical or
symbolic reinterpretations. For Jesus' listeners, on the
other hand, as believing Jews, the question of possibility
was not allowed to get in the way of hearing the promise.
They therefore did not prejudice their sense of what
might happen by knowing ahead of time what Jesus
could not mean.

(b) In correlation with our sense of impossibility we
tend to think of "apocalyptic" promises as pointing "off
the map" of human experience, off the scale of time, in
that they announce an end to history. But the past
deliverances of Israel had been recounted as having taken
place within their own history and on their own Palestinian soil. The whole body of hermeneutic prejudices
linked with the concept of the "interim ethic," as if what
Jesus was predicting was an end to time and space, gets us
off the track right at this point.[11] Jesus' proclamation of

11 In an earlier section we already argued that the haste with which
recent scholars have discounted the realism of Jesus' intentions was the
result of a particular negative philosophical prejudice extraneous to the texts
(p. 22 above); here we observe that Jesus' listeners might well have heard
him with a particular affirmative prejudice intrinsic to their faith and
culture.

the kingdom was unacceptable to most of his listeners *not* because they thought it could not happen but because they feared it might, and that it would bring down judgment on them.

If, with the cultural empathy that is the elementary requisite for honestly understanding any ancient documents, we measure Jesus' meaning not by what *we* can possibly conceive of as happening but by what his listeners can have understood, then we are forbidden to filter his message through our modern sense of reality, of the uniformity of nature and the inconceivability of the extraordinary. "Miracles don't happen" is the one assumption we dare not impose from outside on Jesus or his listeners.

Our modern sense of what may and may not reasonably be expected to happen in our age and in our world will, of course, not avoid coming to terms with the deterministic world view that surrounds us. We may even be driven by the commitment we make to this contemporary view to project it backwards as a judgment as to what can really have happened in the time of Hezekiah, or of Jesus. That is a problem of modern theological self-understanding which the present study does not mean to resolve, nor to pass off lightly. But here our topic is much more modest and much more precise. We are testing whether *what Jesus meant* is properly to be determined under the shadow of our assumption that for him, or for his listeners, or for the Gospel writers and readers, concrete divine intervention was no option, or if conceivable at all, would have meant the end of time and of social-historical process. The evidence is abundant that such a dilemma not only was not self-evident, but was unthinkable. The mighty acts of God in Israel's history had been neither the end of history, nor off the scale of human events. We have every reason to assume that the inauguration of the jubilee was understood by Jesus' hearers with the same concreteness as the Exodus story or the deliverance of Jehoshaphat had for them.

5

The Possibility
of Nonviolent Resistance

Readers of the Gospel story, we have noted, have had difficulty concceiving of Jesus' public ministry as involving any genuine options for social change. This difficulty is reinforced not only by the factors we have thus far been dealing with,[1] but also by the assumption that in his time there were clearly no other ways to resist the Romans than those which the Zealots advocated. We have been giving increased attention to the Zealot option; but thereby we have risked reinforcing this misconception. We have spoken of the pious Israelite's ability to believe in divine intervention[2] but without suggesting how, in the thought of a devout Jew, such an intervention might take place.

To dispel some of this air of irrealism we should therefore be reminded that effective nonviolent resistance was not at all unknown in recent Jewish experience.[3]

---

[1] The logical axioms leading to the claim that the gospel is apolitical are identified especially above, pp. 15ff.

[2] Above, ch. 4, pp. 78ff.

[3] The following exposition parallels and expands a segment of André Trocmé's *Jésus-Christ et la révolution non-violente,* pp. 124ff.

Just before his brief reference to Jesus, the historian Josephus reports this singular episode:[4]

> But now Pilate, the procurator of Judea, removed the army from Caesarea to Jerusalem, to take their winter quarters there, in order to abolish the Jewish laws. So he introduced Caesar's effigies, which were upon the ensigns, and brought them into the city; whereas our law forbids us the very making of images; on which account the former procurators were wont to make their entry into the city with such ensigns as had not those ornaments.[5] Pilate was the first who brought those images to Jerusalem, and set them up there; which was done without the knowledge of the people, because it was done in the nighttime; but as soon as they knew it, they came in multitudes to Caesarea and interceded with Pilate many days, that he would remove the images; and when he would not grant their requests, because it would tend to the injury of Caesar, while yet they persevered in their request, on the sixth day he ordered his soldiers to have their weapons privately, while he came and sat upon his judgment seat, which seat was so prepared in the open place of the city, that it concealed the army that lay ready to oppress them; and when the Jews petitioned him again, he gave a signal to the soldiers to encompass them round, and threatened that their punishment should be no less than immediate death, unless they would leave off disturbing him, and go their ways home. But they threw themselves upon the ground and laid their necks bare and said they would take their death very willingly rather than that the wisdom of their law should be

---

[4] Quoted here from Josephus *Antiquities* xviii.3; a briefer parallel report is found as well in his *Wars* ii.9. The latter source adds that the sit-in lasted five days and nights.

[5] Carl H. Kraeling, "The Episode of the Roman Standards at Jerusalem," *HTR*, 35 (1942), 263ff, tries to spell out something of the fuller meaning of these events: What kind of standards were so offensive? What kind of army unit bore them? If this happened in A.D. 26, as Kraeling and others surmise, then 1290 days, which according to Dan. 12:11 were to separate "the setting up of the abomination of desolation" from the beginning of the end, would have run from then just about to the time of Jesus' public ministry. Kraeling suggests that apocalyptic calculations in this vein might have contributed to an especially tense expectancy in the situation into which John and Jesus came.

transgressed; upon which Pilate was deeply affected with
their firm resolution to keep their laws inviolable, and
presently commanded the images to be carried back from
Jerusalem to Caesarea.

This was evidently not a planned campaign to achieve
a set goal, but rather a spontaneous common response,
effective perhaps partly because it surprised Pilate. It did
not set up a repeatable pattern; for the next effort of
protest, this time against Pilate's confiscation of the consecrated temple treasure to build an aqueduct, was put
down bloodily. The situation in that latter case was quite
parallel, and the Jews' massing unarmed for protest was
the same; but this time Pilate gave them no summons to
withdraw, and thus avoided giving them a signal to throw
themselves on his mercy.[6]

Not much later another threat called forth a concerted
act of resistance which this time had all the marks of a
Gandhian campaign.[7] Gaius Caligula, the first of the
Caesars to demand formal worship of himself, was
incensed at the Jews' refusal to obey, and ordered Petronius, Roman legate of Syria, to install a statue of Caligula
in the temple at Jerusalem. This would have been to
repeat the "abomination of desolation," the profanation
of the temple itself by idolatry, which had been per-
petrated once before by Antiochus Epiphanes and had
triggered the Maccabean wars. This time, however, the
response was a general strike. Fields were left untilled in
the sowing season, and by the tens of thousands the Jews
gathered to entreat Petronius, at Ptolemais and then at

---

[6] This second episode is reported in both Josephus sources, in the
immediately following paragraph. This juxtaposition might indicate more
than time sequence; it might suggest a conscious repetition of the same
strategy by the Jews. Some have conjectured that this latter massacre might
be the same as the event mentioned in Luke 13:1f (above, pp. 43f), where it
is said that Pilate "mingled with that of their sacrifices" the blood of certain
Galileans. But neither the reference to Galilee nor that to sacrifice seems to
fit with Josephus' account.

[7] *Antiquities* xviii.8; *Wars* ii.10.

Tiberias, for over a month.[8] The unity of the people could not be broken; the leaders when summoned privately by Petronius took the same position as the multitudes. Even the heads of the Romanizing royal house, King Agrippa at Rome, and his brother Aristobulus, supported the petition. Disavowing any desire to war against Caesar, the Jews all together as one man could not be moved from the promise to give their lives and those of their wives and children, before permitting the threatened sacrilege. Petronius was finally moved to risk his own standing before Caligula, and became himself the advocate of the Jews' scruples.[9]

Thus collective nonviolent resistance by the Jewry of Palestine was successful against the Roman forces twice within a decade. Called forth by a threat pointed at the heart of the people's religious identity, the reaction founds its own forms of leadership and interpenetration, despite the total absence of any prior training or planning, and without the support of an ethical commitment excluding all violence. This does not suffice to verify the strained hypothesis that if Jesus' message had been accepted by the multitudes he would have led them in such campaigns. It does suffice nonetheless to negate the sweeping assumption that in rejecting the Zealot option Jesus' only other conceivable alternative would have been the end of the world or a retreat to the desert; i.e. that to reject the responsible sword is to withdraw from history.

---

[8] The *Antiquities* account reports forty days, the *Wars* fifty. The economic loss from crop failure seems to have been part of the conscious threat, a threat under which the Jews themselves of course stood to suffer as much as the Romans.

[9] Josephus clearly intends to report that these events included providential intervention. Just after Petronius' decision there came a late, hard rain which made late seeding possible without loss of crops. Caligula, who had first been moved by Agrippa's pleading to withdraw the threat, was nonetheless angered by Petronius' taking the side of the Jews and ordered him to commit suicide. But then Caligula died, and the news of his death reached Petronius before the messengers bearing the order to kill himself (which had been delayed providentially by bad weather on the Mediterranean, thus rewarding him with his life for his sympathy to the Jews).

6

Trial Balance

The reader who has followed us thus far may be ready to grant that, by watching closely the details and the context of the Gospel narrative, we can see reported the work of an ethical-social Jesus whose words and work, life and death, consistently project and make real a particular pattern of presence in the world. But if the reader grants this, and grants as well, hypothetically, that Jesus may have tried to get others to share in that new kingdom reality, does such an argument suffice to reach the present? Did it even reach into the other parts of the New Testament? Did it even survive the translation into the cultural idiom of the early non-Jewish churches?

A sustained, systematic argument would soon become repetitive. We can, however, substantially support our claim in a more episodic or selective way. For our purposes it need not be air-tightly demonstrated that every section of the early church, or of the New Testament, extends in full clarity and fidelity the social stance of Jesus; it suffices to find that at several points, in varied languages and contexts, in more than one style and kind of literature, something of the same posture is found again. The fragmentary essays in the chapters that follow are selected with a view to the variety of semantic and cultural styles into which the Jesus kind of life was

transposed, and with special attention to those points
where it has often been argued or assumed that we are
farthest from his influence, or that his influence is of the
least concrete kind. As before, no original textual insight
will be argued here; we merely summarize scholarly
trends whose relevance, or whose unity, has hitherto not
been exploited for social-ethical thought. To facilitate the
testing of how the "Jesus kind of life was transposed" we
first devote this chapter to a schematic summary.

From Luke to Paul

Assuming that the Jesus of the earliest tradition was
something like the Jesus of Luke, we move to the next
question, that of post-Pentecost ethics, with a certain
momentum. The motif of the disciples' cross is carried
over directly from Luke 14 to the Epistles. The place the
Epistles give to sharing in the sufferings of Christ, as a
key concept in piety and in ethics, has been widely
analyzed in recent study.[1]

Paul can speak of his own ministry as a sharing in the
dying and rising of Jesus (most pointedly in II Cor. 4:10f,
"I carry about in the body the dying of Jesus. . ."; cf.
Col. 1:24: "I will fill out what is lacking in the afflictions
of Christ for his body the church").

Or he can draw the parallel to the sufferings of all
believers (Phil. 1:29, "To you is given not only to believe
in Christ but also to suffer for him"). Christ's self-giving
can be made paradigmatic for the attitude of husband to

---

[1] This "imitation" theme is expanded in ch. 7 below. Here we sketch
only enough to lead into a summary of the conclusions to draw from the
Gospels. It might be asked why in this survey we do not follow Luke's
narrative on into Acts. (a) The Epistles are earlier than either the Acts or the
Gospels, and thereby constitute a corroboration from a source more independent of Luke; (b) our concern is not for Luke's own editorial or
theological contribution (which would lead us to seek its continuation in
Acts) but for the common primitive Jesus story which shows through his
narrative despite his particular editorial concerns.

wife (Eph. 5:25) or for the disposition that enables unity
in the church (Phil. 2:1-5).[2] I Peter speaks of the cross as
an example finding concrete imitation when a slave obeys
a cruel master; Hebrews 12 describes Jesus as the author
and finisher of that faith whose expression in the believers may yet reach to the shedding of blood. I John 3
makes the polarity Cain/Christ, hate/love, killing/laying
down one's life, typical of all the meaning of obedience.[3]

Before drawing any affirmative conclusions let us first
note the absence of the concept of imitation as a *general*
pastoral or moral guideline. There is in the New Testament no Franciscan glorification of barefoot itinerancy.
Even when Paul argues the case for celibacy, it does not
occur to him to appeal to the example of Jesus. Even
when Paul explains his own predilection for self-support
there is no appeal to Jesus' years as a village artisan. Even
when the Apostle argues strongly the case for his teaching
authority, there is no appeal to the rabbinic ministry of
Jesus. Jesus' trade as a carpenter, his association with
fishermen, and his choice of illustrations from the life of
the sower and the shepherd have through Christian his-

[2] By thus moving to the Epistles we do of course leave untouched some
questions which our reading of Luke would lead us to put to Acts: Is the
eschatology of the discourses of Acts different from that of the Gospels?
What has come of the at-hand-ness of the kingdom after Pentecost?

[3] A sample of recently renewed scholarly awareness of the centrality of
the theme of "sharing in the sufferings of Christ" is seen in Edvin Larsson's
Christus als Vorbild (Lund: Gleerup, 1964). The theme "What is lacking in
the sufferings of Christ" is exposited by Henry Gustafson, *BR*, 8 (1963),
28ff. Our observation that Paul saw himself and his church living on in the
line of the sufferings of Jesus, and perhaps as fulfilling in his flesh some
"Words of the Lord" to that effect, would only make more concrete the
other dimensions of corporate personality, eschatological tribulation, and
participation in faithful witness which are Gustafson's leitmotifs.

C. H. Dodd suggests that one of the principles of selection operative in
the writing of the Gospels may well have been the concern to gather
examples that could throw light on Christians' moral choices. "It is probable
that the idea of the *imitatio Christi* had more to say than is commonly
recognized . . . in the selection of incidents from the life of Jesus for record
in the Gospels" (Moffatt commentary on I John, p. 85).

tory given momentum to the romantic glorification of the handcrafts and the rural life; but there is none of this in the New Testament, which testifies throughout to the life and mission of a church going intentionally into the cities in full knowledge of the conflicts which awaited her there. That the concept of imitation is *not* applied by the New Testament at some of those points where Franciscan and romantic devotion has tried most piously to apply it, is all the more demonstration of how fundamental the thought of participation in the suffering of Christ is when the New Testament church sees it as guiding and explaining her attitude to the powers of the world. Only at one point, only on one subject—but then consistently, universally—is Jesus our example: in his cross.

This much could have been said without special attention to our learnings from Luke. But all of this language of imitation and participation, all the pious and pastoral meditation on the believer's cross, takes on a new dimension if we take the measure of the social character of Jesus' cross.

The believer's cross is no longer any and every kind of suffering, sickness, or tension, the bearing of which is demanded. The believer's cross must be, like his Lord's, the price of his social nonconformity. It is not, like sickness or catastrophe, an inexplicable, unpredictable suffering; it is the end of a path freely chosen after counting the cost.[4] It is not, like Luther's or Thomas Müntzer's or Zinzendorf's or Kierkegaard's cross or *Anfechtung,* an inward wrestling of the sensitive soul with self and sin; it is the social reality of representing in an unwilling world the Order to come. The Word:

[4] John J. Vincent, "Discipleship and Synoptic Studies," *TZ,* 16 (1960), 456ff, argues cogently the value of the Synoptic concept of discipleship as foundation for a theologically valid reconception of ethics; what Vincent argues on formal grounds is here worked through in a concrete application. Vincent however does not give to the issue of kingship and cross the central place it seems to have in the Synoptic discipleship sayings.

> *"The servant is not greater than his master.*
> *If they persecuted me they will persecute you."*
>   (John 15:20)

is not a pastoral counsel to help with the ambiguities of
life; it is a normative statement about the relation of our
social obedience to the messianity of Jesus. Representing
as he did the divine order now at hand, accessible; renouncing as he did the legitimate use of violence and the
accrediting of the existing authorities; renouncing as well
the ritual purity of noninvolvement, his people will encounter in ways analogous to his own the hostility of the
old order.

Being human, Jesus must have been subject somehow
or other to the testings of pride, envy, anger, sloth,
avarice, gluttony, and lust; but it does not enter into the
concerns of the Gospel writer to give us any information
about any struggles he may have had with their attraction. The one temptation the man Jesus faced—and faced
again and again—as a constitutive element of his public
ministry, was the temptation to exercise social responsibility, in the interest of justified revolution, through the
use of available violent methods. Social withdrawal was
no temptation to him; that option (which most Christians
take part of the time) was excluded at the outset. Any
alliance with the Sadducean establishment in the exercise
of *conservative* social responsibility (which most Christians choose the rest of the time) was likewise excluded
at the outset. We understand Jesus only if we can em-
pathize with this threefold rejection: the self-evident,
axiomatic, sweeping rejection of both quietism and establishment responsibility, and the difficult, constantly re-
opened, genuinely attractive option of the crusade.

The statement of the problem with which we began
was drawn not from Luke but from the present. Because
Jesus is not meant to be taken as normative for political
ethics, it is said, we must obviously, consciously, properly

get our ethics elsewhere, from a "responsible" calculation of our chances and our duty to make events come out as well as possible. This substitution of nature or history for Jesus as the locus of revelation was justified by the claim that Jesus had nothing to say on this subject. But now we see that he did have something to say; in fact that he said little that was not somehow on this subject. The Gospel record refuses to let the modern social ethicist off the hook. It is quite possible to refuse to accept Jesus as normative; but it is not possible on the basis of the record to declare him irrelevant.

Back to the Present

The fruit of this sketchy survey can be only a global impression, but it is a consistent one. It leaves no room for the prevalent tradition of discounting Jesus' ethic as socially irrelevant either because Jesus' intentions were only on some other level or because the issues he faced were radically different from our own. According to the record, as gathered by witnesses who have never been accused of warping the report to make this point,[5] what

---

[5] If there is any critical consensus on the particular concerns present in Luke's compilation and editing, it is that he meant to give an impression opposed to the one we have been finding here. A resume of the critical conjecture that *all* the Gospel writers slanted their materials, so as to weaken the impression that Jesus' ministry was any threat to society, is offered by Ellis E. Jensen, "The First Century Controversy over Jesus as a Revolutionary Figure," *JBL*, 60 (1941), 261ff. S. G. F. Brandon, *Jesus and the Zealots*, and Neill Q. Hamilton, *Jesus for a No-God World* (Philadelphia: Westminster, 1969), pp. 43-120, make the same sweeping assumption.

The last few years have seen an accumulation of journalistic-type references to "Jesus as a radical," seeking to catch the mood of an age when "revolution" is an in word. With much of what I am saying here, the stance suggested in such texts, e.g. Stephen Rose, "Agitating Jesus," *Renewal* (Oct. 1967); Sebastian Moore, *No Exit* (Paramus, N.J.: Newman, 1968), can be fruitfully compared. Yet the differences are significant. By skipping over the challenge of the collision with traditional interpretations, such claims tend to discredit themselves for novelty-mongering. Often as well (e.g. Willis E. Elliott, "No Alternative to Violence," in *Renewal* [Oct. 1968]) they fail to

Jesus announced was a new stance to be taken by repentant men in the midst of the world: his vocabulary and his picture of what must come to pass were much more "political" than they were "existential" or cultic. His disavowal of Peter's well-intentioned effort to defend him cannot be taken out of the realm of ethics by the explanation that he had to get himself immolated in order to satisfy the requirements of some metaphysically motivated doctrine of the atonement; it was because God's will for God's man in this world is that he should renounce legitimate defense. When Jesus wrestled repeatedly with the tempter, from the desert at the beginning to the garden at the end, this was not a clumsily contrived morality play meaning to teach us that kingship was no temptation; it was because God's Man in this world was facing, and rejecting, the claim that the exercise of social responsibility through the use of self-evidently necessary means is a moral duty.

At the outset of our study we noted the kinds of arguments with which the exemplarity of Jesus' work and the relevance of his teachings are often set aside. They may not unfairly be characterized as seeing Jesus through ebionitic eyes, i.e. limiting his relevance to that which one chooses to attribute to his human status as a radical rabbi. We have observed in the main body of our study that as a radical rabbi Jesus was far more of a political figure than the ebionitic view had been ready to concede; and now we have seen, though only briefly, that the early apostolic church made that political humanness normative for their life. We could support this consideration

---

discern the particular place that the temptation of the sword and his rejection of it has in the *form* and the *substance* of Jesus' social proclamation and impact. They thereby call on Jesus to legitimate their own contemporary revolutionary visions rather than perceiving the uniqueness of his vision. Thereby the risk is great of missing the very core of his originality, namely his rejection (sympathetic, but a clear rejection nonetheless) of the Zealot option.

further if we were to follow the developments which Christian doctrine underwent. When the later, more "theological" New Testament writings formulated the claim to preexistence and cosmic preeminence for the divine Son or Word (John 1:1-4; Col. 1:15ff; Heb. 1:2ff) the intent of this language was not to consecrate beside Jesus some other way of perceiving the eternal word, through reason or history or nature, but rather to affirm the exclusivity of the revelation claim they were making for Jesus. The same must be said of the later development of the classic ideas of the Trinity and the Incarnation. "Incarnation" does not originally mean (as it tends to today in some theologies of history, and in some kinds of Anglican theology) that God took all of human nature as it was, put his seal of approval on it, and thereby ratified nature as revelation. The point is just the opposite; that God broke through the borders of man's definition of what is human, and gave a new, formative definition in Jesus. "Trinity" did not originally mean, as it does for some later, that there are three kinds of revelation, the Father speaking through creation and the Spirit through experience, by which the words and example of the Son must be corrected; it meant rather that language must be found and definitions created so that Christians, who believe in only one God, can affirm that he is most adequately and bindingly known in Jesus.

We did not at the beginning of the paper identify in the same way the other set of alternatives, i.e. the docetic ways of avoiding the political Jesus. These approaches concede unique authority to Jesus, but do so by divorcing him from our humanity.

(a) According to all orthodox doctrines of salvation, Jesus had to die for the sins of men. This was predicted in the prophecies of the Old Testament so that Jesus and Paul could speak of his death as having happened "according to scripture." It was also necessary because of the meaning of man's lostness and the demands of the holiness of God. Jesus had to die—as a ransom to purchase men's liberty from bondage, or as an expiatory sacrifice to purge the stain of sin, or as a substitutionary penalty to pay the price of broken law. Whatever be the imagery, Jesus knew he had to die, for reasons unrelated to his social humanity. Therefore the social humanity of how that necessity came to be carried out is unimportant. The reason he refused to be king or to defend himself was not that there was anything wrong with kingship or self-defense; he just could not have met his destined cross that way.

(b) It is possible to claim that within the space of a generation the concern of the early Christians had moved from the human Jesus of the Gospels to the cosmic Jesus of the letter to the Colossians. In the name of this cosmic Christ the church proclaimed a general acceptance by God of the nature and structures of this world, from which there must flow an ethic of world-affirmation and of creativity. The whole cosmos must be taken as the ultimate revelation of the dimensions of mankind: the Jesus of the Gospel stories is merely a bridge from the cultural isolation of Judaism to the world-encompassing acceptance of the givenness of history and mankind in the deutero-Pauline proclamation.

There was a time earlier in this century when such a contrast between the Jesus of the Gospels and the Christ of Paul was so understood as to prefer the former to the latter. Today, in the most widely publicized thinking on the mission of the church, in the popularization of which Joseph Sittler's 1961 New Delhi poem-sermon[6] and Harvey Cox's 1967 interpretation of "Church and Society"[7] were two landmarks, the current has moved clearly in the

6 Joseph Sittler, "Called to Unity," *Ecumenical Review*, 14/2 (Jan. 1962), 177ff.

7 Harvey Cox, "The Biblical Basis of the Geneva Conference," *CC* (Apr. 5, 1967), p. 435.

other direction. One makes majestic, orthodox-sounding statements about the cosmic significance of Christ; but the effect of this language—just the opposite of what it has for Paul—is to move farther from the claims that could be made for the Palestinian Jesus. The hidden workings of the cosmic Christ throughout the fabric of present history, they assume, will give us more guidance than a bygone Jesus.

(c) The other frequent way of making almost the same point is the appeal to the dogma of the Trinity, most sweepingly and structurally stated in the analysis of H. Richard Niebuhr.[8] An ethic of the Son, guided by either the teachings or the example of Jesus of Nazareth, needs to be completed or even corrected by two other kinds of resource. We first of all need an ethic of the Father, in whose name the structures of the created world must be affirmed. What traditionally was called an ethic of the orders of creation is therefore founded in the will of the Father. Perhaps he might as well be appealed to as the authority underlying the moral teaching of the Old Testament.

Probably still more significant in Niebuhr's intent is the completion or correction which needs to be brought from the perspective of the Holy Spirit. By this is not meant—at least not primarily, not in the thinking of Niebuhr himself—any ecstatic or prophetic insight, mystical or pentecostal, but rather the whole body of decisions and precedents, arrangements and adaptations which have been made between Christ and culture throughout the history of Christendom. These decisions have been made by the churches and may be presumed to have been the work of the Holy Spirit. They have by and large led away from an ethic of the Son.

[8] Initially projected in his *Christ and Culture* (New York: Harper, 1951), pp. 80f, 114, 131, this analysis is extended in "The Doctrine of the Trinity and the Unity of the Church," *TT*, 3/3 (Oct. 1946), 371ff.

It is quite evident that, caught between the universality and the validity of the orders of creation on the one hand and the historical continuity and present relevance of the accumulation of Christian tradition on the other, whatever substantial originality there may have been in the ethic of Jesus is no longer of determining significance. . . . If it still enjoys some kind of symbolic centrality, the gem is nevertheless almost lost within the size of the setting.

(d) Still one other kind of cavil must be recognized. Have we not been admonished for the past three-quarters of a century to be clear in distinguishing between *Historie* and *Geschichte?* Is there not a difference between the historic and the historical Jesus? Can we bypass either the literary questions or the philosophical ones with which our colleagues have been entertaining us since it began to be recognized that the Gospel sources are not neutral chronicles but witnesses of the faith?

As distinct from some of the other questions above, this is one that cannot be resolved simply by reading the sources, since it reflects the modern reader's judgment on the character and authority of the sources. Neither can it be resolved from traditional perspectives, since it reflects a conception of the novelty and authority of the modern mind for which dogmatic study becomes irrelevant. But fortunately for our purposes, this is a question we need not answer in a general, methodological way, since it just happens—or *is* it just happenstance?—that the particular Gospel materials we have been looking at are generally conceded to be those points at which the historic and the historical most nearly coincide; the place where there is the least distinction between what the critic thinks must actually have happened and what the believing witnesses reported.[9] There is widespread debate about the sense in

[9] Rudolf Bultmann's most basic statement on "the relationship of the primitive Christian proclamation of Christ to the historical Jesus," *Das*

which the resurrection reports can be called "history," or about how much the sayings and parables have evolved when we find them in their Synoptic settings. The doubts have not the same depth or breadth when we turn to the narrative skeleton of the Gospels, according to which Jesus gathered disciples, proclaimed the imminence of the kingdom, and was executed accused of insurrection.

To deal with the many ways, ebionitic and docetic, of avoiding the normativeness of Jesus, would call for a different kind of study from the present one. Such questions are of a dogmatic, not exegetical character, and would need to be encountered on that level. From the perspective of our reading of Luke and our brief glance at the Epistles, all that can be said is that these texts themselves provide no demand for such redefinitions and raise no need for them. If we were to carry on that other, traditionally doctrinal kind of debate, we would seek simply to demonstrate that the view of Jesus being proposed here is more radically Nicene and Chalcedonian than other views. We do not here advocate an unheard-of modern understanding of Jesus; we ask rather that the implications of what the church has always said about Jesus as Word of the Father, as true God and true Man, be taken more seriously, as relevant to our social problems, than ever before.

But then relevance must be redefined. If it is not enough to say with the Reformation traditions that Jesus purges our will and dampens our pride, sending us back to follow the dictates of our "office" or "station" with greater modesty and thoroughness; if it is not enough to say with the Puritan traditions that we derive from Josiah and Theodosius the vision of a holy commonwealth con-

Verhältnis der urchristlichen Christusbotschaft zum historischen Jesus (Heidelberg: Carl Winter, 3rd ed. 1962), considers as fully *certain* only that Jesus died the death of a political criminal (p. 12) and as *probable* that he cast out demons, broke the sabbath law, favored the social outcasts, and gathered a small circle of disciples (p. 11).

stantly being reformed to approach increasingly the theocratic ideal; if it is not enough with the "natural law" to find our instructions in the givenness of the fallen world; if it is not enough with the quietist and sectarian traditions to let someone else take care of the world out there, what can then be the shape of a reformulated social responsibility illuminated by the confession that it is Jesus who is Messiah who is Lord? Where are we called to an ethicist's repentance, i.e. to a reformulation of the thought patterns that underlie moral choice? I suggest that this reformulation must take five lines:

1. Recent systematic tradition tells us that we must *choose between the Jesus of history and the Jesus of dogma.*

If Jesus is the divine Word incarnate, then what we will be concerned about is the metaphysical transactions by means of which he saved humanity by entering into it. We will then leap like the creed from the birth of Jesus to the cross. His teachings and his social and political involvement will be of little interest and not binding for us.

If, on the other hand, we seek to understand the "Jesus of history" in his human context, as this is reconstructed by the historical disciplines, this will be in order to find a man like any other, a reforming rabbi fully within the limits attainable by our human explanations, who is sometimes mistaken, especially about the future, and whose authority over us will depend on what we ourselves can consent to grant to his teachings.

The nineteenth century chose the Jesus of history, until Albert Schweitzer showed us that Jesus "as he really was" really did take himself to be an apocalyptic figure and his age to be the one just before the New Order begins. Then the systematic tradition veered back to metaphysics, using literary criticism to demonstrate how the Gospel documents project onto Jesus the existential self-awareness of the young church—an awareness closely tied to the name of Jesus but not to his historical reality, so that if he hadn't really been who he was it wouldn't jeopardize anything of his "meaning for us."

If we confess Jesus as Messiah we must refuse this choice.

The Jesus of history is the Christ of faith. It is in hearing the revolutionary rabbi that we understand the existential freedom which is asked of the church. As we look closer at the Jesus whom Albert Schweitzer rediscovered, in all his eschatological realism, we find an utterly precise and practicable ethical instruction, practicable because in him the kingdom has actually come within reach. In him the sovereignty of Jahweh has become human history.

2. The systematic tradition tells us that we are obligated to *choose between the prophet and the institution.*

The prophet condemns and crushes us under his demand for perfection. He is right, ultimately, both in convincing us of our sinfulness and in pointing us toward the ideal which, although unattainable, must remain our goal. But as far as that social order is concerned which it is up to us to administer today and tomorrow, his demands are without immediate relevance. Love, self-sacrifice, and nonviolence provide no basis for taking responsibility in this world. Dependent upon the grace of God alone, one cannot act in history. Those who are called to assure the survival and the administration of institutions will therefore accept violence in order, one day, to diminish or eliminate it. They will accept inequality and exploitation with the goal of progressively combatting them. This is a very modest task and one in which one dirties oneself, but an indispensable task if something worse is to be prevented. While respecting the prophet, the rest of us will choose the institution.

The new regime instituted by Jesus as Messiah forbids us to make this choice.

The jubilee which Jesus proclaims is not the end of time, pure event without duration, unconnected to either yesterday or tomorrow. The jubilee is precisely an *institution* whose functioning within history will have a precise, practicable, limited impact. It is not a perpetual social earthquake rendering impossible any continuity of temporal effort, but a periodic revision permitting new beginnings.

3. The systematic tradition tells us to *choose between the catastrophic kingdom and the inner kingdom.*

Jesus announced the imminent certain end of history as an event which could happen tomorrow or which was, at the latest, sure to come soon after his death. The apostles maintained this intensity of expectation for a few decades but finally it had to be admitted that there had been a mistake about the date, or perhaps about what they were looking for so soon.

The other option begins by assuming that Jesus could not have been wrong. It must then be concluded that he was speaking of the kingdom of God and its coming only in order to teach, by means of the mythical language which was current in his time, about an inner, spiritual, existential kingdom, whose reality properly will always remain hidden to the eyes of the unbeliever and of the historian.

Once again if Jesus is the Christ we must refuse this choice.

The kingdom of God is a social order and not a hidden one. It is not a universal catastrophe independent of the will of men; it is that concrete jubilary obedience, in pardon and repentance, the possibility of which is proclaimed beginning right now, opening up the real accessibility of a new order in which grace and justice are linked, which men have only to accept. It does not assume time will end tomorrow; it reveals why it is meaningful that history should go on at all.

That men would refuse this offer and promise, pushing away the kingdom that had come close to them, this Jesus had also predicted. He was not mistaken.[10]

[10] André Trocmé's book (*op. cit.*) includes a chapter, "Was Jesus mistaken about the date?" which points to what might be a whole new, specifically biblical grasp of the relation of present and future in moral thought. This extended footnote can only suggest a line of argument worthy of far fuller treatment.

A. Strobel, *Untersuchungen zum eschatologischen Verzögerungsproblem* (Leiden: Brill, 1961), makes a careful study of this "problem" from the standpoint of Jewish understanding of Hab. 2. The not-having-come and the having-come of the Rule of God were both present in the faith of each biblical epoch. The concept of a purely future coming, so firmly dated that at a certain time its failure to arrive becomes a clear disappointment, is foreign to the biblical mind. Thus the concept that the specific character of Jesus' ethic was conditioned upon the imminence for him of a purely future end of human history is likewise unthinkable. This study confirms that the problem of the delay of the parousia is one that scholars have imported into the New Testament. It is certainly one that did not trouble the early church to any degree, to say nothing of providing motive for theological redefinition in the next century, as especially the school of Martin Werner (*The Formation of Christian Dogma* [New York: Harper, 1957]) would claim.

Similar argument is made by Ethelbert Stauffer, *Jesus and His Story*, p. 59, and in greater exegetical depth by Hans Werner Bartsch, "Zum Problem der Parusieverzögerung bei den Synoptikern," *EvT,* 19 (1959), 116ff. " . . . The problem of the delay of the parousia is a problem only in so far as the early community misunderstood and literalized the apocalyptic form." Graydon F. Snyder, "The Literalization of the Apocalyptic Form in the New Testament Church," *BR,* 14 (1969), 7.

This concept of the adjustment to the kingdom's non-arrival is inapt also in its unspoken assumption about the development of New Testament literature. Reading through the New Testament in narrative sequence, we find first the human-social Jesus, who calls men to follow him about in a real community in a real Palestine; then we move on to Paul's cosmic Christ, whose risen glory transfigures the cross and dispenses with the earthly career. It is then thinkable that in this movement there was a necessary dehistoricizing, de-Judaizing process, indispensable if the church was to spread beyond Palestine into the Hellenistic world. But this is to forget that Paul wrote before, not after the Gospel writers. *First* there was the bare resurrection message; *then* there was the Lordship proclamation; *then* it was filled out with the body of memories of the words and works of Jesus of Nazareth. The movement in the formation of the New Testament literature was toward, not away from, filling out the picture of Jesus' humanity. This point is made helpfully by Eric Lane Titus, "The Fourth Gospel and the Historical Jesus," in F. T. Trotter, ed., *Jesus and the Historian* (Philadelphia: Westminster, 1968), pp. 98ff. This consideration applies to the point at issue in our present study. The sources that make most clear the social-apocalyptic

4. The systematic tradition tells us we must *choose between the political and the sectarian.*

In the tradition of Ernst Troeltsch, Western theological ethics assumes that the choice of options is fixed in logic and for all times and places by the way the Constantinian heritage dealt with the question. Either one accepts, without serious qualification, the responsibility of politics, i.e. of governing, with whatever means that takes, or one chooses a withdrawn position of either personal-monastic-vocational or sectarian character, which is "apolitical."[11] If you choose to share fully in

realism of Jesus' claims are those whose authors or editors had had the most time to know that the end of history had not yet come. Fittingly, Titus lifts up the Servanthood episode of John 13 as expressive of the concretization of glorification-Christology with human history.

Of the respected senior scholars in the New Testament field, it is perhaps Amos Wilder who comes closest to holding the door open for the concern of this study. His *Eschatology and Ethics in the Teaching of Jesus* (New York: Harper, 2nd ed. 1950) competently dissects the Schweitzerian argument that the radicality of Jesus' call can be understood only if one posits a very brief "interim" before the parousia. Yet Wilder does not finish his sketch of a coherent alternative. He retains a conceptual division in Jesus' teachings between those of general validity and others characterized as "extraordinary," "drastic," "desperate," "hasty," i.e. as limited to a *kairos* or a crisis or the "exigencies of his work." Sometimes this distinction seems to suggest after all the legitimacy of a lower-voltage discipleship for run-of-the-mill believers in noneschatological times or places. If this line of thought were carried through we would have once again what Schweitzer meant by his "interim ethic" concept, namely the priority in our noneschatological context of a nonheroic and nonchristological standard for "normal" Christian ethics. John Knox deals with the "interim" theme under the fitting label, "Ways of Escape," in his *The Ethics of Jesus in the Teaching of the Church* (Nashville: Abingdon, 1961), esp. pp. 45ff.

11 Troeltsch has obtained a wide following in American thought through the brothers Niebuhr; it is very difficult for an American Protestant ethicist even to conceive that questions might be posed in other terms. H. Richard Niebuhr's classic *Christ and Culture* presupposes it, reinforces it with the trinitarian language we have already noted, and has propagated it widely. Paul Ramsey's *Basic Christian Ethics* uses this formulation of the problem to provide his outline. If we had space for a wider excursion in the byways of hermeneutic theology, we might link this dichotomy (or that of B above) with those others which often separate history from meaning, *Historie* from *Geschichte,* the course of world events from the concern of religion, or "revelation" from "fact," or "faith" from "science."

the duties and the guilt of government, you are exercising responsibility and are politically relevant; if you choose not to, it is because you think politics is either unimportant or impure, and are more concerned for other matters, such as your own salvation. In so doing you would have Jesus on your side,[12] but having Jesus on your side is not enough, for there are issues to which Jesus does not speak (here this view overlaps with and appeals to the other three already sketched). We must therefore supplement and in effect correct what we learn from him, by adding information on the nature and the goodness of the specifically "political" which we gain from other sources.[13]

If Jesus is confessed as Messiah this disjunction is illegitimate. To say that any position is "apolitical" is to deny the powerful (sometimes conservative, sometimes revolutionary) impact on society of the creation of an alternative social group, and to overrate both the power and the manageability of those particular social structures identified as "political." To assume that "being politically relevant" is itself a univocal option, so that in saying "yes" to it one knows where one is going, is to overestimate the capacity of "the nature of politics" to dictate its own direction.

Because Jesus' particular way of rejecting the sword and at the same time condemning those who wielded it *was* politically relevant, both the Sanhedrin and the Pro-

12 The strongest statement of the concession that Jesus is really on the other side from one's own is in Reinhold Niebuhr's writings, beginning with his *Interpretation of Christian Ethics,* where this problem of the sword is the basic one. Niebuhr does not deal in this book with work, or sex, or truthtelling or education; the problem of faithfulness and compromise in dealing with power in politics and economics, as best portrayed by what we do with the Sermon on the Mount, is for him the central ethical issue (as it was for Jesus). Paul Ramsey (*op. cit.,* esp. pp. 35ff: "In What Way, Then, Are the Teachings of Jesus Valid?") makes the same admission.

13 See above, pp. 19ff and 100ff, concerning the "other sources." Cf. also my *Original Revolution,* pp. 132ff with reference to "other lights."

curator had to deny him the right to live, in the name of both their forms of political responsibility. His alternative was so relevant, so much a threat, that Pilate could afford to free, in exchange for Jesus, the ordinary Guevara-type insurrectionist Barabbas. Jesus' way is not less but more relevant to the question of how society moves than is the struggle for possession of the levers of command; to this Pilate and Caiaphas testify by their judgment on him.[14]

One can sympathize with those who think that problems of substance can be swept away by semantic conventions. Some would say there is such a difference of character between what the whole world considers as politically relevant that we should grant the definition of the "political" as best represented by what Jesus rejects. Then Jesus would be after all "apolitical," taking for himself and his disciples a withdrawn stance. After thus agreeing on definitions, we could then go on to argue the moral justification, and perhaps also the political relevance on some other level, of the apolitical stance;[15] but at least we would not need to stumble over diversities of definition. But Jesus chose not only to stumble over diversities of definition but to be crucified on them. He refused to concede that the men in power represent an ideal, a logically proper, or even an empirically acceptable definition of what it means to be political. He did not say

[14] "This denial that the human exercise of violent power is necessary to existence was not a withdrawal from political concerns. . . . Yahweh's leadership in history had to do with political order, both for the community's external and internal relationships." Millard Lind, *ASTI*, VII, 4ff.

[15] Reinhold Niebuhr himself devoted half a chapter of his *Interpretation of Christian Ethics* to affirming the "relevance of an impossible ideal." There is the relevance of the ideal's indiscriminate criticism, which by condemning all man's achievements as insufficient takes us off the scale of ethical options and drives man to repentance; there is also the discriminate criticism whereby the ideal, impossible in itself, still helps to determine which of the real options is preferable. There is the prophetic relevance of the minority whose vocation it is to represent that double critique by withdrawing from the political realm. Yet all of this relevance can only be had at the cost of admitting first that Jesus' way is not *really* for here and now.

(as some sectarian pacifists, or some pietists might), "you can have your politics and I shall do something else more important"; he said, "your definition of *polis,* of the social, of the wholeness of man in his socialness is perverted."

5. The tradition tells us we must *choose between the individual and the social.*

The "ethics of the Sermon on the Mount" is for face-to-face personal encounters; for social structures an ethic of the "secular vocation" is needed. Faith will restore the individual's soul, and Jesus' strong language about love for neighbor will help with this; but then how a restored man should act will be decided on grounds to which the radical personalism of Jesus does not speak.

But Jesus doesn't know anything about radical personalism. The personhood which he proclaims as a healing, forgiving call to all is integrated into the social novelty of the healing community.[16] This is clear from the Lucan text we have read; it would be even more clear if we

---

16 A few steps in the direction of our concern are made by George S. Hendry in his *The Gospel of the Incarnation* (Philadelphia: Westminster, 1958). Hendry seeks to move beyond the older polarizations of Christology around Bethlehem, the cross, Easter and Pentecost, finding the center of them all and the rootage of a renewed two-natures doctrine in a vision of the Christ of Galilee. If contemporary man now perceives reality as personhood-in-relation, then it is in that form that we must cast our vision of the divine originality of Jesus. Jesus is the other-centered man *par excellence,* servant of men and of God. The kernel of this double other-centeredness is Jesus' action in forgiving men, not so much in providing the metaphysical prerequisites for forgiveness as in telling specific men, now, personally, convincingly, that they are freed.

Fully in key with this approach, I need only suggest that if Hendry's question: "If we survey the human life of Christ as a whole, what is the chief characteristic it exhibits?" had been asked with a fuller cultural realism, then the resulting view of Jesus could not have been limited to his one-to-one forgiving relationships, but would have had to englobe as well the social-institutional community-creating aspect of Jesus' ministry. The forgiveness of sins is not, for Jesus, a mere assuaging of personal guiltiness or of interpersonal estrangement; it is the sign of the new age and the presupposition of a new possibility of community.

could read the Jesus story with a stronger sense of the Jewishness of his context and with Amos ringing in our ears. The more we learn about the Jewishness of Jesus (from archeology and the new textual finds, as well as from growing respect for rabbinical studies on the part of Christian theologians), the more evident it becomes that he could not have been perceived by his contemporaries otherwise than as we here have portrayed him. In fact, to be fully honest we must turn the point around: the idea of Jesus as an individualist or a teacher of radical personalism could arise only in the (Protestant, post-Pietist, rationalist) context where it did; i.e. in a context which if not intentionally anti-Semitic, was at least sweepingly asemitic, stranger to the Jewish Jesus.

We could extend the list of traditional antinomies of which we must repent if we are to understand. Tradition tells us to choose between respect for persons and participation in the movement of history; Jesus refuses because the movement of history is personal. Between the absolute *agape* which lets itself be crucified, and effectiveness (which it is assumed will usually need to be violent), the resurrection forbids us to choose, for in the light of resurrection crucified agape is not folly (as it seems to the Hellenizers to be) and weakness (as the Judaizers believe) but the wisdom and power of God (I Cor. 1:22-25).

7

The Disciple of Christ
and the Way of Jesus

The question with which our study began was whether
Jesus' teaching or example can have been of such character as to provide the substance of guidance in social
ethics. We concluded, according to the Gospel accounts
and counter to the prior assumptions of many modern
interpreters, that his deeds show a coherent, conscious
social-political character and direction, and that his words
are inseparable therefrom.

But that is not yet the whole story. The traditional
axioms can be rephrased so as to place between Jesus and
the early church the gap that previously was posited
between Jesus and social ethics. Jesus, the reformulated
argument may now run, may after all have conceived his
ministry as a socially relevant messianity; and the Gospels
are honest enough not fully to have hidden this fact. But
still, it is possible to argue, early Christianity turned out
to be a far cry from the kingdom he had announced.
There must be a hiatus somewhere between the human
Jesus' proclaimed kingdom at Jerusalem and the worship
of the heavenly Christ in the Gentile churches of Greece
and Asia Minor.

The second phase of our study turns therefore to

several strands of the apostolic ethical tradition. The thesis we have just posited shall find its response not in detailed debate on its own terms (it is no longer being argued thus simply by New Testament scholars) but by independent induction from the texts. Looking one by one at several distinct themes of apostolic ethics, each for itself, we shall ask how each related to the Jesus to whom we have seen the Gospels testifying.

One very pervasive such theme, perhaps the most widespread, is the one we here may call "participation" or "correspondence," in which the believer's behavior or attitude is said to "correspond to" or reflect or "partake of" the same quality or nature as that of his lord. A more careful analysis than we can here undertake[1] would discern great varieties of shading and substance within this one theme, yet without any substantive contradiction.

In addition to numerous expressions where the concept of correspondence/participation appears with no fixed technical label, there are two distinguishable sets of firm images or verbal traditions visible in the traditions. One which we might call "discipleship" centers upon the noun "disciple" and the verb "follow after" or "learn." The image is spatial: the Israelites "following after" the pillar of cloud; a prophet or a rabbi or Jesus being followed around Palestine by his pupils.[2]

The other tradition might be called "imitation." Its

---

[1] The most thorough studies of the theme are Hans Dieter Betz, *Nachfolge und Nachahmung Jesu Christi im Neuen Testament* (Tübingen: Mohr, 1967) and Anselm Schulz, *Nachfolgen und Nachahmen* (Munich: Loesel, 1967). Both Schulz and Betz survey and digest a very wide field of detailed studies. An earlier exposition of the core concepts was Eduard Schweizer, *Lordship and Discipleship* (*SBT*, 28, 1960). A more systematic statement is that of E. J. Tinsley, *The Imitation of God in Christ* (Philadelphia: Westminster, 1960).

[2] Despite the identity of language, when Dietrich Bonhoeffer uses the term "discipleship" it carries a different shade of meaning. The accent falls less on sharing the Master's way or nature, and more on the unquestioning willingness to obey.

imagery is more structural or perhaps mystical; it affirms an inner or formal parallelism of character or intent beneath the similar behavior. Such a concept is found in many religions; it is present in the Old Testament despite its warnings against conceiving of God as comparable to man. The idea, not specifically Christian, that man somehow corresponds to or reflects the nature of God, or should seek to do so, was quite current in the Old Testament.[3] However we understand the statement that man was created "after the image of God," in any case it says at least this much: that in that which he is and that which he should do or become, man corresponds somehow to God's own being. This status of "image of God" is not questioned. The Old Testament neither preaches nor teaches it, but simply presupposes it universally.[4] The founding of the sabbath law in the reminder of God's resting after creation (Exod. 20) or through reference to how "humane" God was to free Israel from slavery (Deut. 5) is meaningful only if we presuppose some sort of correspondence between God and man. "Be holy, for I am holy" (Lev. 19:2) might initially have pointed more to the ritual than to a moral sanctity; nevertheless there begins with this text a tradition of "following God" which stretches through the prophets and through Judaism all the way to Martin Buber.[5] What in the Old Testament is a universally presupposed fundamental con-

---

[3] Walther Eichrodt in his *Theology of the Old Testament* (Philadelphia: Westminster, 1967), II, 373, characterizes as the basic theme of the Holiness code, "The forming of human nature after the pattern of the divine." Edmond Jacob in his *Theology of the Old Testament* (New York: Harper, 1958) designates the imitation of God as "the principle of the moral and spiritual life" (pp. 173ff). We cannot deal here with the numerous analogous concepts in nonbiblical faiths, or how they differ.

[4] Johann Jakob Stamm, *Die Gottebenbildlichkeit des Menschen im Alten Testament, ThSt,* 54 (1959).

[5] Martin Buber, "Nachahmung Gottes," in *Der Morgen,* I (1925), 368ff; cf. S. Schechter, *Aspects of Rabbinic Theology* (London, 1909; New York: Schocken, 1961), ch. 14, pp. 199ff.

cept becomes in the New Testament a new reality with the gift of the Holy Spirit. The two patterns of "discipleship" and "imitation" overlap sufficiently in substance that we properly treat them here together.[6]

I. The Disciple/Participant and the Love of God

A. Sharing the divine nature as the definition of Christian existence

> God is light, and in him there is no darkness at all. . . . If we walk in the light as he himself is in the light, then we share together a common life. . . . (I John 1:5-7)
> We were called God's children, and such we are. . . . What we shall be has not been disclosed, but we know that when it is disclosed we shall be like him, because we shall see him as he is. Everyone who has this hope before him purifies himself as he[7] is pure. (I John 3:1-3)
> The One who called you is holy: like him, be holy in all your behavior, because Scripture says, "You shall be holy, for I am holy. (I Pet. 1:15f, citing Lev. 19:2)
> Even in this world we are as he is. (I John 4:17)
> You have discarded the old nature with its deeds and have put on the new nature, which is being constantly renewed in the image of its Creator. . . . (Col. 3:9; cf. Eph. 4:24)[8]

B. Forgive as God has forgiven you

> Be generous to one another, tender-hearted, forgiving one another as God in Christ forgave you. (Eph. 4:32)

[6] Both Betz and Schulz, after having carefully disentangled the same two strands of thought and analyzed each independently, come to the conclusion that the substantial meaning of both is parallel. Edvin Larsson, *Christus als Vorbild,* pursues this theme by way of a very thorough study of the Pauline texts dealing with baptism and with the word *eikon* (image). He is driven to challenge the neat distinction between "following" and "imitation" which had long held sway in Lutheran theology.

[7] The context (cf. 2:23f) would suggest that "he" here points not only to the Father but also to the Son. NEB translates: " . . . as Christ is pure."

[8] The concept of transformation (*metamorphosis*) is one of the shadings of meaning which could be pursued further: II Cor. 3:18; Rom. 12:2; 8:24; Phil. 3:21; I Cor. 15:49. Still other expressions of the same concept are "image" (II Cor. 4:14; Col. 1:15) and "firstborn" (Col. 1:15, 18).

*Be forebearing with one another, and forgiving, where any
of you has cause for complaint: you must forgive as the
Lord forgave you.* (Col. 3:13 NEB)[9]

*Forgive us the wrong we have done, as we have forgiven
those who wronged us.* (Matt. 6:12; cf. Luke 11:4)

*For if you forgive others . . . your heavenly Father will also
forgive you; but if you do not forgive others then the
wrongs you have done will not be forgiven by your Father.*
(Matt. 6:14f)

*I remitted the whole of your debt when you appealed to
me; were you not bound to show your fellow servant the
same pity as I showed to you?* (Matt. 18:32f)

C. Love indiscriminately as God does

*If you love only those who love you, what credit is that to
you. . . ? But you must love your enemies, and do good and
lend without expecting return; . . . you will be sons of the
Most High, because he himself is kind to the ungrateful and
wicked. Be compassionate as your Father is compassionate.*
(Luke 6:32-36)

*Love your enemies and pray for your persecutors; only so
can you be children of your heavenly Father who makes his
sun rise on good and bad alike, and sends the rain on the
honest and dishonest. . . . You must therefore be all goodness, just as your heavenly Father is all good.* (Matt.
5:43-48 NEB)[10]

The AV rendering of verse 48: "be perfect as your
Father is perfect," has for years been made the key to the
whole Sermon on the Mount. Perfectionist preachers saw
there the promise of an accessible sinlessness; mainstream
ethicists turned it around as the proof that the sermon's
intent is not at all to be obeyed but to prepare men for
grace by crushing them under the demand of an unattainable Godlikeness.[11]

---

[9] The reference here to "the Lord" would in predominant Pauline usage
refer specifically to Jesus as the one who had forgiven. Thus to be as precise
as possible this usage could have been entered as well below under II.

[10] We need not enter the scholarly debate about which of these roughly
parallel texts more faithfully reflects the original words of Jesus. Both state
the same imperative and both root it in the Father/child resemblance.

[11] Cf. my fuller analysis of "The Political Axioms of the Sermon on the
Mount" in *The Original Revolution*, pp. 34ff.

Both extremes are wrong because they import a modern concept of "perfection" where it has no place. "All goodness" (NEB) does not make the point quite clear either. The parallel in Matthew 5:45 and in Luke makes it clear that "perfect" here means "indiscriminate" or "unconditional"—a quite conceivable, even attainable imperative. Modern (or Hellenistic or medieval) concepts of "perfection" as meaning that one has gone beyond finite limitations, as being flawless or living up perfectly to every demand of the law, or having a nature devoid of temptation or self-concern, are brought into this text by those who want to use it to prove a point of their own. All such side meanings distract from the simplicity of the gospel demand, which is no more (and no less) than that because God does not discriminate, his disciples are called upon likewise not to discriminate in choosing the objects of their love.

> Everyone who loves is a child of God and knows God. . . . The love I speak of is not our love for God, but the love he showed to us in sending his Son[12] as the remedy for the defilement of our sins. If God thus loved us . . . we in turn are bound to love one another. . . . God himself dwells in us if we love one another; his love is brought to perfection within us. (I John 4:7-12 NEB; emphasis mine)

II. The Disciple/Participant and the Life of Christ

A. Being in Christ as the definition of Christian existence

> Here is the test by which we can make sure that we are in him: whoever claims to be dwelling in him, binds himself to live as Christ himself lived. (1 John 2:6)

B. Having died with Christ and sharing his risen life

---

12 Cf. II/C below.

> *The man we once were has been crucified with Christ, for the destruction of the sinful self. . . . We shall also come to life with him. . . . In dying as he died, he died to sin . . . and in living as he lives, he lives to God. In the same way you must regard yourselves as dead to sin and alive to God, in union with Christ Jesus.* (Rom. 6:6-11 NEB)

> *If the Spirit of him who raised Jesus from the dead dwells within you, then the God who raised Jesus Christ from the dead will also give new life to your mortal bodies. . . .*(Rom. 8:11)

> *I have been crucified with Christ: the life I now live is not my life, but the life which Christ lives in me. . . .* (Gal. 2:20; cf. 5:24)

> *But that is not how you learned Christ.*[13] *For were you not told . . . that, leaving your former way of life, you must lay aside that old human nature which . . . is sinking toward death. You must be made new in mind and spirit, and put on the new humanity of God's creating.* (Eph. 4:20-24)

> *In your baptism you were buried with him, in baptizing also you were raised to life with him through your faith in the active power of God. . . . Did you not die with Christ and pass beyond the reach of the elemental spirits of the world . . . ? Were you not raised to life with Christ? Then aspire to the realm above. . . .*(Col. 2:12-3:1)

C. Loving as Christ loved, giving himself

> *I give you a new commandment: love one another. As I have loved you so you are to love one another.* (John 13:34)

> *This is my commandment: love one another as I have loved you. There is no greater love than this, that a man should lay down his life for his friends.* (John 15:12)

> *The message you have heard from the beginning is this: that we should love one another; unlike Cain, who was a child of the evil one and murdered his brother. . . . It is by that that we know what love is: that Christ laid down his life for us. And we in our turn are bound to lay down our lives for our brothers.* (I John 3:11-16; cf. 4:7-10 cited above)

---

[13] It is perhaps significant that the concept of "learning" is still present in the writings of Paul. This indicates that the "discipleship" terminology, i.e. the language of learning and following, still is vestigially present, continuing to overlap the imagery of transformation.

It is often mistakenly held that the key concept of Jesus' ethic is the "Golden Rule": "do to others as you would have them do to you." This is stated by Jesus, however, not as the sum of his own teaching but as the center of the law (Mark 12:28f; Matt. 22:40, citing Lev. 19:15).[14] But Jesus' own "fulfillment" of this thrust of the law, which thereby becomes through his own work a "new commandment" (John 12:34 cited above; 15:12; cf. I John 2:18), is different, "Do as I have done to you" or "do as the Father did in sending his Son."[15] It is striking how great is the mass of writings on religious ethics seeking to deal specifically with whether the teaching of Jesus is any different from that of the rabbis (or Confucius), which still fails to note this very evident structural change.

D. Serving others as he served

> *If I, your Lord and Master, have washed your feet, you also ought to wash one another's feet. . . . A servant is not greater than his master, nor a messenger than the one who sent him.* (John 13:1-17)
>
> *Those of us who have a robust conscience must accept as our own burden the tender scruples of weaker men, and not consider ourselves. Each of us must consider his neighbor . . . for Christ too did not consider himself. . . . In a word, accept one another as Christ accepted us.* (Rom. 15:1-7; emphasis mine)
>
> *His purpose in dying was that all men . . . should cease to live for themselves and should live for him who for their sake died and was raised to life.* (II Cor. 5:14ff)
>
> *Surely you should show yourselves equally lavish in this generous service. . . . For you know how generous our Lord Jesus Christ has been: he was rich, yet for our sake he became poor, that through his poverty you might become rich.* (II Cor. 8:7-9)[16]

14 That "love thy neighbor as thyself" is the heart of *the Law* is said as well in Matt. 19:19; Luke 10:27; Rom. 13:9; Gal. 5:14 and James 2:8.

15 T. W. Manson, *Ethics and Gospel* (London: SCM, 1960), pp. 60ff.

16 This is but one of the places where Phil. 2:1-11 might be cited. That Christ "became poor" is not unrelated to the actual economic practice of

> *Husbands, love your wives, as Christ also loved the church*
> *and gave himself up for it. . . . In the same way men also are*
> *bound to love their own wives.* (Eph. 5:25-28)

E. Subordination

This last citation, carrying Christ's model of servant-hood into the concreteness of family life, links us to another body of apostolic thought which is dealt with at greater length in a separate chapter (cf. below, pp. 163ff). All of the substance of that chapter could well have been digested here as well.

III. The Disciple/Participant and the Death of Christ

A. Suffering with Christ as the definition of apostolic existence[17]

> *All I care for is to know Christ, to experience the power of*
> *his resurrection, and to share his sufferings, in growing*
> *conformity with his death, if only I may arrive at the*
> *resurrection from the dead.* (Phil. 3:10f)
> *Wherever we go we carry death with us in our body, the*
> *death that Jesus died, that in this body also life may reveal*
> *itself, the life that Jesus lives . . . for continually . . . we are*
> *being surrendered into the hands of death, for Jesus' sake,*
> *so that the life of Christ may also be revealed in this mortal*
> *body of ours.* (II Cor. 4:10)[18]

Jesus among his disciples; yet the "he was rich" indicates a wider, even a cosmic reference, in the condescension of the Lord, parallel to the "form of God" or the "equality with God" of Phil. 2:6.

[17] Cf. Erhardt Güttgemanns, *Der Leidende Apostel und sein Herr* (Göttingen: Vandenhoeck & Ruprecht, 1966). A constant theme of Güttgemanns' work is what he calls "christological distance," i.e. the objectivity of the reference to the earthly Jesus, as over against tendencies (both in the early church and in modern scholarship) to redefine Christ in some more "contemporary" meaning, less dependent on just who the crucified Jesus was.

[18] Paul almost always uses "Christ" as a proper name; the usage here of the name Jesus standing alone is a significant pointer. Either Paul is echoing a distinct usage prior to his own adoption of the tradition, or his own free use of the name Jesus must be understood as placing special emphasis on the historical career of the Man of Nazareth, as contrasted to the more general functional title "Christ."

> *As we share abundantly in Christ's sufferings, so through*
> *Christ we share abundantly in comfort too.* (II Cor. 1:5)
> *It is my happiness to suffer for you. This is my way of*
> *helping to complete in my poor human flesh the full tale of*
> *Christ's afflictions,*[19] *still to be endured.* (Col. 1:24)[20]

Only the artifice of our classification separates the Apostle's self-interpretation from what he considers binding on other Christians. He is merely an exemplary follower of the true example.[21]

> *For my part, I always try to meet everyone halfway,*
> *regarding not*[22] *my own good but the good of many. . . .*
> *Follow my example, as I follow Christ's.* (I Cor. 10:33f)
> *You, in your turn, followed the example set by us and by*
> *the Lord; the welcome you gave the message meant grave*
> *suffering for you, yet you rejoiced in the Holy Spirit.* (I
> Thess. 1:6)

B. Sharing in divine condescension

> *Rivalry and personal vanity should have no place among*
> *you, but you should humbly reckon others better than*
> *yourselves. . . . Let your bearing toward one another rise*

---

[19] It should be noted that Paul does not distinguish between the sufferings of Christ and those of the apostles; it is the suffering of Christ, namely in his body the church, that the Apostle bears.

[20] Literally: "what is lacking in the sufferings of Christ."

[21] Cf. again Güttgemanns, *op. cit.* One of the omissions of this outline is the thought of Jesus about his own suffering; we have picked up from the Gospel accounts only Jesus' words about the disciples' cross. In view however of the intimate linkage which Paul here affirms, careful analysis should also move farther back. Eduard Lohse, *Maertyrer und Gottesknecht* (Göttingen: Vandenhoeck & Ruprecht, 2nd ed. 1963), and Nils Dahl, *Volk Gottes,* p. 251, suggest that the fusion of the images of the Suffering Servant as community and as messianic figure would not have been possible in the standard Jewish exegesis of Isa. 53, and must have been Jesus' own creative reinterpretation. Paul also speaks of himself as example in I Cor. 4:16; Phil. 3:17; II Thess. 3:7ff; and Heb. 6:12 speaks as well of other human models. Victor Paul Furnish, *Theology and Ethics in Paul* (Nashville: Abingdon, 1968), pp. 218ff, discusses especially those passages where the imitation of the Apostle illuminates the imitation of Christ.

[22] The "regarding" is parallel to the "considering" which was underlined in II/D.

> *out of your life in Christ. For the divine nature was his*
> *from the first; yet he . . . made himself nothing, assuming*
> *the nature of a slave. . . . (Phil. 2:3-14)*

This passage, by widespread scholarly consensus,[23] is built around a pre-Pauline hymn of praise to the condescension of the divine Son. The initial humiliation praised in the hymn was not that of the cross but of abandoning the prerogatives of "the divine nature."[24] Yet in Paul's application the image takes on new dimensions.[25] The reference to humiliation becomes not simply "human form" but "the form of a servant," and this even to the extremity of death on a cross.[26] By its insertion in the larger context of the exhortation addressed to the Philippians, this already doubled meaning of humiliation/exaltation takes on yet a third level of meaning: the self-denial which fosters the unity of the church.

Donald G. Dawe[27] interprets the Philippians hymn at

[23] Archibald M. Hunter, *Paul and His Predecessors* (Philadelphia: Westminster, 1961), p. 36; R. P. Martin, *Carmen Christi* (Cambridge U. P., 1967).

[24] The thought of "seizing equality with God" may be in contrast to the example of Lucifer or of Adam. In the very earliest stages of christological thinking the concept of "grasping equality with God" might not have presupposed the preexistence of the Son; cf. above II/D n. 14. It may originally have referred to his renunciation of Zealot kingship.

[25] Betz, *op. cit.*, says the imitation imagery is "ethicized" in Paul's application of it to the problem at Philippi. Protestant interpretation has generally sought to ward off the idea that "having the mind of Christ" would be in any way a reflection of the human posture of Jesus. Protestant interpreters have generally preferred more complicated concepts like "having the kind of attitude which befits one who is in Christ," so as to undermine any possibility of moralism. As Schulz points out, however, the simpler conception of imitation is dictated by the context.

[26] The Phillips translation is not literal, but renders well the sense of offense or scandal that belongs here, with the paraphrase, "the death of a common criminal." It is widely supposed, following Lohmeyer, that this phrase "even the death on the cross" was an insertion by Paul in the extant hymn text. The reader acquainted with the original hymn would have been more struck by the insertion than we are.

[27] *The Form of a Servant* (Philadelphia: Westminster, 1968).

some length, but his understanding of the "kenotic motif" is focused upon the metaphysics of incarnation and how this can be updated. Neither the possibility that Jesus' renouncing the seizure of Sonship might also have meant concretely his decision in the desert, nor the possibility that the call to unity of Philippians 2:1-4 might throw light back upon the motive of the example being appealed to, is dealt with.

C. Give your life as he did

> *As God's dear children, try to be like him, and live in love as Christ loved you, and gave himself up on your behalf. . . .* (Eph. 5:1f; cf. I John 3:16, cited above II/C)

D. Suffering servanthood in place of dominion[28]

> *In the world the recognized rulers lord it over their subjects, and their great men make them feel the weight of authority. That is not the way with you; among you, whoever wants to be great must be your servant. . . . For even the Son of Man did not come to be served but to serve, and to surrender his life as a ransom for many.* (Mark 10:42-45; Matt. 20:25-28)

In the accounts of Matthew and Mark this word was provoked when, just after Jesus' most detailed prediction of his coming passion, two of his disciples (or their mother) expressed their desire for a place of privilege in his kingdom. Luke records an almost identical statement in the midst of the Last Supper conversations, thus making it in effect a parallel to John 13:1-13 (cited above II/C). The content differs in two details in Luke's report. Luke adds (22:25), "those in authority are called 'benefactors' "—a recognition, perhaps ironic, of government's claim to moral accreditation. The imperative is founded not in the Son of Man's imminent sacrifice of his life (as

---

[28] This section is very similar to II/D. It differs in that: (a) the specific alternative to servanthood, namely lordship, is looked at, and rejected; and (b) the servanthood goes all the way to death.

in Mark and Matthew) but in Jesus' present posture: "Here I am among you as a servant" (22:27).[29]

Only at two points, here and in III/F, do we include materials from the Synoptic Gospels as testimony to the mind of the apostolic church. Both words are somewhat independent of any particular point in the Gospel narrative and are spoken to the continuing career of the church beyond Pentecost. It is thus not improper to draw them into our summary on the thought of the church.

E. Accept innocent suffering without complaint as he did

> When you have behaved well and suffer for it, your fortitude is a fine thing in the sight of God. To that you were called, because Christ suffered on your behalf, and thereby left you an example. It is for you to follow in his steps. (I Pet. 2:20f NEB)
> It is better to suffer in well-doing ... than for doing wrong. For Christ also died for our sins. ... He, the just, suffered for the unjust. ... (3:14-18)
> Do not be bewildered by the fiery ordeal that is upon you. ... It gives you a share in Christ's sufferings, and that is cause for joy. (4:12-16)

F. Suffer with or like Christ the hostility of the world, as bearers of the kingdom cause.

> No one who does not carry his cross and come with me can be a disciple of mine. (Luke 14:27-33)

Luke's statement of the call to the cross is preceded by the call to forsake family loyalties and is followed by

---

[29] Although the several Gospel accounts vary in the way they place this text, all of them relate it to the mandate Jesus is giving to his church. Most commentators fail to note the anti-Zealot and anti-Roman thrust of the text. Jesus is not simply telling his disciples to be servants. He is pointedly contrasting this command with any way of being "lord" which his listeners are assumed to have in mind. The contrast is meaningful only if the desire for lordship is assumed to be real, as it was in the request of James and John to which he is responding.

the warning against making a commitment to Jesus' cause
without counting the cost. In Matthew (10:37ff) the
setting is the sending of the twelve. In Mark (8:34ff; also
10:39f) it follows Peter's confession "You are the Messiah" and the first prediction of the passion. Each setting
makes it a foundational statement. Each is in a wider
context emphasizing the social suffering of rejection by
one's family. It points not to a special elite moral vocation for Jesus or for a spiritual elite, but to a condition
for salvation. This is one of the places where the "Disci-
ple/follow" and the "Imitate/partake" language com-
plexes overlap. To follow after Christ is not simply to
learn from him, but also to share his destiny.

> *"A servant is not greater than his master." As they perse-
> cuted me, they will persecute you.* (John 15:20f)
> *Persecution will come to all who want to live a godly life as
> Christians.* (II Tim. 3:12)
> *You have been granted the privilege not only of believing in
> Christ but of suffering for him.* (Phil. 1:29)
> *You share in Christ's sufferings, and that is cause for joy.* (I
> Pet. 4:13)

Christian thought is accustomed to conceiving of "persecution" as a ritual or "religious" matter independent of
any immediate ethical import. Christians are made to
suffer because they worship the true God; what has this
to do with our study's concern with an attitude to
government, to violence, war, conflict? Is not being persecuted for the faith quite independent of social ethics?

Such a dichotomy between the religious and the social
must be imported into the texts; it cannot be found
there. The "cross" of Jesus was a political punishment;
and when Christians are made to suffer by government it
is usually because of the practical import of their faith,
and the doubt they cast upon the rulers' claim to be
"Benefactor."

We cannot quote in full the text of Hebrews
11:1-12:5, which forms a coherent series of examples or

"witnesses" of fidelity, from Abel through to the prophets. "Faith" or "fidelity" in each case meant the readiness to obey amidst suffering, trusting God for a not yet discernible vindication.[30] The culmination of this series ("Pioneer and Perfecter," or "Author and Finisher") is Jesus, "who for the sake of the joy that lay ahead of him endured the cross" and whose disciples should be ready to resist to the point of shedding their blood (12:2-4).

G. Death is liberation from the power of sin

> Since therefore Christ suffered in the flesh, arm yourself with the same thought, for whoever has suffered in the flesh has ceased from sin. . . . (I Pet. 4:1f; cf. II/B above)
> Those who belong to Christ Jesus have crucified the flesh with its passions and desires. (Gal. 5:24)

H. Death is the fate of the prophets; Jesus, whom we follow, was already following them

> Matt. 23:24; Mark 12:1-9; Luke 24:20; Acts 2:36; 4:10; 7:52; 23:24; I Thess. 2:15ff.

I. Death is victory

> On the cross he discarded the cosmic power and authorities like a garment; he made a public spectacle of them and led them in his triumphal procession. (Col. 2:15)[31]
> Jews call for miracles, Greeks look for wisdom; but we proclaim Christ—yes, Christ nailed to the cross; and though this is a stumbling block to Jews and folly to Greeks, yet to those who have heard this call, Jews and Greeks alike, he is the power of God and the wisdom of God. (I Cor. 1:22-24)

[30] When the author defines "faith" as assurance of the hoped-for and conviction of the unseen, the "hoped-for" and "unseen" realities are not some otherwise unknown truth, proposition, or prediction but the concrete vindication of obedience. "Faith" is obeying when it is not "visible" that it "pays" or "works."

[31] The imagery of the triumphant procession may be interpreted as placing the Christians either in the position of captives (God's former enemies) or of soldiers.

> *This is the hour of victory for our God, the hour of his sovereignty and power, when his Christ comes to his rightful rule. . . . By the sacrifice of the Lamb they have conquered him . . . for they did not hold their lives too dear to lay them down.* (Rev. 12:10f; cf. 5:9ff)
> *They* [ten kings] *will wage war upon the Lamb, but the Lamb will defeat them . . . and his victory will be shared by his followers. . . .*(17:14)

Summing Up

What can be said of the total impact of this great bulk of textual evidence? Our pigeonholes are not neat. The subcategories used here do not separate really distinct thoughts; they rather spread out before us a rich variety of shadings and emphases within one pervasive thought pattern. In some expressions the reference to the earthly ministry, especially the death of Jesus, is definite; in others the "descending and ascending" Christ is portrayed in less concrete, more Hellenistic images. In some the element of suffering is not spoken of, in some it is focused upon the cost of ministering to one's brethren, but more often it centers upon the renunciation of Lordship, the abandonment of earthly security, the threat which the Suffering Servant poses to the powers of this world, and the antagonism of the world's response. Thus the Epistles repeat the Gospel narratives' center points of Mark 8:34 ("let him take up his cross and follow me") and 10:42 ("but let it not be so among you").

As long as readers could stay unaware of the political/ social dimension of Jesus' ministry (which most of Christendom seems to have done quite successfully), then it was also possible to perceive the "in Christ" language of the Epistles as mystical or the "dying with Christ" as psychologically morbid. But if we may posit—as after the preceding pages we must—that the apostles had and taught at least a core memory of their Lord's earthly ministry in its blunt historicity, then this centering of the apostolic ethic upon the disciple's cross evidences a sub-

stantial, binding, costly social stance. There have perhaps
been times when the issues of power, violence, and peo-
plehood were not at the center of ethical preoccupations;
but in the waning twentieth century they certainly are,
and the rediscovery of this ethic of "responsibility" or of
"power" can no longer at the same time claim to be
Christian and bypass the judgment or the promise of the
Suffering Servant's exemplarity.

Yet this affirmation encloses some serious negatives.
Seldom has the exemplary quality of Jesus' social humanity been perceived as a model for our social ethics; [32]
yet the large body of New Testament traditions represented by the texts we have analyzed has not gone
unnoticed. It has been perceived, but interpreted differently. To these other interpretations we must now
turn. [33]

[32] Carl F. H. Henry, in a chapter "Jesus as the Ideal of Christian Ethics,"
in *Christian Personal Ethics* (Grand Rapids: Eerdmans, 1957), pp. 398ff,
gathers a wealth of material to reaffirm an orthodox loyalty to the exemplarity of Jesus. Yet the description of Jesus is strikingly selective. It centers
upon motivational virtues (unselfishness, compassion, resisting temptation,
meekness, obedience) rather than on ethical specifics. There is no reference
to the specific temptation of the Zealot option, and it is expressly denied
that Jesus' poverty or celibacy might have any exemplary value (p. 411).
Henry's later *Aspects of Christian Social Ethics* (Eerdmans, 1964) makes no
use of this theme. Henry thus represents faithfully the tradition that has
been able to appropriate much of the New Testament idiom without catch-
ing its central historical thrust.

[33] In his article, "Von der Imitatio Dei zur Nachfolge Christi" (*Aus
Frühchristlicher Zeit* [Tübingen, 1950], pp. 286ff), Hans Joachim Schoeps
supports this chapter's understanding of the meaning of discipleship with an
analysis of the term's backgrounds. He emphasizes that Jesus' call to "follow
me" (Mark 2:14) is a messianic claim; that the invitation to discipleship is
founded in Jesus' own claim to be following the Father. Although John's
Gospel states this identity with the Father in Greek substantial terms, and
although the Apostle Paul chooses another set of terminology, that of
mimesis, they are still all basically within this Jewish framework. Schoeps is
concerned to point out that later interpretation of the imitation of Christ
took on quite foreign meanings. It could focus upon an ecstatic experience
(stigmatization); upon a symbolic repetition of details of the earthly life of
Jesus (barefoot itinerancy); or it can claim to partake of the deification of
mankind of which the incarnation is the beginning. It is characteristic of all
these deviations that they move away from the realm of personal and social
conflict within which Jesus originally gave the phrase its meaning.

The "Cross" in Protestant Pastoral Care

One universal demand which the church as an agency of counsel and consolation must meet is the need of men and women of all ages for help in facing suffering: illness and accidents, loneliness and defeat. What more fitting resource could there be than the biblical language which makes suffering bearable, meaningful within God's purposes, even meritorious in that "bearing one's cross" is a synonym for discipleship? Hosts of sincere people in hospitals or in conflict-ridden situations have been helped by this thought to bear the strain of their destiny with a sense of divine presence and purpose.

Yet our respect for the quality of these lives and the validity of this pastoral concern must not blind us to the abuse of language and misuse of Scripture they entail. The cross of Christ was not an inexplicable or chance event, which happened to strike him, like illness or accident. To accept the cross as his destiny, to move toward it and even to provoke it, when he could well have done otherwise, was Jesus' constantly reiterated free choice; and he warns his disciples lest their embarking on the same path be less conscious of its costs (Luke 14:25-33). The cross of Calvary was not a difficult family situation, not a frustration of visions of personal fulfillment, a crushing debt or a nagging in-law; it was the political, legally to be expected result of a moral clash with the powers ruling his society. Already the early Christians had to be warned against claiming merit for any and all suffering; only if their suffering be innocent, and a result of the evil will of their adversaries, may it be understood as meaningful before God (I Pet. 2:18-21; 3:14-18; 4:1, 13-16; 5:9; James 4:10).

Another transposition makes the cross an inward experience of the self. This is found in Thomas Müntzer, in Zinzendorf, in revivalism, and in Christian existentialism. An excellent modern statement is that by Carl Michalson,

"How Our Lives Carry Christ's Death and Manifest His Resurrection."[34]

The other direction in which "cross" language can evolve is that of subjective brokenness, the renunciation of pride and self-will. Bonhoeffer's *Life Together* [35] speaks of "breaking through to the cross" as occurring in confession. "In confession we affirm and accept our cross." Our sharing in Christ's death, he continues, is the "shameful death of the sinner in confession." A similar thrust is typical of the Keswick family of renewal movements in Anglo-Saxon Protestantism. We may agree that the humility of confession may be quite desirable for mental health, for group processes, and for the creation of community; but this should not keep us from realizing that "cross" is not the word for it in the New Testament.

Kierkegaard is another thinker who makes incisive use of the "cross" and "imitation" motifs; I am less sure than my friend Vernard Eller[36] that this includes the concreteness of enablement for discipleship.

Imitation and Renunciation

A long history of interpretation and application which we might designate as "mendicant" has centered its attention upon the outward form of Jesus' life; his forsaking domicile and property, his celibacy or his barefoot itinerancy. Again, without disrespect for the nobility of the monastic tradition and its needed critique of comfortable religion, we must be aware that it centers the renunciation at another point than the New Testament. Both the few who seek thus to follow Jesus in a formal mimicking

---

[34] *Encounter* (organ of Christian Theological Seminary, Indianapolis), 20/4 (Autumn 1959), 410ff.

[35] New York: Harper, 1954, p. 113.

[36] *Kierkegaard and Radical Discipleship* (Princeton U. P., 1968), especially the chapter "Christ as Savior and Pattern."

of his life style and the many who use this distortion to
argue Jesus' irrelevance, have failed to note a striking gap
in the New Testament material we have read. As we
noted before more briefly: there is no *general* concept of
living like Jesus. According to universal tradition, Jesus
was not married; yet when the Apostle Paul, advocate *par
excellence* of the life "in Christ," argues at length for
celibacy or for a widow's not remarrying (I Cor. 7), it
never occurs to him to appeal to Jesus' example, even as
one of many arguments. Jesus is thought in his earlier life
to have worked as a carpenter; yet never, even when he
explains at length why he earns his own way as an artisan
(I Cor. 9), does it come to Paul's mind that he is imitating
Jesus. Jesus' association with villagers, his drawing his
illustrations from the life of the peasants and the fishermen, his leading his disciples to desert places and moun-
taintops, have often been appealed to as examples by the
advocates of rural life and church camping; but not in the
New Testament. His formation of a small circle of disciples whom he taught through months of close contact has
been claimed as a model pastoral method; his teaching in
parables has been made a model of graphic communication; there have been efforts to imitate his prayer life or
his forty days in the desert: but not in the New Testament.

There is thus but one realm in which the concept of
imitation holds—but there it holds in every strand of the
New Testament literature and all the more strikingly by
virtue of the absence of parallels in other realms: this is at
the point of the concrete social meaning of the cross in
its relation to enmity and power. Servanthood replaces
dominion, forgiveness absorbs hostility. Thus—and only
thus—are we bound by New Testament thought to "be
like Jesus."

8

Christ and Power

One of the strands in the argument against the normative claims by or for Jesus has always been that his radical personalism is not relevant to problems of power and structure. Sometimes this ground for rejection has been covered over by more evident arguments such as the "interim" theme, that the ethic of Jesus is disqualified because he expected history not to continue very long, or by the "clenetic" theme, that the high demands of the ethic of Jesus are meant not to be obeyed but to bring man to sorrow for his sin; but often this broader negation on the grounds of personalism shows through as well in the argument. In line with the personal appeal which has been so central in Protestant faith since Luther, even more since Pietism, and especially since the merging of Protestant existentialism with modern secular personalism—and even more especially since Freud and Jung imposed upon everyone in our culture the vision of man as a self-centered reacting organism—it has seemed quite evident that the primary message of Jesus was a call most properly perceived by an individual, asking the hearer for something that can be done most genuinely by an individual standing alone. Whether this something that he can do standing alone be a rare heroic ethical performance like loving one's enemies, or a response more accessible to the

135

common man, like sorrow for his sins, it is a response
each individual can make only for himself. It has nothing
to do with the structures of society.[1]

When then in the fourth century Christians found
themselves in positions of social responsibility, so the
argument continues, they had to go for their ethical
insight to other sources than Jesus. This should not
surprise us. This happened not only because the writers
and readers of the New Testament were culturally naive
people without much conception of social institutions

[1] One of the classic modern expressions of this understanding is that of
Rudolf Bultmann: "unlike the prophets' preaching, His preaching is directed
not primarily to the people as a whole, but to individuals. . . . Thus Jesus in
His thought of God—and of man in the light of this thought—'dehistoricized'
God and man." *Theology of the New Testament* (New York: Scribner,
1951), p. 25. Bultmann goes on to say that Jesus "released the relation
between God and man from its previous ties to history."

The assumption that biblical language is not immediately socially relevant
is by no means made only by those who do not care about social issues. Also
among those who are quite committed to "relevance," the assumption can
still be made that this is not a properly biblical concern but must be
approached somehow indirectly through the generalities of a philosophy of
history or a concept of Christian vocation. In the editorial preface to a
collection of "biblical passages on power and its use," a part of the special
number of the *Student World* on the Problem of Power (57 [1964]), the
unnamed editor commented (p. 169): "Our subject is part of a contemporary discussion, and is therefore brought to the Bible rather than lifted from
it. . . . The opposite is true of dogmatic questions, which come to us from
the records of God's revelation; we would not ask them if it were not for the
Biblical text."

I would suggest, if I may, that what have traditionally been thought of as
"dogmatic questions" are more foreign to the import of the original texts in
many cases than is the problem of power. We have the record of Jesus'
dealing explicitly with whether he should be king or whether we should love
our enemies, with what we should do with wealth; only very indirectly can
we get from his teachings any help on the metaphysics of incarnation.

A very representative more recent statement of this same view is the
contribution of Roger Mehl, "The Basis of Christian Social Ethics," in
Bennett, ed. *Christian Social Ethics in a Changing World.* Mehl's purpose is to
lay the base for an understanding of social ethics, but he does it by setting
the New Testament's concern uniquely on a personal level so that the
problematic of social ethics is how to get there from Jesus. A major part of
the answer will be trying to apply individual categories ("personalization,"
"responsibility") to social structures.

and power, although this was also the case and reinforces
this consideration. It occurred not only because Christians in the first century were so few in number and so
unimportant in terms of social class that they could very
well live their lives without paying attention to such
issues, although this as well was true and likewise had a
reinforcing effect. The real reason we should not be
surprised that the church at the age of Constantine had to
resort to other models for the construction of a social
ethic in Christendom was that, quite simply and logically,
Jesus had nothing much to say on the subject. And if,
perchance, Jesus might be said to have spoken in this
area, due to vestiges of the prophetic tradition which he
took up only to transmute them into something more
existential, then at least it is clear that by the time of the
Pauline churches any such dimension was lost.

We have already spoken to the *substance* of this portrayal, by reading again the Gospel story. There we have
found a view of Jesus that refutes the whole line of
argument. Yet we have not spoken as precisely to its
form, by asking whether one actually does find in the
biblical literature some equivalents of the concepts of
"power" or "structure," in the sense in which these terms
are used by modern thinkers in the social and political
sciences. Does not the preoccupation with the transcen-
dent and with the soul, with justification, revelation, and
reconciliation, center our attention so powerfully upon
the inner structures of the unique, the individual, that no
bridge is possible to that other realm?

Even though the interdisciplinary agenda has not been
able to make much of it, it happens to be the case that
biblical scholarship in the last generation has come to a
rather striking degree of clarity at this point. A body of
exegetical literature has been building up, slim in quantity but impressive in the consistency with which several
different readers come to basically similar results. Stated
most systematically and concisely by Hendrik Berkhof

and G. B. Caird, supported in detailed studies or incidentally by G. H. C. MacGregor and Markus Barth, this
renewed understanding has the sympathy of a whole
generation of scholars working in the mood of "biblical
realism," but its idiom is not yet understood across the
borders of the disciplines. The effort of this chapter must
therefore be devoted not to explicating the Pauline doctrine of the powers—for this exposition is by now widely
understood and accepted by scholars in the field—but to
illuminating the way in which this doctrine meshes with
modern understandings and questions.

The Clarity and Ambiguity of the Language of Power

It is quite evident in contemporary conversation that
one can very well agree on the nature or location of a
problem without being sure just how to "get hold of" it.
When in modern social analysis such terms as "power"
and "structure" are used, everyone knows just about
what is meant; but still a logician would have little
trouble in demonstrating that not everyone means exactly all the same things and nothing else. Sometimes the
term "power" is clearly distinguished from "authority,"
including in the latter term a special reference to some
kind of legitimacy or validation of the exercise of power;
other times the two are merged. Sometimes "power" is
distinguished from "force" as being somehow more
general or more justified or less overt; again they are
sometimes identified. The concern for precision and the
concern to observe generalities and commonalities constantly cross over and overlap, with the linkages being
different from every school of thought and every language.

Something of the same stimulating confusion is present in the thought of the Apostle Paul as he applies some
of the same thought patterns to different challenges in
different contexts. He speaks of "principalities and

power," and of "thrones and dominions," thus using
language of political color. But he can also use cosmological language like "angels and archangels," "elements,"
"heights and depths." Or the language can be religious:
"law," "knowledge." Sometimes the reader perceives a
parallelism in all these concepts, sometimes not.[2]

The most fruitful illustration of the complexity of this
language for the modern reader would probably be a
meditation on the variety of meanings of the word
"structure" as it is currently widely used in American
English. Sometimes it refers to a particular network of
persons and agencies able to make decisions or exert
pressure, as in the phrase "power structure." When this
term is used it may refer to a group of persons who are
known or can be found. A civil rights worker may, for
example, use the phrase to refer to the editor of the local
newspaper, the banker, the sheriff, the chairman of the
school board, and the owner of the largest department
store in a Southern town. Other times the "power structure" is not so visible but one is no less sure that it is
there, as when Marxists speak of "Wall Street" to sym-
bolize a phenomenon that is no less real for being difficult to localize with exactitude.

Yet other times, "structure" is present only in the
mind of the one analyzing it. When a psychologist speaks
of the "structure of the personality" or the "structure of

---

[2] Berkhof (*Christ and the Powers* [Scottdale: Herald, 1962]) suggests
that probably for Paul each of these several terms had its own very precise
and technical meaning; that they are not simply synonyms standing parallel.
Still the best we can do today is to come to some understanding about the
general trend of meaning which the total body of thought has for us. We
may quite agree with Berkhof that Paul probably had such a very precise
understanding in mind; but it could be well pointed out that it would hardly
matter if he had not. A contemporary sociologist or psychologist can very
well use such phrases as "power" or "structure" in different ways when
dealing with different audiences or different topics and yet be no less clear
or systematic in dealing with his thought. To use several terms with roughly
synonymous meaning or to use one term with different meanings and
different contexts is not necessarily a sign of unclear thinking.

a response," he does not mean to point our attention most precisely to a certain set of nerve endings and connections; he perceives rather a pattern in reactions and perceptions which has its character as "structure" quite independently of our knowledge of the actual chemistry and electro-mechanics of the nerve network. Yet again, for the architect, "structure" means the physical artifact. The structure of a language is its grammar and syntax and logic, the way words function following unwritten laws located somewhere in the common mental process of the race.

In all of these many ways and more we could add, the concept "structure" functions to point to the patterns or regularities that transcend or precede or condition the individual phenomena we can immediately perceive. The bridge is more than the cables and girders that compose it; the psychic "complex" or "syndrome" is much more than the thoughts and reflexes it organizes; the "class" is much more than the individual persons who make it up; a "religion" is much more than a bagful of assorted practices. It is this patternedness that the word "structure" tries to enable us to perceive within all the varieties of its appearance. Similarly, "power" points in all its modulations to some kind of capacity to make things happen.

We have already identified a body of vocabulary, especially in the thought of the Apostle Paul, that deals with power and structure. What does he say with this vocabulary? And are the things he says translatable into the concepts of modern social science?

Christ and the Powers in Contemporary Theology

One of the significant advances of theological understanding in the last generation has been the juxtaposition of a gap in theological ethics with a puzzle in New Testament interpretation. Since the onset of critical New Testament studies it has practically been taken for granted that when the Apostle speaks about angels or demons

or powers this is a dispensable remainder of an antique
world view, needing not even to be interpreted or translated, but simply to be dropped without discussion. And
on the other hand, as we have just observed, under the
shadow of Protestant individualism it was assumed that
the Apostle did not deal with structural problems. What
we now behold is that the unmanageable imagery has the
same shape as the missing piece in the ethical puzzle.
Driven by the events that shook Europe between 1930
and 1950, Protestant theology sought a more adequate
theological understanding of the power of evil which had
been seen breaking through the crust of the most civilized
of societies. No longer can it be taken for granted that
man and his institutions can solve his problems. Theologians began anew to ask what their faith in Jesus Christ
could say to a society in disarray.

At the same time the techniques of contemporary
erudition had given to theologians a greater capacity to
conceive the meaning of scriptural thought within its own
original cultural context, a capacity for cultural empathy
probably greater than has obtained at any time since the
end of the Apostolic Age. So we became able to take up
more successfully the task of understanding those New
Testament passages which hitherto had been the least
"interesting." Instead of asking what those texts mean in
the modern world, scholars learned to ask first, more
carefully, what the writer, speaking to his own age in its
own language, was seeking to say *then,* by his use of
concepts not immediately understandable to us. This new
question and the new technique for putting such a question to the biblical text coincided in such a way as to fit
the Pauline answer into the ethical puzzle. The part of
the gospel world view which we had been unable to read
was found to speak precisely to those questions which we
had earlier been taught the gospel did not speak to.[3]

---

[3] The positive emphasis of this present discussion on the relevance of the
Apostle's powers language to the institutions and ideologies of our times

The present portrayal of this teaching leans gratefully and heavily on the way Paul is interpreted by Hendrik Berkhof, one of the creative thinkers responsible for this analysis. His statement is, however, only the most transparent and accessible of several whose major thrusts are mutually reinforcing.[4]

The Origin of the Powers in the Creative Purpose of God

> He is the image of the invisible God, the firstborn of all creation. For in him were created all things, those in heaven and those on earth, visible and invisible; whether thrones or dominions or principalities or powers; all was created through him and by him. And he is before all things, and all things subsist in him. (Col. 1:15-17)

need not imply the rejection of all the more literal meanings which the language of the demonic and of bondage can also have (occultism, astrology, possession, exorcism). That these two areas or two kinds of definitions of "the demonic" are quite distinct from one another would probably have been much less evident to Paul than it seems to be to some moderns.

[4] H. Berkhof, op. cit. Next to the Berkhof text, which we are here reflecting extensively, the most helpful other studies, all of them substantially parallel in their interpretation, are the following: G. B. Caird, Principalities and Powers (Oxford: Clarendon, 1956); G. H. C. MacGregor, "Principalities and Powers: the Cosmic Background of Paul's Thought," NTS, 1 (1954), 17-28; also in H. McArthur, ed., New Testament Sidelights (Hartford, 1960), p. 101; E. Gordon Rupp, Principalities and Powers: Studies in the Christian Conflict in History (London: Epworth, 1952); W. A. Visser 't Hooft, The Kingship of Christ (New York: Harper, 1948), pp. 136ff; D. E. H. Whitely, The Theology of Saint Paul (Oxford: Blackwell, 1964), ch. 2, pp. 18-30; Amos N. Wilder, Kerygma, Eschatology and Social Ethics (Philadelphia: Fortress, 1966).

Supportive comments are provided also by: James S. Stewart, "On a Neglected Emphasis in New Testament Theology," SJT, 4 (1951), 292; and Anders Nygren, "Christ and the Forces of Destruction," ibid., p. 366. The related studies of Clinton Morrison and Heinrich Schlier deal less directly with the possibility of contemporary "translations" of the Pauline concepts. Cf. n. 5 for an ethics text in the Pauline idiom. Graydon F. Snyder (op. cit., pp. 8f) suggests that the use of the "powers" language to describe the origin and the defeat of evil is rooted in what he calls the "watcher myth." Markus Barth surveys recent scholarship concerning the Powers in his Acquittal by Resurrection (New York: Holt, 1964), p. 159 n. 21.

The word translated "subsist" in verse 17 has the same root as the modern word "system." The Apostle Paul says that this is the share of Christ (John would have spoken of the preexisting Word) in creation; namely, in him everything "systematizes," everything holds together. This "everything" that Christ maintains united is the world powers. It is the reign of order among creatures, order which in its original intention is a divine gift.

Most of the references to the "Powers" in the New Testament consider them as fallen. It is important therefore to begin with the reminder that they were part of the good creation of God. Society and history, even nature, would be impossible without regularity, system, order—and this need God provided for. The universe is not sustained arbitrarily, immediately, and erratically by an unbroken succession of new divine interventions. It was made in an ordered form and "it was good." The creative power worked in a mediated form, by means of the Powers that regularized all visible reality.

The Fallen Powers in the Providence of God

Unfortunately, however, we have no access to the good creation of God. Man and his world are fallen, and in this the powers have their own share. They are no longer active only as mediators of the saving creative purpose of God; now we find them seeking to separate us from the love of God (Rom. 8:38); we find them ruling over the lives of those who live far from the love of God (Eph. 2:2); we find them holding man in servitude to their rules (Col. 2:20); we find them holding men subject under their tutelage (Gal. 4:3). These structures which were supposed to be our servants have become our masters and our guardians.

Yet even in this fallen and rebellious state the working of the Powers is not simply something limitlessly evil. The Powers, despite their fallenness, continue to exercise an ordering function. Even tyranny (which according to Rom. 13:1 is to be counted among the powers) is still better than chaos and we should be subject to it. The law (which according to Gal. 4:5 prevents us from attaining to filial maturity) is nevertheless righteous and good and we should obey it. Even the pagan and primitive forms of social and religious expression, although obviously unworthy of being imitated, remain a sign of the preserving patience of God toward a world that has not yet heard of its redemption (Acts 17:22-28). Thus, before moving on to declare the impact of the work of Christ, Paul has made three fundamental declarations, in the language of his time, concerning the structures of creaturely existence:

(a) These structures were created by God. It is the divine purpose that within human existence there should be a network of norms and regularities to stretch out the canvas upon which the tableau of life can be painted.

(b) These powers have rebelled and are fallen. They did not accept the modesty that would have permitted them to remain conformed to the creative purpose, but rather they claimed for themselves an absolute value. They thereby enslaved man and his history. Man is bound to them; "slavery" is in fact one of the fundamental terms used in the New Testament to describe the lost condition of man outside of Christ. To what is man subject? Precisely to those values and structures which are necessary to life and society, but which have claimed the status of idols and have succeeded in making men serve them as if they were of absolute value.

(c) Despite their fallen condition the Powers cannot fully escape the providential sovereignty of God. He is still able to use them for good.

Before continuing the analysis of "values" and of "structures," let us follow Berkhof in suggesting some concrete modern phenomena which he considers to be structurally analogous to the Powers. At one point (p.

22) he enumerates: "Human traditions, the course of earthly life conditioned by the heavenly bodies, morality, fixed religious and ethical rules, the administration of justice and the ordering of the state." In another list (p. 25) there appear: "The State, politics, class, social struggle, national interest, public opinion, accepted morality, the ideas of decency, of democracy...." And in still another list (p. 27) we find: "The place of the clan or the tribe among primitive peoples, the respect for ancestors and the family ... [in] Chinese life, the Hindu social order..., the astrological unity of ancient Babel..., the manifold moral tradition and codes of which moral life is full..., the powers of race, class, state and *Volk*."

If we can analyze more abstractly this wealth of allusions, we might say that we have here an inclusive vision of religious structures (especially the religious undergirdings of stable ancient and primitive societies), intellectual structures ('ologies and 'isms), moral structures (codes and customs), political structures (the tyrant, the market, the school, the courts, race, and nation). The totality is overwhelmingly broad.[5] Nonetheless, even here with careful analysis we observe that it can be said of all of these "structures" what the Apostle was saying concerning the powers:

(a) All these structures can be conceived of in their general essence as parts of a good creation. There could not be society or history, there could not be Man without

[5] Borrowing explicitly and expressly from the thought structure of Berkhof, Albert H. van den Heuvel wrote what he calls a "funny book" on mission for young adults. Under the heading, *These Rebellious Powers* (New York: Friendship, 1965), van den Heuvel sketches an approach to social ethics in what he considers a modern translation of the thought structure of Paul. William Stringfellow, in his *Free in Obedience* (New York: Seabury, 1964), esp. pp. 49ff, makes more extensive use of the "principalities" language in a similar intent. Both demonstrate the fruitfulness of the Pauline imagery to render the idolatrous-demonic claims of the fallen powers; Stringfellow gives less attention to what can be said affirmatively about them from the perspective of creation and redemption, and van den Heuvel gives less note to their collective and structural nature.

the existence above him of religious, intellectual, moral
and social structures. *We cannot live without them.* These
structures are not and never have been a mere sum total
of the individuals composing them. The whole is more
than the sum of its parts. And this "more" is an invisible
Power, even though we may not be used to speaking of it
in personal or angelic terms.

(b) But these structures fail to serve man as they
should. They do not enable him to live a genuinely free,
human, loving life. They have absolutized themselves and
they demand from the individual and society an unconditional loyalty. They harm and enslave man. *We cannot
live with them.* Looking at the human situation from
within, it is not possible to conceive how man once
unconditionally subjected to these Powers can ever again
become free.

(c) Man is lost in the world, in its structures, and in
the current of its development. But nonetheless it is in
this world that man has been preserved, that he has been
able to be himself and thereby to await the redeeming
work of God. His lostness and his survival are inseparable,
both dependent upon the Powers.

Thus, far from being archaic or meaningless, the
"exousiology" of the Apostle, i.e. his doctrine of the
Powers, reveals itself to be a very refined analysis of the
problems of society and history, far more refined than
the other ways in which theologians have sought to
describe the same realities in terms only of "creation" or
"personality." Some traditional theologies have sought to
treat this theme under the heading of "orders of creation." But rarely, if ever, has it been possible under this
heading to combine with such clarity and precision the
simultaneous recognition of man's fallen condition and
the continuing providential control. Nor has it generally
been the case within traditional thought regarding the
orders of creation that religion or ideology has been
included. Nor has it generally been affirmed that it is in

Christ that these values all find their meaning and coherence. As a matter of fact, the theology of the orders
of creation has generally affirmed that Jesus Christ has
little directly to do with them, but that rather these
several orders (the state, family, economy, etc.) have an
autonomous value unrelated to redemption and the
church, by virtue of their having been created by the
Father.[6]

The Work of Christ and the Powers

If the lostness of man consists in his subjection to the
rebellious powers of a fallen world, what then is the
meaning of the work of Christ? Man's subordination to
these Powers is what makes him human, for if they did
not exist there would be no history nor society nor
humanity. If then God is going to save man *in his humanity*, the Powers cannot simply be destroyed or set aside
or ignored. Their sovereignty must be broken. This is
what Jesus did, concretely and historically, by living
among men a genuinely free and human existence. This
life brought him, as any genuinely human existence will
bring any man, to the cross. In his death the Powers in
this case the most worthy, weighty representatives of
Jewish religion and Roman politics—acted in collusion.
Like all men, he too was subject (but in his case quite

---

[6] Perhaps the most explicit contemporary statement of this view is the
"trinitarian" ethical argument of H. Richard Niebuhr: "The Doctrine of the
Trinity and the Unity of the Church," *TT*, 3/3 (Oct. 1946), 371ff. Here the
distinction of persons in the Trinity is correlated with the distribution of
different kinds of ethical thought, with God as Father the specific authority
behind what an earlier theology would have called "the orders of creation"
or "providence." This appeal to the trinitarian formulas has as its special
polemical point an effort to counteract what Niebuhr called a "unitarianism
of the second person," namely an ethic too directly oriented around Christ.
Well before Niebuhr, much Lutheran theology made a similar point by
affirming the moral autonomy (*Eigengesetzlichkeit*) of the several realms of
culture.

willingly) to these powers. He accepted his own status of
submission. But morally he broke their rules by refusing
to support them in their self-glorification; and that is why
they killed him. Preaching and incorporating a greater
righteousness than that of the Pharisees, and a vision of
an order of social human relations more universal than
the Pax Romana, he permitted the Jews to profane a holy
day (refuting thereby their own moral pretensions) and
permitted the Romans to deny their vaunted respect for
law as they proceeded illegally against him. This they did
in order to avoid the threat to their dominion represented
by the very fact that he existed in their midst so morally
independent of their pretensions. He did not fear even
death. Therefore his cross is a victory, is the confirmation
that he was free from the rebellious pretensions of the
creaturely condition. Differing from Adam, Lucifer, and
all the Powers, Jesus did "not consider being equal with
God as a thing to be seized" (Phil. 2:6). His very obedience unto death is in itself not only the sign but also
the firstfruits of an authentic restored humanity. Here we
have for the first time to do with a man who is not the
slave of any power, of any law or custom, community or
institution, value or theory. Not even to save his own life
will he let himself be made a slave of these Powers. This
authentic humanity included his free acceptance of death
at their hands. Thus it is his death that provides his
victory: "Wherefore God has exalted him highly, and
given him the name which is above every name . . . that
every tongue might confess that Jesus Christ is Lord"
(2:9-11).

> And you, who were dead in trespasses and the uncircum-
> cision of your flesh, God made alive together with him,
> having forgiven us all our trespasses, having cancelled the
> bond which stood against us with its legal demands; this he
> set aside, nailing it to the cross. He disarmed the princi-
> palities and powers and made a public example of them,
> triumphing over them in him.[7] (Col. 2:13-15)

7 Or: "in it [the Cross]."

The Apostle uses three complementary verbs to describe what Christ and his death did to the Powers. The way these three terms fit together reciprocally is masterfully summarized in the words of Berkhof (pp. 30f):

> By the cross (which must always, here as elsewhere, be seen as a unit with the resurrection) Christ abolished the slavery which, as a result of sin, lay over our existence as a menace and an accusation. On the cross He "disarmed" the Powers, "made a public example of them and thereby triumphed over them." Paul uses three different verbs to express more adequately what happened to the Powers at the cross.
>
> He "made a public example of them." It is precisely in the crucifixion that the true nature of the Powers has come to light. Previously they were accepted as the most basic and ultimate realities, as the gods of the world. Never had it been perceived, nor could it have been perceived, that this belief was founded on deception. Now that the true God appears on earth in Christ, it becomes apparent that the Powers are inimical to Him, acting not as His instruments but as His adversaries. The scribes, representatives of the Jewish law, far from receiving gratefully Him who came in the name of the God of the law, crucified Him in the name of the temple. The Pharisees, personifying piety, crucified Him in the name of piety. Pilate, representing Roman justice and law, shows what these are worth when called upon to do justice to the Truth Himself. Obviously, "none of the rulers of this age," who let themselves be worshipped as divinities, understood God's wisdom, "for had they known, they would not have crucified the Lord of glory" (I Cor. 2:8). Now they are unmasked as false gods by their encounter with Very God; they are made a public spectacle.
>
> Thus Christ has "triumphed over them." The unmasking is actually already their defeat. Yet this is only visible to men when they know that God Himself has appeared on earth in Christ. Therefore we must think of the resurrection as well as of the cross. The resurrection manifests what was already accomplished at the cross: that in Christ God has challenged the Powers, has penetrated into their territory, and has displayed that He is stronger than they.
>
> The concrete evidence of this triumph is that at the cross Christ has "disarmed" the Powers. The weapon from which they heretofore derived their strength is struck out of their hands. This weapon was the power of illusion, their ability to convince men that they were the divine regents of

the world, ultimate certainty and ultimate direction, ultimate happiness and the ultimate duty for small, dependent
humanity. Since Christ we know that this is illusion. We are
called to a higher destiny: we have higher orders to follow
and we stand under a greater protector. No powers can
separate us from God's love in Christ. Unmasked, revealed
in their true nature, they have lost their mighty grip on
men. The cross has disarmed them: wherever it is preached,
the unmasking and the disarming of the Powers takes place.

The Work of the Church and the Powers

If this victory over the powers constitutes the work of
Christ, then it must be also a message for the church to
proclaim. "To me, less than the least of all the saints,"
says Paul, "was given the grace to proclaim among the
Gentiles the gospel of the inscrutable riches of Christ, and
to declare to all what is the dispensation of the mystery
hidden since the ages in God, who created all things; so
that the manifold wisdom of God should henceforth be
made known by means of the church to the principalities
and powers in heavenly places, according to the eternal
purpose which he set in Jesus Christ our Lord" (Eph.
3:11). Again here I cannot improve on the resume of
Berkhof (pp. 41f):

> Paul's statement is made in connection with the truth that
> since Christ a new force has made its entry on the stage of
> salvation history: the church. She is something quite differ-
> ent from Israel as God's people. She is an undreamed of
> synthesis of the two sorts of men who people the world,
> Jews and Gentiles. That Christ has brought together both
> into one body is the mystery, which for ages had remained
> hidden (v. 9) but has come to light, thanks to Paul's
> ministry. In this ministry is manifested "the unsearchable
> wealth of Christ" (v. 8) and the "manifold wisdom of God"
> (v. 10).
>   This is what the church announces to the Powers. The
> very existence of the church, in which Gentiles and Jews,
> who heretofore walked according to the *stoicheia*[8] of the

---

[8] Or "elements"; the components of which reality is composed: H.
Berkhof, p. 58 n. 6.

world, live together in Christ's fellowship, is itself a proclamation, a sign, a token to the Powers that their unbroken dominion has come to an end. Thus even this text says nothing of a positive or aggressive approach to the Powers. Such an approach is superfluous because the very presence of the church in a world ruled by the Powers is a superlatively positive and aggressive fact. We have already dealt with what this fact means to the Powers, for whom it is a sign of the end time, of their incipient encirclement and their imminent defeat.

This same fact is also freighted with meaning for the Christians. All resistance and every attack against the gods of this age will be unfruitful, unless the church herself is resistance and attack, unless she demonstrates in her life and fellowship how men can live freed from the Powers. We can only preach the manifold wisdom of God to Mammon if our life displays that we are joyfully freed from his clutches. To reject nationalism we must begin by no longer recognizing in our own bosoms any difference between peoples. We shall only resist social injustice and the disintegration of community if justice and mercy prevail in our own common life and social differences have lost their power to divide. Clairvoyant and warning words and deeds aimed at state or nation are meaningful only insofar as they spring from a church whose inner life is itself her proclamation of God's manifold wisdom to the "Powers in the air."

It is thus a fundamental error to conceive of the position of the church in the New Testament in the face of social issues as a "withdrawal," or to see this position as motivated by her weakness, by her numerical insignificance or low social class, or by fear of persecution, or by scrupulous concern to remain uncontaminated by the world. What can be called the "otherness of the church"[9] is an attitude rooted in her strength and not in her weakness. It consists in her being a herald of liberation and not a community of slaves. It is not a detour or a waiting period, looking forward to better days which she hopes might come a few centuries later; it was rather her victory when the church rejected the temptations of

9 Cf. my "The Otherness of the Church," *MQR,* 35 (Oct. 1961), 286.

Zealot and Maccabean patriotism and Herodian collabora-
tion. The church accepted as a gift the fact that she was a
"new humanity" created by the cross and not by the
sword. Once more Berkhof (p. 43):

> This is not to say that Paul is ignorant of a more direct
> encounter between the faithful and the Powers. Ephesians
> 6:10-18 proves the contrary. The believer strives ultimately
> not against tangible men and objects ("flesh and blood," v.
> 12), but against the Powers they obey. This war with the
> Powers must be waged seriously. A man must arm himself
> for it. The arms named (truth, righteousness, the readiness
> of the Gospel of peace, faith, salvation, and the Word of
> God) show that Paul is not contemplating an offensive
> against the Powers. Though surely the believer must assure
> his defense against them, he can do this only by standing,
> simply, by his faith. He is not called to do more than he can
> do by simply believing. His duty is not to bring the Powers
> to their knees. This is Jesus Christ's own task. He has taken
> care of this thus far and will continue to do so. We are
> responsible for the defense, just because He takes care of
> the offense. Ours it is to hold the Powers, their seduction,
> and their enslavement, at a distance, "to be able to stand
> against the wiles of the devil" (v. 11, cf. 13). The figurative
> allusion to weapons points to this defensive role. Girdle,
> breastplate, shoes, shield, helmet, and sword (*machaira*, the
> short sword) are all defensive arms. Lance, spear, bow and
> arrow are not named. They are not needed; these are the
> weapons Christ Himself bears. Our weapon is to stay close
> to Him and thus to remain out of the reach of the drawing
> power of the Powers.

The Priority of the Church in Christian Social Strategy

We have asked whether the New Testament provides
any concept with which it would be possible to interpret
the structures and the history of a secular society. In the
Pauline understanding of the powers we have discovered a
line of thought very apt to deal with this kind of matter.

In this view of things the condition of man as creature,
his fallen state, the continual providential care of God
which preserves him as man, the saving work of Christ,

and the specific position of the Christian community in the midst of history are all described in terms of social structure and their inherent dynamics. Thus there can be easily established a correlation with contemporary ways of understanding man's society and his history. This in turn drives us to suggest that we observe more specifically the place of the church within the larger society.

For Paul, as interpreted by Berkhof, the very existence of the church is her primary task. It is in itself a proclamation of the Lordship of Christ to the powers from whose dominion the church has begun to be liberated. The church does not attack the powers; this Christ has done. The church concentrates upon not being seduced by them. By her existence she demonstrates that their rebellion has been vanquished.[10]

This Pauline vision of the place of the church in the world bears decisive implications for the contemporary ecumenical discussion of the place of the church in a world in the midst of rapid social change. The phrase "responsible society" became very current since its occurrence in the preparatory documents for the Amsterdam Assembly of 1948. In these documents it was strongly

[10] Scholarly debate about the sense in which the early church's expectations of the parousia may or may not have been disappointed (cf. p. 109 n. 10) has diverted attention from the unanimity of conviction about the novelty of what had already come. "Thus the confession of Jesus as Lord and Savior, and the claim of Christ over the whole civilized world as dramatized in Paul's far-reaching missionary goals, represented a continuation of the hopes of the prophet, psalmist and the devout poor for the time when God's will would be done on earth as in heaven. . . . It is true that the early church looked for the imminent parousia of Christ. This was an inevitable aspect of their picture of history. But this cannot set aside the fact that the believers were shaping a new pattern of the human community and realizing very concrete social values in a widening movement which collided increasingly with existing institutions and vested interests, economic, social and political." Amos Wilder, *Otherworldliness and the New Testament* (New York: Harper, 1954), p. 116. The entire life work of Wilder, in his rehabilitation of New Testament language and imagery, lies generally along the lines of the present study.

affirmed that if the church is to have a ministry to society in general, the first step of this duty would have to be to herself, the church. "Let the church be the church," was the slogan. Let the church be a restored society," we could have said equally well. The church must be a sample of the kind of humanity within which, for example, economic and racial differences are surmounted. Only then will she have anything to say to the society that surrounds her about how those differences must be dealt with. Otherwise her preaching to the world a standard of reconciliation which is not her own experience will be neither honest nor effective.[11]

The position paper from which was taken the phrase "responsible society" was drafted by J. H. Oldham.[12] He began his discussion of "the practice of common life" by declaring that:

> The first indispensable task is to restore substance to the human person through the revitalization of personal life in the living give-and-take, the mutual obligation and responsibility of a society of persons. If our diagnosis is true, the world cannot be set right from the top but only from the bottom upwards.
>
> There is no way of restoring substance and depth to the life of man except by living. . . . Human living is living in relations with other persons and can acquire meaning and

[11] Franklin H. Littell, *From State Church to Pluralism* (New York: Doubleday Anchor, 1962), p. 120, points out how Protestant church leaders condemn themselves when they seek to use political sanctions to enforce upon all society moral obligations which they cannot with theological and ecclesiastical motivations commend to their own membership. Littell says this of the prohibition and evolution controversies; he could say it of open housing. " . . . Politicians in the churches attempted to secure by public legislation what they were unable to persuade many of their own members was either wise or desirable. . . . Lacking the authenticity of a genuinely disciplined witness, the Protestant reversion to political action was ultimately discredited, and the churches have not to this day recovered their authority in public life."

[12] J. H. Oldham, "A Responsible Society," in *The Church and the Disorder of Society*, vol. III in the Amsterdam Assembly Series *Man's Disorder and God's Design* (New York: Harper, 1948). The internal quotation within the following passage is from an article by G. D. H. Cole in the *Christian News-Letter*.

depth only in those relations. Since the number of persons with whom an individual can have direct and close relations is limited, the art of social living has to be learned and practiced in small groups, of which the family is the chief.

". . . These little groups are the forces out of which the new Europe must be built, if democracy is to be its ruling spirit. They are the nuclei of the new social consciousness on which alone the practical architects of the social order of tomorrow can hope to build a society in which men's higher faculties of love and creative service will have soil to grow."

The church is concerned with the primary task of re-creating a true social life in two ways. In the first place, its greatest contribution to the renewal of society is through the fulfillment of its primary functions of preaching the Word and through its life as a worshipping community. It is the worship of God that is the source of all genuine renewal. It is only in response to the demands of His perfection that it can reach out to new tasks. It is His grace and truth which in the last resort guarantee and sustain the personal and cultural values which are essential to the health of society.

There is nothing greater that the Church can do for society than to be a center in which small groups of persons are together entering into this experience of renewal and giving each other mutual support in Christian living and action in secular spheres. Such groups will find their vital inspiration in Word and Sacrament and in the fellowship of such gatherings as the parish meeting.

This centrality of the church continued to be affirmed in the basic documents of ecumenical social strategy in succeeding years. But it did not remain equally clear when studies on specific social problems came into view.[13] These concrete studies were necessary to relate

[13] Since 1961 (New Delhi) the phrase "responsible society" has dropped out of currency in ecumenical meetings and journals. A few ethicists, notably H. D. Wendland and Walter Muelder, had adopted the term, giving it their own meaning. A few others, notably Keith Bridston, Max-Alain Chevallier, and Charles West, had raised doubts on the level of systematic-theological logic. Perhaps an equally significant, though less apparent reason for the phrase's failure to find permanent usefulness and conceptual clarity might be its rootedness in the Christendom or post-Christendom context, where it is natural for Christians to conceive of themselves as holding a determining power in society and the state.

to problems of social organization concerning which often it appeared that there would not be such a thing as a specifically *Christian* point of view. It seemed that in such cases there would exist only the *correct* point of view of the expert—the economist, the agronomist, the sociologist, who could not necessarily be found within the church. Furthermore, it seemed that the basis of social cooperation between Christians and non-Christians would have to be something other than a specifically Christian standard. We cannot be sure that in all this process of study the central importance of the Christian community as a new humanity was kept in view, not only as a verbal affirmation, but also as an instrument of social change.

In the published documents arising from the ecumenical conversation on social ethics since 1948 there has been a degree of success in avoiding the temptations of the Pharisees. There is little tendency to seek to resolve these problems by trusting in some kind of immutable law or a loophole-free casuistry. But one cannot be so sure that there has been equal success in discerning and avoiding the temptation of the Sadducees, which is also a form of servitude to the Powers. By this we mean the assumption that the forces which really determine the march of history are in the hands of the leaders of the armies and the markets, in such measure that if Christians are to contribute to the renewal of society they will need to seek, like everyone else—in fact in competition with everyone else—to become in their turn the lords of the state and of the economy, so as to use that power toward the ends they consider desirable.[14]

14 The form in which this thought pattern gathered the most attention recently was the proposal that violent revolution might be justified if directed against hopelessly unjust social situations in (for instance) Latin America. Jacques Ellul in his study of *Violence* (New York: Seabury, 1969) has effectively punctured the logic of the assumption that violence, while wrong in the oppressor, becomes right when used by Christians for desirable social change. What the hasty, theologically conservative critics of this

The "Pietistic" Misunderstanding

Let us avoid with great care the two possible misunderstandings of this critical statement about social pressure to which the Apostle Paul has led us. What he says is not, as some conservative religious groups would say, that the gospel deals only with personal ethics and not with social structures. Nor does he say that the only way to change structures is to change the heart of an individual man, preferably the man in power, and then see that he exercises his control of society with more humility or discernment or according to better standards. What needs to be seen is rather that the primary social structure through which the gospel works to change other structures is that of the Christian community. Here, within this community, men are rendered humble and changed in the way they behave not simply by a proclamation directed to their sense of guilt but also by genuine social relationships with other persons who ask them about their obedience; who (in the words of Jesus) "bind and loose."

Neither should we be understood as stating here the extreme application of particularly radical ethical commitment, such as the argument that everything having to do with the structure of this world is impure or unworthy for the Christian because of the coercion or violence that governs society.[15] There may well be certain circum-

"theology of revolution" often fail to notice is that it constitutes only a modest reformulation of the concepts of the just war that are held to by most nonrevolutionary Christian groups. One of the earliest very perceptive criticisms of this kind of theological affirmation of revolution was made by the contributions of Max-Alain Chevallier and Keith Bridston to the World Student Christian Federation study, *The Christian in the World Struggle* (Geneva: WSCF, 1952), ed. M. M. Thomas and D. J. McCaughey.

15 There is widespread agreement among the historians of ethics, in the wake of Ernst Troeltsch, Max Weber, and H. Richard Niebuhr, that such a "withdrawn" or "purist" position is represented by the General Epistles of the New Testament, by Tertullian, the Anabaptists, and Tolstoy. Niebuhr's description of what he calls the "Christ against Culture" position, in his

stances in which the Christian, in order to be morally faithful, would refuse certain functions within society. Every ethical system draws some kind of lines. But if the disciple of Jesus Christ chooses not to exercise certain kinds of power, this is not simply because they are powerful; for the Powers as such, power in itself, is the good creation of God. He chooses not to exercise certain types of power because, in a given context, the rebellion of the structure of a given particular power is so incorrigible that at the time the most effective way to *take* responsibility is to refuse to collaborate, and by that refusal to take sides in favor of the men whom that power is oppressing. This refusal is not a withdrawal from society. It is rather a major negative intervention within the process of social change, a refusal to use unworthy means even for what seems to be a worthy end.

Frequently the faithfulness of the church has been put to the test the moment she was asked to follow the path of costly conscientious objection in the face of the world's opposition. Yet we should not overdramatize the normal expression of her mission in and through society. Her calling is to be the conscience and the servant within human society. The church must be sufficiently experienced to be able to discern when and where and how God is using the Powers, whether this be thanks to the faithful testimony of the church or in spite of her infidelity. Either way, she is called to contribute to the creation of structures more worthy of man. But the church will also need to be sufficiently familiar with the manifest ways in which God has acted to reconcile and call together a people for himself that she will not fall prey to the Sadducean or "German Christian" temptation to read off

vastly influential *Christ and Culture,* is seriously distorted by his prior polemical stance. Whether or not such a characterization be fair to the persons and movements just named, it in any case does not describe the position of the present study.

the surface of history a simple declaration of his will. [16] God is working in the world and it is the task of the church to know how he is working. She should be the first to distinguish between this kind of divine work—which can be discerned definitively and faithfully, not only in the light of faith—and the to and fro on the surface of current events, concerning which many, even many in the church, will exclaim, "Behold, here is the Christ." "This is where God is at work!" This task of discernment is much less simple than seems to be assumed by many who in the last decade have been encouraging us to look for God at work in "the World Revolution" (whatever that is).

The Relevance of Christ to the Powers Today

It is often said that the Christian understanding of the human individual, which considers him at the same time fallen yet redeemable, offers a point of departure more adequate, i.e. more correct and more realistic, than that which was provided by the Utopian idea, where man is seen as almost ready to complete his own redemption, or by the mechanistic idea, where man is nothing but the product of his circumstances. We are now ready to affirm that the biblical understanding of the powers in history can give us a more adequate intellectual framework of the task of *social* discernment to which we are especially called in our age. This discernment is not simply a way of

[16] Lest it be assumed that this temptation is one that besets the church especially in unique fascist situations, we should remember that it probably happens far more often in the situation of a comfortable establishment (like the churches of the American Bible Belt) or in the crusade, the revolution proclaimed by very good people to be a holy cause because of the nobility of the purposes to which it is committed. The accommodation of the Bible Belt is fittingly denounced by Samuel S. Hill, "Culture-Protestantism in the South," *CC* (Sept. 12, 1962), and by George H. Shriver, "When Conservatism is Liberalism," *CC* (Aug. 6, 1969).

helping the needy with their social problems, a kind of updated philanthropy, nor does it mean simply to guide individual Christians by helping them to do good deeds or to avoid sin. It is rather a part of the Christians' proclamation that the church is under orders to make known to the Powers, as no other proclaimer can do, the fulfillment of the mysterious purposes of God (Eph. 3:10) by means of that Man in whom their rebellion has been broken and the pretensions they had raised have been demolished. [17] This proclamation of the Lordship of Christ is not a substitute for nor a prerequisite to the gospel call directed to individuals. Nor is it the mere consequence within society of the conversion of individuals one by one. Nor does it dispense with, or guarantee, or always necessarily facilitate such conversions. Such phrasings of alternatives are commended to us by traditional Protestant thought. But the New Testament does not begin at such a dilemma nor do we need to be hobbled by it. [18] That Christ is

[17] The use Charles West makes of "powers language" is typical of the taken-for-granted meaning it has for a few, yet without having been exposited or tested widely. In his *Ethics, Violence, and Revolution* (New York: Council on Religion and International Affairs, 1969), pp. 45f, West speaks of "the continual de-mythologizing and disarming of the powers by God—more specifically by Christ—in order that they may be legitimized as servants of his purpose for man." The term "legitimized" risks being understood too simply and affirmatively, forgetting the note of continuing struggle, relapse, and worse, rebellion; but our point in citing West here is simply as a document of the agreed (yet not fully exposited or tested) fruitfulness of the *exousia* imagery.

[18] Protestant theology has long been divided about the sense in which the work of Christ is "objectively" real as over against the sense in which it depends for its reality upon being "appropriated" by the believer. Is the victory over the powers something that has happened "out there" whether or not everyone knows it or believes it? Has the shape of the universe really been changed? Or is there only a change in the orientation of the individual believer or the church, so that we should say that the sovereignty of the powers is broken "only for faith" and that its continuing defeat is dependent upon the faithfulness of the church in living out her liberation? As Graydon Snyder has argued in an unpublished paper, this set of alternatives is foreign to the apocalyptic and mythic literary context in which these statements are found. This kind of language is not interested in dealing with realities that are "out there" but do not transform our situation, nor can it conceive of our situations as being transformed by the mere force of our own believing. This set of alternatives, which echoes down the halls of Christian controversy

Lord, a proclamation to which only individuals can respond, is nonetheless a social, political, *structural* fact
which constitutes a challenge to the Powers. It thus
follows that the claims such proclamation makes are not
limited to those who have accepted it, nor is the significance of its judgment limited to those who have decided
to listen to it. It was Johann Christoph Blumhardt who
rediscovered for German Protestantism a century ago the
wondrous power of the gospel in individual lives and at
the same time the eschatological foundation of Christian
involvement in politics. We may echo his battle cry:
"Dass Jesus siegt ist ewig ausgemacht. Sein ist die ganze
Welt!" "That Jesus is conqueror is eternally settled: the
universe is his!" This is not a statement concerning the
benevolent disposition of certain men to listen or of
certain Powers to be submissive. It is a declaration about
the nature of the cosmos and the significance of history,
within which both our conscientious participation and
our conscientious objection find their authority and their
promise.

It cannot be the task of this chapter to spell out at
length samples of the relevance of this kind of approach
for concrete social and ethical thought. Berkhof himself
suggests only very sketchily some directions, especially
with reference to the foreign missionary enterprise of the
church and to that particular Western totalitarianism
which arises when the Powers are no longer cowed by the
proclamation that had originally humbled them. Probably
Jacques Ellul, in his writing on money, the law, violence,
and technology, thinks the most consistently within the
framework of this approach, though often without direct
allusion to the Pauline vocabulary.[19] Scientifically ori-

in social ethics, from the classic Lutheran-Catholic debate through the
Lutheran-Reformed debate to the contemporary "evangelical-liberal" debate, is the fruit of a warped initial phrasing in the question. This dilemma is
a product of the modern Protestant individualistic ontology, not a conceivable distinction within the biblical text itself.

[19] Perhaps the earliest effort to make sense of the concept of the powers
in modern theology was that of Otto Piper, *Die Grundlagen der Evangel-*

ented Westerners are poorly equipped to perceive other points of relevance which this approach might have to occultism, psychodynamics, or the mass media. The creative translation of the Pauline mood into the language of today, however, need not be completed for us to be able to perceive that such a translation would be not only conceivable but natural.

With this observation we have found one more point at which the ethical relevance of the stance of Jesus breaks through in a segment of the apostolic literature with which for generations most Protestants did not know how to deal. The Powers have been defeated not by some kind of cosmic hocus-pocus but by the concreteness of the cross; the impact of the cross upon them is not the working of magical words nor the fulfillment of a legal contract calling for the shedding of innocent blood, but the sovereign presence, within the structures of creaturely orderliness, of Jesus the kingly claimant and of the church who herself is a structure and a power in society. Thus the historicity of Jesus retains, in the working of the church as she encounters the other power and value structures of her history, the same kind of relevance that the man Jesus had for those whom he served until they killed him.

ischen Ethik (Gütersloh, 1928), pp. 122ff, "Die Mächte." The book is preoccupied, however, with theodicy and with philosophical anthropology, locating the awareness of the rebelliousness of the powers in "believing contrition" rather than in history itself. It does not attempt to unfold in any detail the actual inner structure of the thinking of Paul about the powers, nor to sketch contemporary relevance. In Piper's later writings on *God in History* (New York: Macmillan, 1939), there is a continuing accent upon the reality of a satanic power, but the same is not done with the wider realm of distinct rebellious created powers. Without being so labelled, the "principalities and powers" thought pattern is present in Piper's *Christian Meaning of Money* (Englewood Cliffs, N.J.: Prentice-Hall, 1965); it is not explicit in his *Biblical View of Sex and Marriage* (New York: Scribner, 1960). Cf. the more popular treatments above, n. 4. John Swomley in his *Liberation Ethics* (Macmillan, 1972), esp. chs. 3 and 10, interprets "principalities and powers" as oppressive social structures.

9

Revolutionary Subordination

We began this book by taking issue with the recent scholarly consensus about the relevance of Jesus, according to which he took such a short view of the existence of society that he taught no relevant social ethic. We sought to provide an alternative to the reading of the Gospels which that consensus both assumes and reinforces. Yet our argument is not concluded with a new reading of the Gospels. Another major segment of the case for a low view of Jesus' relevance argues from the interpretation of the ethical teaching that actually arose in the early church. Since Jesus did not provide a social ethic relevant to the continuing life of human communities, it is claimed, the early church found itself obliged to borrow one from somewhere else.

A key aspect of this claim as it relates to the ethic of the early church is symbolized by that particular type of ethical instruction which scholars have come to refer to as the *Haustafeln*.[1] The New Testament has numerous

---

[1] The German term *Haustafeln*, literally "house tables" or "household tablets," has usually been rendered "household precepts." The term "tables" is cognate to the English usage which refers to the "two tables" of the Decalog; i.e. a listing of rules. "Household precepts" is not an accurate rendering, since it points to a plurality of individual rules, whereas *Tafel* identifies the format of a *series* of stated rules standing in some parallel

163

traces of a particular type of ethical teaching, most purely represented by Colossians (3:18-4:1):

> *Wives, be subject to your husbands,*
> *As is fitting in the Lord.*
> *Husbands, love your wives.*
> *Children, obey your parents in everything,*
> *for this pleases the Lord.*
> *Fathers, do not provoke your children,*
> *lest they become discouraged.*
> *Slaves, obey in everything those who are your*
> *earthly masters,*
> *. . . fearing the Lord.*
> *Masters, treat your slaves justly and fairly,*
> *Knowing that you also have a master in*
> *heaven.*

A similar line of instruction is found in Ephesians
(5:21-6:9):

> *Be subject to one another out of reverence for*
> *Christ.*
> *Wives, be subject to your husbands,*
> *As to the Lord.*
> *Husbands, love your wives,*
> *As Christ loved the church and gave himself up*
> *for her. . . .*
> *Children, obey your parents in the Lord,*
> *For this is right. . . .*
> *Fathers, do not provoke your children to anger,*
> *But bring them up in the discipline and instruc-*
> *tion of the Lord.*
> *Slaves, be obedient to those who are your earthly*
> *masters,*

---

relationship to each other. The present study does not seek to establish a
new standard usage, but will use sometimes the German term and sometimes
the various English paraphrases.

> *As to Christ. . . .*
> *Masters, do the same to them,*
> *. . . knowing that he was both their Master and*
> *yours.*

Very similar again in thought content, but differing in detail, is the admonition of I Peter (2:13-3:7). Here the reference to children and parents is lacking but a reference to government is found instead:

> *Be subject for the Lord's sake to every human*
> *institution, . . .*
> *For it is God's will that by doing right you should*
> *put to silence*
> *the ignorance of foolish men. . . .*
> *Servants, be submissive to your masters in all re-*
> *spect. . . .*
> *Likewise you husbands, live considerately with*
> *your wives,*
> *bestowing honor on the woman as the weaker sex.*

Any effort to reconstruct imaginatively the life of the churches from which these texts arose will surmise that when we find thoughts and even expressions this nearly parallel in quite distinct literary contexts, the only sensible hypothesis is that there must have been some patternedness in the moral teaching of the earliest churches.[2] At least since Martin Luther these outlines

---

[2] This essay borrows heavily, with permission, from the unpublished dissertation of David Schroeder, *Die Haustafeln des Neuen Testaments, Ihre Herkunft und ihr theologischer Sinn,* accepted by the Evangelical Theological Faculty of the University of Hamburg in 1959, and from a series of lectures *New Testament Ethics* (unfortunately also unpublished) derived from the dissertation. Schroeder makes clear on critical grounds that no literary dependence of these texts upon each other can be demonstrated or assumed; the parallelism is explainable only by assuming that there was in the pre-literary life of the earliest churches a far-reaching commonality in the use of this pattern of moral instruction. Schroeder's writings will henceforth be referred to as *Die Haustafeln* and *Ethics.*

have come to be discerned by scholars as representing a particular literary form.[3] Whether the practical focus of the use of these phrases was in a catechism or a baptism liturgy,[4] the parallelism in content and in logic fully supports the surmise that there was a regular way of thinking about these questions in the early church.

If we have once established the probable existence of a recurrent pattern of thought and instruction, what does this then mean for the question with which we began? Here we may turn to the classic statement of the widely accepted thesis by Martin Dibelius, father of the form-critical analytical method.

> These collections of proverbs intend to define the duties of the several groups [i.e. categories of persons] in the household. Their existence in the early Christian writings testifies to the need of the young Christian movement to establish itself within ordinary daily life. This need is not self-evident; for that [particular kind of] Christianity which burst into the world and especially into the Hellenistic world (I Thess. 1:9f) could apparently do without any basic attitude to the cultural communities of Family and Father-land, as toward Culture itself. (Cf. Paul's personal attitude to marriage, I Cor. 7:29ff.) Thus Christianity was unprepared for meeting these needs, or to say the least, could not adequately deal with them in terms of the gospel of Jesus. Resort to the moral instructions which Hellenistic and Jewish propaganda had developed was inevitable. . . . Thus early Christianity began, by a very gradual process, to come to grips with the World. The *Haustafeln* are especially fitting specimens of this process. They do show that Christian paraenese preserved for the common ethic of the West both the moral family principles of Greek popular philosophy and those of Jewish halakah.[5]

[3] Luther may be the creator, and at least was a major popularizer of the label *Haustafeln*.

[4] After reviewing the various scholarly conjectures as to the place of the *Haustafeln* in early church life, Schroeder (*Ethics*, ch. 3) concludes that they must have arisen within the ethical preaching/teaching life of the congregations rather than from a particular liturgical setting.

[5] *An die Kolosser, Epheser, und Philemon, HzNT,* XII (3rd ed. 1953), pp. 48f.

We have here again, in classic form, the statement that the ethic derived from the meaning of Jesus was inadequate or irrelevant to meet the practical needs of the church as she went on living in society while the kingdom did not arrive, so that the stuff of moral discrimination and discernment had to be borrowed elsewhere, wherever it could be found, namely from both Jewish and Gentile thinking. In the case of the *Haustafeln* it is from Stoicism that such borrowing must have come.[6]

The fact of this borrowing, if it be a fact, has three significant implications. One of them has to do with the relationship of revelation and nature, or of Jesus on one hand and reason on the other, as sources of ethical organization. If the early church could borrow from nonbiblical sources of moral insight, then our accepting the appropriateness of such free borrowing (in any age), and the inadequacy (which this demonstrates) of the resources we have available if we do not resort to borrowing, will go a long way toward setting the ground rules for Christian ethical thought.

Second: not only does this demonstrate that borrowing ethical guidance from nonbiblical, non-Christian sources is necessary, possible, and legitimate; it also suggests what kind of insight we will find there. In seeing ethical obligations as defined by the *status* of persons (wives and husbands, children and parents, slaves and

---

[6] In the Dibelius text just quoted, the Jewish ethical tradition (*halakah*) and the Hellenistic (*stoa*) were mentioned as parallels. They were properly parallel in Dibelius' mind, in the sense that he could appeal to either to fill in the gap where the overheated eschatology of Jesus had failed to provide an ethic. They may also have been somewhat parallel in content, since any ethical teaching that reckons with social continuities must say some of the same things. They were not parallel, however, in their literary and logical form. Schroeder makes clear (*Die Haustafeln*, pp. 29ff) that the Jewish tradition provides no immediate literary models for the *Haustafeln;* it is too clearly bound to specific commands of God, their application and interpretation, to be guided by lists of given social structures. We thus appropriately shall restrict our continuing discussion to the Stoic side of the alleged borrowing.

masters. . .), the *Haustafeln* are saying in effect that it is
possible to ascertain one's duties by finding out who one
is, what is one's *role*. At this point, as did Dibelius, many
others have pointed out that the Stoics offered a very
similar kind of instruction:

> He [the philosopher] should bring his own will into har-
> mony with what happens, so that neither anything that
> happens happens against our will, nor anything that fails to
> happen fails to happen when we wish it to happen. . . . The
> result of this . . . [is] that each person passes his life to
> himself, free from pain, fear, and perturbation, at the same
> time maintaining with his associates both the natural and
> the acquired relationships, those namely of son, father,
> brother, citizen, wife, neighbor, fellow traveller, ruler, and
> subject.[7]
>
> The second field of study deals with duty; for I ought
> not to be unfeeling like a statue, but should maintain my
> relations, both natural and acquired, as a religious man, as a
> son, a brother, a father, a citizen.[8]
>
> See whether they [those who get ahead of you] observe
> what becomes them as men, as sons, as parents, and then, in
> order, through all the other terms for the social relations.[9]

The third lesson that would follow is that by moving
from the radicality of the ethic of Jesus to the guidance
the early church found in the structures of society in
their givenness, the early church took on a position that
was essentially conservative. It chose not to challenge the
subjugation of woman or the institution of slavery.[10]

---

[7] *The Discourses of Epictetus as Reported by Arrian,* trans. W. A.
Oldfather, Loeb Classical Library, CIV, 308f.

[8] *Ibid.,* CV, 23.

[9] *Ibid.,* CV, 355. Similar listings can be found as well in Marcus An-
tonius, Plutarch, Diogenes Laertius, Cicero, Horace, and others; Schroeder,
Die Haustafeln, pp. 32ff.

[10] A full statement of the traditional interpretation of Paul's failure to
challenge the institution of slavery is: P. R. Coleman-Norton, "The Apostle
Paul and the Roman Law of Slavery," in his anthology, *Studies in Roman
Economic and Social History* (Princeton U. P., 1951), pp. 155ff. Coleman-
Norton gathers a wealth of background material for the interpretation of

Thereby it prepared itself gradually to become the religion of the established classes, a development that cul-
minated in the age of Constantine three centuries later.

This development can be evaluated either positively or
negatively. Martin Dibelius considered it a kind of progress that the church moved away from the timeless
radicality of Jesus and began coming to grips with "the
world"—by which he meant what Martin Luther earlier
had called the "orders of creation."

One strand of social ethical thought ever since the
Reformation has accordingly taken the borrowings of
Paul from Stoicism as representing a precedent or a mandate for the continued legitimacy in Christian ethics of
insights drawn from "the nature of things" as any philosopher can see them.[11] More recently, especially within
the context of "progressive" Protestantism, the evalua-
tion has often turned the other way; the apostles, and
Paul in particular, can be rapidly and vigorously condemned for having such a low view of women or for
having failed to attack the institution of slavery head-on
as we now know he should have.

The same kind of negative judgment can also be
reached in another way: it can be claimed from the

slavery as an institution and the treatment of runaway slaves. He wrongly
suggests that the *Haustafeln* type of teaching appears only once in the NT (p.
164). By failing to ask in any historically relevant way what it would have
meant for Paul to challenge the institution of slavery, he keeps himself from
observing the extent to which both the *Haustafeln* and the Epistle to
Philemon do provide an alternative to the contemporary way slavery func-
tioned as an institution. Cf. below, n. 32.

[11] Probably the most perceptive interpretation of the *Haustafeln* in the
framework of these assumptions is that of Heinz-Dietrich Wendland, "Zur
Sozialethischen Bedeutung der Neutestamentlichen Haustafeln," in Otto
Michel and Ulrich Mann, eds., *Die Leibhaftigkeit des Wortes, Festgabe Adolf
Köberle* (Hamburg: Furche Verlag, 1958), pp. 34ff. Through careful analysis Wendland comes to many insights parallel to those argued for later in this
present text; but he does not question the basic axiom of borrowing and
"Christianizing" pagan principles; this thought structure of course is very
much at home in his Lutheran understanding of law and gospel and the Ethic
of the Orders.

perspective of the radical Protestant "theology of the
word of God" that in borrowings like this we see the
beginning of a relapse into "natural theology," an evalua-
tion that would support a critical conviction that these
texts are not genuinely representative of the theology of
the Apostle Paul, and were probably written by some of
his later disciples who no longer had his deep grasp of the
meaning of revelation as an alternative to human wisdom.

These lines of argument, despite their differing conclusions, begin by agreeing in their reading of what actually
happened in the early church, and therefore in their
understanding of the way we must approach the problems. For both views there is in the midst of the canon a
chasm separating the ethic of Jesus from that of the
apostolic church, of such a nature that one must choose
between the two. The reason for the church's leaping
over the chasm was the lack of any adequate moral
equipment on Jesus' side of the gap.

Second Thoughts

The assumption of the Stoic origin of the *Haustafeln*
was accepted so rapidly and sweepingly by scholars that
only recently have serious doubts come to the surface.
More careful reading now sees more clearly to what
extent the polarity of Jesus and Paul was imposed on
New Testament criticism in the last century by the
Hegelian philosophical assumptions of F. C. Baur, rather
than rising necessarily out of the text.[12] The material is
after all not wholly in the Pauline writings, but in I Peter
as well, an indication that no one apostle dictated this
way of teaching.[13] Nowhere in the texts is there any

[12] The landmark study which most pointedly called into question the
axiom of the chasm in the canon was Edwyn Hoskyns and Noel Davey, *The
Riddle of the New Testament* (London: Faber & Faber, 1947, 3rd ed. 1957).

[13] For some scholars, like Hans Lietzmann in his *Beginnings of the
Christian Church* (New York: Scribner, 1937), the Petrine Epistles represent

literary basis for the claim that the moral exhortations to wives and husbands, children and parents, slaves and masters, calling them to behave fittingly toward one another, are derived as a kind of makeshift substitute from the failure of the kingdom to come. Quite other reasons are given in these texts, as we shall observe shortly, for the behavior the *Haustafeln* call for.

Thus already on the level of careful logic and skeptical reading of sources we must begin to doubt Dibelius' view. But more serious doubts—and perhaps more helpful learnings—come to the surface if we actually look more closely and respectfully at the instructions in question. We shall discover that although in the widest sense the *Haustafeln* are vaguely like Stoicism, in that they call upon a person to fulfill the meaning of his special role, there are other very significant differences which forbid any simple explanation such as that of direct borrowing from an extant Stoic source.

(a) The call of Stoic morality is to live up to *my own nature*. This nature or role or function, of course, has a social side; it relates me to other persons. But the fulfillment of the authenticity of my living my role is seen by Stoic thought as centered in my person. In the *Haustafeln*, on the other hand, it is the relationship itself that we are called upon to live up to. This is evident in the literary form. Whereas the Stoic functions of father, friends, brother, friend, are listed one by one, in the *Haustafeln* the listing occurs in *pairs:* both the woman and her husband are spoken to; both the slave and the

---

"early Catholicism," i.e. a degeneration subsequent to the early more correct insights of the Pauline gospel. For others, like Vincent Taylor in his *The Atonement in New Testament Teaching* (London: Epworth, 1940), the level of development in the thought of the church which is represented by I Peter is—whatever the date of actual writing—more "primitive" or less "evolved." In either case it would be hard to explain the parallel appearance of the *Haustafeln* in both Pauline and Petrine writings as proof of a radical shift in ethical thought in the midst of the New Testament canon.

master. Not only does this reciprocity of relationship show in the literary structure of the listing; it is also a part of the imperative. The call to be "subject" or to "love" or to "respect" always uses a verb which relates this person not to himself, or to his image of himself, or to his nature or role, but to the other member of that pair.

(b) Stoic thinking uses all of these nouns in the singular, and discerns in one person as many different roles as possible. Amidst the multiplicity of all these roles, it is the freedom and self-determination of the individual that shows through. It is the man himself, in a given decision, who will determine which definition of his role is to apply. There are so many such roles, and they are combined in such varied ways, that the listing of roles amounts to a relativizing of all ethical bindingness.

The *Haustafeln* on the other hand speak in plural terms. The admonitions are addressed to all wives or all servants or all parents in the churches receiving these Epistles. There are also a limited number of such relationships to which the *Haustafeln* always speak. Thus there is in the ethical admonition of the *Haustafeln* the possibility of community discipline, of common insight and standards, around which it is possible for a whole group of persons, and not simply a meditative elite, to develop a shared moral commitment.

(c) The Stoic pattern of reasoning seeks simply to unfold or to get *insight into what is.* Its tool is reason and the basis of moral obligation is "the nature of things." If a man can see what the nature of things truly is, it is assumed that he will act accordingly. The Stoic discourse is not in the imperative mood. In the *Haustafeln,* on the other hand, the grammatical form is uniformly imperative.

In its form, the *Haustafeln* ethic is patterned most closely on the style of the so-called "Apodictic law" of the Old Testament. This is not only the case where in

Ephesians 6:2 there is explicit reference to Exodus 19:25; but the imperative style is generally parallel to the construction of the ethical appeals of the Old Testament.[14] The borrowing—by the testimony of syntactic style—is not from Hellenistic Judaism (although the substance would not be greatly different therefrom) but from the prophetic imperatives recorded in the Old Testament as received from the mouth of God himself. This view is further demonstrated by the grammatical peculiarity of the imperative participle.[15]

(d) Still further demonstration of the difference between Stoic and apostolic thought shows in the vocabulary itself. Even where almost the same point is being made, the most usual terms are not the same. For the concept of obedience the New Testament uses *hypakouein* where the Stoics would use *peithesthai;* for the relation of servant and master the New Testament uses *doulos* and *kyrios* whereas the Stoics used *oiketai* and *despotai.* For love the New Testament uses *agapan* and the Stoics *philein.*[16] If the apostles had been borrowing directly from Stoic usage and counting on the terms they used to be already familiar to their readers, one would have expected a greater correlation in the actual words used.

(e) Stoicism addresses *man in his dignity* and calls upon him to live up to the highest vision of himself. This call is addressed to the dominant man in society, especially to the prince or freedman or father, to the person

[14] Deut. 16:21f; 17:1; 22:5; 23:7f; Lev. 17:10; Amos 5:4; Prov. 3:1f (Schroeder, *Die Haustafeln,* pp. 92ff).

[15] In addition to the *Haustafeln* of I Peter, this same imperative use of the participle is found in Rom. 12:9ff. Its origins are not Greek but rabbinic: Schroeder, *Ethics,* II, 11; David Daube, *The New Testament and Rabbinic Judaism* (London: Univ. of London, 1956), pp. 90ff; and W. D. Davies, *Paul and Rabbinic Judaism* (London: S.P.C.K., 2nd ed. 1955), pp. 329f.

[16] Schroeder, *Die Haustafeln,* p. 124. Schroeder adduces other linguistic and literary grounds as well for denying any direct verbal borrowing from Stoic sources (pp. 86ff).

who had time and leisure and capacity to meditate on his nature and its fulfillment.[17]   Self-control and a measure of dominion over others is itself a virtuous posture. The free man should avoid coming into bondage to a woman or to his subordinates.

This concentration upon the dignity of the addressee is missing in the New Testament. The admonition of the *Haustafeln* is addressed *first to the subject:* to the slave before the master, to the children before the parents, to the wives before the husbands.[18]

Here begins the revolutionary innovation in the early Christian style of ethical thinking for which there is no explanation in borrowing from other contemporary cultural sources. The *subordinate* person in the social order is *addressed as a moral agent.* He is called upon to take responsibility for the acceptance of his position in society as meaningful before God. It is not assumed, as it was in both Jewish and Hellenistic thought, that the wife will have the faith of her husband, or that the slave will be part of the religious unity of his master's household. Here we have a faith that assigns *personal moral responsibility to those who had no legal or moral status* in their culture, and makes of them decision-makers. It gives them responsibility for viewing their status in society not as a simple meaningless decree of fate but as their own meaningful witness and ministry, as an issue about which they can make a moral choice.

(f) Not only does Stoicism address itself to the domi-

[17] More accurately: it is only the philosopher who can be taught to understand himself in these roles. There is no concept of an ethical vision accessible to a community or to those who have no claim on the philosopher's help.

[18] The priority of the address to the subordinate party of the pair is further reinforced by Schroeder's hypothesis (*Die Haustafeln,* p. 89; *Ethics,* III) concerning the pre-literary history of these admonitions. On the grounds that they are more uniform in written traditions he argues that they must also have become routinized in the preaching of the early churches at an earlier date.

nant or noble man and the high or noble element within
man; its vision of what man truly is and should become is
concentrated upon his *dignity and detachment;* his being
free from bondage and obligation.[19] Subordination may
apply in his relationship to God or to the state but not
among men.[20] In the *Haustafeln,* on the other hand, the
center of the imperative is a call to willing subordination
to one's fellow man. The term *hypotassesthai* is not best
rendered by *subjection,* which carries a connotation of
being thrown down and run over, nor by *submission,*
with its connotation of passivity. Sub*ord*ination means
the acceptance of an *order,* as it exists, but with the new
meaning given to it by the fact that one's acceptance of it
is willing and meaningfully motivated.

Why does this need to be said? Why was there any
point, in that ancient time, in directing an imperative to
children and women to subordinate themselves? Was this
not taken for granted? Was there any other choice in that
society? Here we find the second revolutionary axiom
underlying our texts. It is not enough, if we want to
understand a text, that we seek the meaning of an answer
it gives to the question it deals with. If we are truly to
understand any answer, we must also understand the
meaning of the question to which it is addressed. For the
apostles to encourage slaves and women to be subordinate, there must have been some specific reason for them
to have been tempted to behave otherwise. What could
that have been? There must have been something in the
experience of their becoming Christians, or in their edu-

[19] It is noteworthy that although Epictetus was a slave, he does not list
"slave" as one of the roles to live up to.

[20] The root meaning of the very *hypotassein* is "to set in line under"; in
the middle voice it then means "to accept one's lower place." The verb is
used 31 times in the Greek version of the Old Testament, where it renders
ten different Hebrew terms—enough to indicate that there was not one such
clearly focused concept in Hebrew usage. In this Old Testament usage
subordination is normal in relation to God or to the king, but not generally
to other men.

cation as new members of the Christian community, or in their experience in the life of that group, which had given to these subjects a vision or a breath of a new kind of dignity and responsibility. This must already have occurred if they were tempted to rise above their station. Only if something in the life or the preaching of the church had given them the idea that their subordinate status had been challenged or changed, would there be any temptation to the kind of unruliness to which these texts are addressed.

A widespread tradition, present ever since the age of Lincoln but propagated still more sweepingly with the currency of civil rights and women's liberation rhetoric, sees in Paul's teaching about subordination one of the causes for Christianity's failure to seek social justice more aggressively, or more successfully.

Our present study does not focus upon the history of Christianity as a force for social justice[21] but a parenthetical detour may be justified for the light it throws on how easily Paul is misunderstood. Those whose Christian commitment does not permit them simply to mock or ignore the Apostle feel they can "excuse" or "understand" his subordination teaching (which, not understanding its fundamentally revolutionary character, they do not intend to accept) on the ground that he had not yet "matured" or "advanced" to the "higher"[22] insights

[21] Ever since Ernst Troeltsch, it has been commonplace to see that *indirectly* a minority Christian movement with a nonconforming ethic can have considerable social impact.

[22] An example of this condescending approach is the (in other respects quite helpful) study of Krister Stendahl, *The Bible and the Role of Women* (Philadelphia: Fortress, 1966). In order to overcome the uncritical woodenness of certain traditional interpretations, Stendahl plays off the Paul he agrees with against the one he disagrees with in the way just suggested, thereby cutting off the possibility that any new light might be received by hearing the apostolic witness at those points where it says something that does not reinforce what we already believe. Stendahl mocks the naive exegesis that would try to "play first-century Semite" or "out-do the Amish," but does not (in this text) clarify the ground rules of another

expressed in Galatians 3:28, namely the modern-sounding equalitarianism which denies all differences between "Jew and Greek, slave and freeman, male and female."[23]

Paul still gets the credit for finally reaching that height, which we can recognize as a height by its modern sound; and thus we can credit the New Testament with a personalistic view which by implication was to determine slavery and subordination; but in order to be thus indulgent with the Apostle we must forgive his retention of the vestiges of the subordination idea and (for our purposes) cut them out of the canon.

Careful discussion of this kind of supercilious approach to Scripture would have to deal both with the general issue of scriptural interpretation[24] and with the

approach which would better enable Scripture to play a needed role in the life of the churches. There would seem to be other ways to make room for the ministries of women in the Church of Sweden without simply excising those elements of Scripture which seem out of step with contemporary convictions. What if, for instance, the sweeping, doctrinaire egalitarianism of our culture, which makes the concept of "the place of woman" seem either laughable or boorish, and makes that of "subordination" seem insulting, should turn out really (in "the intent of God," or in long-run social experience) to be demonic, uncharitable, destructive of personality, disrespectful of creation, and unworkable? Must we still assume that in order properly to "play twentieth-century occidentals" we must let this modern myth keep us from hearing what the Apostle says about the christological basis of mutual subordination?

23 It should be noted that the point of Gal. 3:28 is not *equality*, in the sense of overruling all variety of roles and rights, but unity. The reference to "slave and free, man and woman" simply reinforces the "Jew and Greek" concern which is the topic of the whole book. Jew remains Jew, Greek Greek in this unity. Equality of *worth* is not identity of *role*. To make of Gal. 3:28 a "modern" statement on women's liberation, from which one can then look down on the rest of Paul's thought, not only misplaces this text logically (as is said in the text above); it also misreads the text itself.

24 Such modern judges of NT ethics generally do not bother to suggest what Paul in his situation should have done differently. What should an Emancipation Proclamation have looked like then? Did Lincoln's way really work? Nor do they generally note that the "established" forms of "Christendom" which legitimized slavery were not obeying the ethics of either Jesus or Paul as we find them in this study. Nor do they generally bother to test whether some other available option (Islam?) would have had over the

character of the implicitly egalitarian personalism which it approvingly finds in Galatians 3:28.[25] Here, however, it must suffice to stay by the context of our texts. The call to willing subordination is not explainable unless there has been a temptation to insubordination. Such a temptation to insubordination is not thinkable unless some kind of message affirming the dignity of the subordinate one had already been heard. Then the call to subordination must, in any thinkable reconstruction of the social context of Paul's message, result from—not deny or fall short of—some kind of proclamation of the dignity of every man and woman.

Thus whereas Stoicism speaks to the man who is already respectable, and encourages him to live up to the dignity he already sees in his role, the *Haustafeln* admonition is addressed first to persons on the bottom side of the social order, and assumes that they have heard a message which calls into question the subjection they have hitherto not been able to challenge.[26] Where had they heard such a message if not from Paul?[27]

centuries a more liberating effect. How can there be any corrective or challenge to our self-sufficiency, any continuity in the Christian community—to say nothing of any judging and redeeming Word of God—if the present insight of the bearer is to be sovereign judge of any new communication he will accept?

[25] The egocentric modernity of the contemporary reader distorts the texts he likes as much as the ones he doesn't (cf. above, note 23). Not only the text of Gal. 3:28 but also its nearly literal parallel Col. 3:11 affirms not the equality of isolated individuality but the complementary unity of diverse people in one body (see below, "justification" and "new creation," pp. 215, 228).

[26] The idea that Paul had "retained a vestige" of subordinationist thought is false also at the point of its assumption that the duty of subordination ever was being taught. Slaves and women were kept subject by superior power, and by the absence of alternatives, not by moral teaching. We have already observed that moral teaching was not addressed to subordinate people. Paul did not "borrow" or "fail to overcome" his subordinationist thought. He (or the church before him) created it, by the application to a universal human problem of the central theme of Christology: that Jesus' suffering is the law of his disciples' life.

[27] We noted that Gal. 3:28 and Col. 3:11 are almost literal parallels, even though the points being argued in the two contexts are quite different. This

How had they heard it if not in the form of the report that in Jesus' messianity a new age had begun in which men are freed for obedience by the resurrection of the Crucified?

(g) The only "sanction" or "motivation" undergirding the Stoic ethic is the self-evident appropriateness of giving in to the way things are and living up to what one is. There is no promise of reward, there is no moving in the heart, there is no pleading. Ethical meditation counts on the readiness of the upright man to do the right, once by insight and reason he knows what that is. He is presumed to be the kind of healthy person who without discussion or question does what is fitting.

In the *Haustafeln,* on the other hand, there are several reasons, not only one, which are given to interpret and to motivate. All of them are *substantial* arguments, i.e. they not only say that the right is imperative but also explain why this kind of action is right. They are all related specifically to the person of Christ and the work of the church. Sometimes the example of Jesus is specifically referred to. This allusion has maximum clarity in I Peter 2:18 with regard to the slave who should subordinate himself even to the unjust master, because of the example of Christ who did the same when unjustly accused, and in Ephesians 5:22 where the readiness of the husband to give himself for his wife is both motivated and given substance by Christ's giving himself for his church.[28]

At other points there is a wider reference to participation in the person and the character and the movement

gives some room for the hypothesis that in each case the writer was quoting an earlier dictum or slogan already known to his readers. If so, this would indicate that the "new-humanity" or "new-creature" or "new-person" imagery, including its illustration by the denial of differences, Jew/Greek, slave/free, was pre-Pauline tradition.

[28] The concept of imitation of, conformity to, or participation in the servanthood of Christ is of course widespread in New Testament thought apart from the *Haustafeln.* Cf. above, pp. 122, 126.

of Christ with such phrases as "as befits one in the Lord."[29]

In still other circumstances there is additional reference to the *testimony* which the Christian seeks to give to the non-Christian. The wife is motivated in her subordination partly by the concern to win to faith in Christ her unbelieving husband.[30] In addition the parallels to the *Haustafeln* in Timothy have considerable reference to the life of the church. Then there are also references to reward or to the results of one's obedience.[31]

Once more it becomes clear at this point that the ethic of the apostles cannot possibly be defined by borrowings from either Jewish or Greek sources. Neither the general imperative to be subordinate nor the specific rooting of this call in the example of Christ, or in the nature of Christ as it is shared by the believer, can have any other explanations than that they arose within the original teaching of the apostles in the earliest common life of the Christian community.

(h) After having stated the call to subordination as addressed first to those who are subordinate already, the *Haustafeln* then go on to turn the relationship around and repeat the demand, calling the *dominant* partner in the relationship to a kind of subordination in his turn. Parents are asked not to irritate their children, husbands are called upon to love (*agapan*) their wives. Philemon is invited to receive Onesimus "no longer as a slave, but

[29] Eph. 5:21, "out of reverence for Christ"; Col. 3:18, "as is fitting in the Lord." Schroeder, *Die Haustafeln*, pp. 161-170, pursues extensively the meaning of the formula *in Christ* or *in the Lord* as it is used to sanction the believer's subordination. Far from being a pagan borrowing, this call is shown by this usage to be rooted in the very center of the Christian's confession and piety.

[30] I Pet. 2:12, 15; 3:1, "so that some may be won without a word by the behavior of their wives"; cf. I Cor. 7:16.

[31] Eph. 6:3, "That it may be well with you" (from Deut. 5:16); 6:8, "whatever good any one does, he will receive the same again"; Col. 3:24, "knowing that from the Lord you will receive the inheritance"; I Pet. 3:7, "in order that your prayers may not be hindered."

more than a slave, as a beloved brother, both in the flesh and in the Lord," as he would receive Paul himself.

That the call to subordination is reciprocal is once again a revolutionary trait. If this acceptance of the existing social order and the call to those who are subordinate to remain there were all that was said, then it might be correct when Lutheran tradition sees in these texts a reaffirmation of the creation order, which has about it the authority of revelation because God has made society thus. That same tradition could then also be right in concluding that the Christian social ethic must always be basically conservative because of the rootage of the present order in the divine imperative. But the *Haustafeln* do not consecrate the existing order when they call for the acceptance of subordination by the subordinate person; far more they relativize and undercut this order by then immediately turning the imperative around. For a first-century husband to love (*agapan*) his wife or for a first-century father to avoid angering his child, or for a first-century master to deal with his servant in the awareness that they are both slaves to a higher master,[32] is to make a more concrete and more sweeping

---

[32] This study does not deal directly with the Epistle to Philemon, since the particular language of the *Haustafeln* does not appear there. The interpretation of that text would, however, only support the rest of the present study. Paul's convert Onesimus, as a part of the meaning of his conversion, voluntarily returns to his master. By leading Onesimus to take this step, Paul went beyond the prescriptions of Deut. 23:15f. (Coleman-Norton, *op. cit.*, pp. 172ff, after surveying considerable material, still is not able to say whether Paul was obeying any particular Roman legal obligation to return Onesimus.) Paul's instruction to Philemon is to receive Onesimus "no longer as a slave, but as a beloved brother, both in the flesh and in the Lord," as Paul himself would be received. This amounts to Paul's instructing Philemon, in the kind of noncoercive instruction which is fitting for a Christian brother (even with the offer of Paul's payment), that Onesimus is to be set free. American experience since 1865 has demonstrated that summary release from chattel slavery is not necessarily an improvement in the status of the slave if not accompanied with a new and honorable relationship to the former master and the prevalent social structure. Then this way of dealing with Onesimus, by instructing that he be treated as a brother and a guest, documents not the conservatism but the innovative character of Paul's ethic.

difference in the way that husband or father or master
behaves than the other imperative of subordination
would have made practically in the behavior of the wife
or child or servant.

The biblical scholar would pause at this point to
concentrate on the possible origins of this particular
fragment of tradition. Where did Peter and Paul get this
set of imperatives which they thus worked into their
Epistles? If the evidence seems to be against their having
devised it by simple borrowing from either Hellenistic or
Jewish sources,[33] and if the evidence seems to be against
the likelihood that one of them borrowed it from the
other, then one has hardly any other choice but to
conclude that this kind of teaching was present in the
very earliest years of the church and that it grows directly
out of the meaning for the young church of her confession of Christ as Lord and the impact that proclamation had upon its listeners. The only remaining source
we very logically suspect is that somehow this tradition
comes from Jesus.[34]

But although leaning most gratefully upon the work
of the biblical critic, it is with a more systematic ethical
concern that we have read these texts. We have now
tested, at another quite distinct point in the New Testament literature, the systematic axiom of modern Protestant ethics, the contrast between the ethic of stable
society in the late teachings of Paul and the ethic of the
immediate kingdom in Jesus. Right where we had been

[33] One most careful study of the relationship between New Testament
thought and Stoicism is J. N. Sevenster's *Paul and Seneca* (Leiden: Brill,
1969). Without setting out to deal specifically with the *Haustafeln,* Sevenster
(esp. pp. 167-218) finds differences between Paul and Seneca very similar to
those we have been observing.

[34] For interpretation of the significance of the chain of tradition reaching back to Jesus, to which the Apostle Paul refers explicitly a few times, but
indirectly still more often, compare Oscar Cullmann, "The Tradition," in
The Early Church (Philadelphia: Westminster, 1956), pp. 59ff; and Archibald M. Hunter, *Paul and His Predecessors* (Westminster, 1961).

told that the systematic split between two kinds of ethical thought is located and symbolized, in the reasoning with which the Apostle Paul speaks to the relation of persons to each other within the most stable functions of society, the family and the economy, we find an ethic that is derived in its shape and in its meaning, and even in its language, from the novelty of the teaching and the work and the triumph of Jesus.

Widening the Circle

Now that we have become familiar with the central structure of ethical thought expressed in the *Haustafeln*, we are able to observe its presence elsewhere in the New Testament as well.[35] In his first letter to the Christians at

---

[35] A most penetrating statement of this wider logic is that of Johannes Hamel:

"The instruction, 'Let everyone be subordinate . . . ' has been so seriously misunderstood, and then abused, because of the failure to respect the complete context in which both the word *hypotassesthai* and the other similar invitations to obedience, honor, to humiliation are found. All of these words give expression to an essential mark of Christian relations to one's fellow man: in the congregation, in the family and in the city, for brethren, for non-Christians, and also (in political contexts) toward the bearers of power. The call to 'be subordinate,' to 'obey,' to 'regard another as higher than oneself' is addressed to men with regard to their wives and vice versa, slaves toward their masters (and again vice versa, compare Philemon), children toward their parents (and the parents should honor their children by not irritating them), the young toward the old, and the elders toward the congregation which they lead.

"If then one does not regard the imperative, 'Be subordinate,' in isolation, it immediately loses the bad taste which the word 'subject' has taken on in German history and literature. *Hypotassesthai* then does not mean playing along at every price, not slavish obedience, not bowing before the throne and the altar. It is not the attitude of the loyal citizen in the time of national absolutism. It is rather founded, in accord with an ethical theme which runs clear through the New Testament, in the person and the way of the Lord, who is at the same time the norm and the realization of this self-abasement; cf. I Tim. 2:3-7; Titus 3:3-7; 2:11-14; I Pet. 2:21-25, 3:18; Eph. 5:25-27; 4:32-5:2; Phil. 2:5-11; Col. 2:18ff; 4:1; Eph. 6:1-9; I Cor. 7:20ff; 8:11f; Rom. 14:7ff; 15:3f; Gal. 5:24; 6:2, and many other texts.

"The best-known example, the christological Psalm of Phil. 2:5ff,

Corinth, Paul has occasion more than once to speak to specific ethical problem cases in the realm of the household, and we can observe the same thought patterns at work.

One of the ways in which the Christian women at Corinth had felt it would be appropriate to dramatize the new dignity given to them in Christ was the gesture of throwing off, in the course of the worship service, the veiling or the head covering which was standard accouterment for a woman appearing in public (cf. I Cor. 11:2ff). This veiling was a sign of protection (Paul calls it a "power") when she went out of the home, in that it indicated that she belonged somewhere in society; that her father or her husband was her protector; but at the same time it was a symbol of subjection.

In reading this passage, as with the *Haustafeln*, some

grounds the imperative to the church to 'regard one another as higher than oneself' by pointing to the self-abasement of the Lord of our salvation. The concrete definition of the meaning of *hypotassesthai* comes from the crucified and risen Lord who, being free, abased himself for our sake and gave himself for us. Since we receive our life from this deed of this Lord, it is fitting that we subordinate ourselves to one another in a way that corresponds to this gift and this example. The form of love among us is defined by *that* love which was shown toward us by the Lord who served us and rescued us.

"If on the other hand one understands *hypotassesthai* in isolation, then one has made of this root word for discipleship a formal and a passive obedience which takes from the 'subject' his own arbitrariness. But the blame for this misunderstanding does not belong to the New Testament but to our unbelief, which has made out of the call to freedom and discipleship and the way of the cross an invitation to duck out of danger, to get out of the way, for the benefit of whatever group may be in power. . . .

"If then *hypotassesthai* (and the other substantially synonymous terms) is in principle a posture 'befitting' the gospel of the self-abasing Lord of the world, then it is in every situation a free, extremely aggressive way of acting, taking very clear account of the situation, including feeling and understanding and will, always including the possibility of a spirit-driven resistance, of an appropriate disavowal and a refusal, ready to accept suffering at this or that particular point."

Johannes Hamel, "Erwägungen zur unchristlichen Paraenese . . . " in Ernst Wolf, ed., *Christusbekenntnis im Atomzeitalter? ThEx,* 70 (1959), 159-161.

interpreters conclude that it is regrettable that Paul had not yet come to the vision that there is equality of all kinds of persons in Christ. But if we are to understand the point of this passage we must assume that the women in Corinth *had* heard that message. Otherwise they would not be taking off their veils, especially not during the worship service. Thus the retention of the veil when a woman would rise to speak in the congregation (to "pray or prophesy") also became a symbol of that double movement: first of the enfranchising impact of the gospel upon women, in that she may rise to speak and can function religiously as far more than simply a member of the household of her father or husband, and secondly of her acceptance of the order of society within which her role is to be lived out.

Here again as in the *Haustafeln* there is a clear reminder that this relationship of subordination and superordination is not a difference in worth: "in the Lord woman is not independent of man nor man of woman; for as woman was made from man so man is now born of woman" (I Cor. 11:11f). To accept subordination within the framework of things as they are is not to grant the inferiority in moral or personal value of the subordinate party. In fact the opposite is true; the ability to call upon the subordinate party to *accept that subordination freely* is, as it was in the *Haustafeln,* a sign that this party has already been ascribed a worth that is fundamentally different from what any other society would have accorded.

In chapter 7 of the same letter, Paul speaks to the specific decisions faced by two categories of subordinate persons: the woman and the slave. His counsel is illustrative both of the *freedom* with which the gospel speaks to specific ethical cases and of the *consistency* within its freedom of application. His first element of counsel is to remain in the social status within which one is; "in whatever state each was called, there let him remain with God" (v. 24). This applied to the slave's remaining a slave, to the single person's remaining single, to the married woman's remaining with her unbelieving husband, to the forsaken married woman's remaining unmarried without her husband as long as he lives; to accepting one's status as circumcised or as not circumcised. The reasoning supporting this general admonition is not that to change in any of these ways would be sinful or wrong, in the sense of an infraction of the law of God. The concern of the Apostle is rather to assist everyone to remain "free from anxieties" (v. 32), in a world whose structures are impermanent, and not so important that we should concentrate our efforts upon changing our status with regard to them. ("The appointed time has grown very short; from now on let those who have wives live as though they have none, those who mourn as though they were not mourning . . . for the form of this world is passing away": vv. 29-31.)

Yet right alongside this concern for that freedom which is maintained by not being rebellious about one's status in the present, there runs a second strand of instruction which seems at first to be opposed to it. If a slave can become free, he should avail himself of this opportunity (v. 21).[36] If the husband of the forsaken woman dies she is free to remarry (v. 39); if anyone is strongly inclined toward marriage that is quite proper (v. 36), but a freed man must not become a slave since that would be to move away from rather than toward freedom (vv. 22f). Thus the Christian is called to view his social status from the perspective of maximizing his freedom. If

---

[36] In order not to open too many arguments at once, we have here accepted the predominant understanding of v. 21: "Get free if you can." This meaning is, however, by no means clear. There are good grammatical arguments supporting the opposite reading: "Even if a choice of liberation should come, it is still better to make use of your servitude" (cf. Sevenster, *op. cit.*, p. 189; Stendahl, *op. cit.*, p. 33). This reading would reinforce the main thrust of this chapter, yet without fully removing the permissiveness toward a change in status where it is imperative.

an opportunity is given him to exercise more freedom he shall do so because it is to freedom that we are called in Christ. But that freedom can already be realized within his present status by voluntarily accepting subordination, in view of the relative unimportance of such social distinctions when seen in the light of the coming fulfillment of God's purposes.

The same attitude toward society occurs again when we move to one still wider circle, the teaching of the New Testament with regard to the state. In I Peter 2, the *Haustafeln* text began: "subordinate yourself for the sake of the Lord to every human institution," and then spoke first of civil government, then of servants, then of wives. Again in I Timothy 2, which some scholars would con sider as also belonging to the list of *Haustafeln*, there is a call first to subjection to government, then subordination of women, and then acceptance by Christians of the orderly office of the bishop and the deacon in the church. Without linkage to the *Haustafeln* texts, the call to subordination to government is clear again in Romans 13. Thus government is, like the order of the family, one of the given structures of human relations within which the Christian is called to live up to his role. This subordination is again motivated and sanctioned by its relationship to the mission of Christ.[37]

There is one striking difference, however, at this point. After the invitation to wives we saw that the *Haustafeln* addressed a similar and immensely more novel call to husbands to love their wives; after calling slaves to

---

[37] Rom. 12:1f sets the entire ethical passage in the context of "the mercies of God"; 12:4-8 explains its imperatives as living up to one's assigned role; 12:17-21 commands the renunciation of vengeance, which coordinates with the acceptance of the powers that be as avengers (13:4). Markus Barth, *Acquittal by Resurrection,* pp. 43ff, exposits fully how the submission of Rom. 13 is rooted in the work of Christ. "He [Paul] reasons not from an order of creation or toward an easy life, but from the humiliation and exaltation of Christ" (p. 46).

be subject, the early Christian moralists called upon the masters to be equally respectful; after calling children to remain subordinate to parents, the admonition was turned about and addressed to parents as well. When, however, the call to subordination is addressed to the Christian in his status as a political subject, then in these texts exhortation is not reversed. There is no invitation to the king to conceive of himself as a public servant. Was this only because, as a matter of course, the apostolic preachers and authors recognized that there were no kings in their audiences? Or was it that, in line with the teaching of Christ, which had been preserved in several forms, Jesus had instructed his disciples specifically to reject governmental domination over others as unworthy of the disciple's calling of servanthood?[38]

In his landmark study of NT tradition criticism, *The Primitive Christian Catechism,*[39] Archbishop Philip Carrington places the *Haustafeln* in a wider context of tradition. He lifts out didactic texts[40] in which the same sequence of imperatives recurs:

> (a) put off . . .
> (b) be subject . . .
> (c) watch . . .
> (d) resist . . .

It would seem reasonable to conjecture that this parallelism in sequence (which is much fuller than just these four verbs) might point back to a commonality in the oral catechetical tradition of the earliest churches. It would then follow that such teaching was received by every new Christian and accepted as a part of his baptismal commitment, a part of "having learned Christ"

---

38 Mark 10:42f; Matt. 20:25ff; Luke 22:25ff.

39 Cambridge U. P., 1940.

40 Col. 3-4; Eph. 3-6; I Pet. 2:1-4:11; I Pet. 4:12ff; James; Heb. 12-13.

(Eph. 4:20; Col. 2:6). Carrington further surmises that the early churches, as they were dealing with the Gentile problem or with Gentiles' problems,[41] were concerned to find common instructional forms (verbal and social) reaching back to pre-Christian (i.e. Jewish) models. He does not point up the novelty whereby these common patterns were Christianized. Regarding the imperative of subordination, which for the NT writers is explicitly measured and motivated by the example of Christ, Carrington[42] retains its (Jewish?) foundation in the acceptance of "the godlike status of the elders and fathers." We can agree with Carrington in finding Jewish precedent for this instructional pattern, without following him in reducing the instructional content to the foundations present in the Jewish parallel.

A Whole New Order[43]

As scattered as are the ethical instructions of the New Testament writers, as freely as they flex to fit the varied positions of the addressees, nonetheless one finds tying them together the link of a common clear logic. The liberation of the Christian from "the way things are," which has been brought about by the gospel of Christ, who freely took upon himself the bondages of history in our place, is so thorough and novel as to make evident to the believer that the givenness of his subjection to the

41 *Ibid.*, pp. 68, 88ff.

42 Pp. 64, 68.

43 This subtitle is borrowed from another Pauline context: "If one is in Christ, behold a whole new world!" (II Cor. 5:17). There is no linguistic justification for the "new creation" in this text to be taken as referring to the regenerate individual personality, as Protestant preaching has so often done; cf. below, p. 226. To confess Jesus Christ as Lord is to make a statement not only about the confessor but about the world. The Christian can transform human relationship through voluntary subordination not because (a la Troeltsch or Dibelius) Jesus did not change the world, but because he did.

enslaving or alienating powers of this world is broken. It
is natural to feel Christ's liberation reaching into every
kind of bondage, and to want to act in accordance with
that radical shift.

But precisely because of Christ we shall not impose
that shift violently upon the social order beyond the
confines of the church. Following his example of accepting subordination (I Pet. 2:18; Eph. 5:22) we shall not
do this because the new world or the new regime under
which we live is not a simple alternative to present
experience but rather a renewed way of living within the
present (I Cor. 7:20; John 17:15f). We may have reason
to hope that the loving willingness of our subordination
will itself have a missionary impact; "the unbelieving
husband is consecrated through his wife, and the unbelieving wife is consecrated through her husband. . . .
Wife, how do you know whether you will save your
husband?"[44] The voluntary subjection of the church is
understood as a witness to the world.

The pattern is thus uniformly one of creative transformation. The early Christians accepted the common
sense analysis of Stoicism that the ethical duties of the
Christian could best be stated with reference to living up
to the meaning of one's role in society. Yet the meaning
of that role was changed in its form by the encounter
with the apodictic imperative style of Old Testament law,
and changed in substance by the stance of servanthood
derived from the example and the teaching of Jesus
himself. His motto of revolutionary subordination, of
willing servanthood in the place of domination, enables
the person in a subordinate position in society to accept
and live within that status without resentment, at the
same time that it calls upon the person in the super-
ordinate position to forsake or renounce all domineering
use of his status. This call is then precisely not a simple

[44] Cf. above, n. 30.

ratification of the stratified society into which the gospel has come.[45] The subordinate person becomes a free ethical agent when he voluntarily accedes to his subordination in the power of Christ instead of bowing to it either fatalistically or resentfully. The claim is not that there is immediately a new world regime which violently replaces the old: but rather the old and the new order exist concurrently on different levels. It is because she knows that in Christ there is no male or female that the Christian wife can freely accept that subordination to her unbelieving husband which is her present lot. It is because Christ has made all men free and the freed man is on the same level with his slave, that their relationship may continue as a humane and honest one within the framework of the present economy, the structure of which is passing away (I Cor. 7:31).

Troeltsch and his disciples were right; the early church had to develop an ethic for living within the structures of society which was not immediately apparent within the discourses of Jesus himself, pervaded as they are by the expectation of the imminent kingdom. But they were wrong in assuming that it must follow from that observation that the ethic the early church did then develop was contradictory to or unrelated to the ethic of Jesus.[46] It is far more accurate to say that it is the ethic of Jesus

[45] The understanding that Paul's teaching did in fact ratify uncritically the social structures of his time, and that Christians following his guidance today would do the same, is prevalent both among social conservatives and among would-be "revolutionaries" who turn away from the New Testament for just this reason. This misapprehension is due partly to the readers' failure to read in the text the elements of moral conscientization and of reciprocity (e and h above) but also to the modern mythical belief that righteous violence on the part of the oppressed is normally a means of liberation.

[46] We referred above (p. 109 n. 10) to the demonstration by Hans Werner Bartsch that, *if* any changes can be discerned in the Gospel *texts* (e.g. between Mark and Luke), those changes represent not the abandon, but rather reaffirmation of the eschatological expectancy of Jesus' preaching. Luke's editing rephrased some details *in order to keep* testifying to his lively hope, not because he had lost it.

himself that was transmitted and transmuted into the
stance of the servant church within society, as indicated
precisely in the *Haustafeln*. Since in the resurrection and
in Pentecost the kingdom which was imminent has now
in part come into our history, the church can now live
out, within the structures of society, the newness of the
life of that kingdom. The early church did not need to
borrow from Stoicism the concept of living one's own
role; she rather transformed the concept of living within a
role by finding how in each role the servanthood of
Christ, the voluntary subordination of one who knows
that another regime is normative, could be made concrete. The wife or child or slave who can accept subordination because "it is fitting in the Lord" has not forsaken
the radicality of the call of Jesus; it is precisely this
attitude toward the structures of this world, this freedom
from needing to smash them since they are about to
crumble anyway, which Jesus had been the first to teach
and in his suffering to concretize.

This chapter might be understood as assuming that for
any question of social ethics a direct solution can be
sought in the casuistic teachings of the New Testament.
We have picked up one segment of these teachings and
found it both relevant to issues of social order and
coherent with the ethic of Jesus. We were especially
concerned to test—and as it turns out, to negate—the
widespread view that the ethic of the apostles betrays
that of Jesus. But this should not be taken as suggesting
that for other questions—the welfare state, or the meaning of property in an industrialized society, ethical dilem-
mas in modern medicine—we could do without broader
generalizations, a longer hermeneutic path, and insights
from other sources. We are not affirming a specific biblical ethical content for modern questions; we are observing that where the New Testament offered specific guidance for its own time, that guidance confirms and applies
the messianic ethic of Jesus.

10

Let Every Soul Be Subject:
Romans 13
and the Authority of the State

Until the crisis of Nazism struck into the heartland of Protestant theological scholarship, there was little question about the centrality and adequacy of Romans 13:1-7 as the foundation of a Christian doctrine of the state. It seems to be said here quite unambiguously that government is established by God and that Christians are therefore to obey their government, not only because they fear its sanctions but because they conscientiously support its function of repressing evil and encouraging good. Especially within the post-Constantinian context which Catholic and Protestant theology had long been taking for granted, this text served as a sort of capsule constitution to guide the Christian statesman (who should punish evil and reward good) and the Christian citizen (who should conscientiously obey). When a government thus divinely instituted wields the sword, this action is therefore excepted from the general prohibition of killing. There might remain some imaginable borderline problems, such as a government waging an unjust war, or a government asking its citizens to commit sins; but within

Christendom such eventualities were not definite enough
to demand that the borders be traced concretely. This
definition presumably would apply to all states, but pre-
eminently of course to the governments of Christian
Europe and America.

New Testament exegesis has long since abandoned
such a simple concept of divine institution in the order of
creation; but it persists in the systematic-theological and
ethical thought of Protestants, especially of theologically
conservative Protestants. It is therefore important that
the traditional commonplaces be challenged in a systematic, even polemic way, in addition to the verse-by-verse
rereading done by the textual scholars.[1] This outline
must run the risks of simplification in order to point up
the polemic issues. Let us then put most precisely the
challengeable claim of the tradition we intend to challenge; it is that by virtue of the ·divine institution of
government as a part of God's good creation, its mandate
to wield the sword and the Christian's duty to obey the
state combine to place upon the Christian a moral obligation to support and participate in the state's legal killing
(death penalty, war), despite contrary duties which other-

[1] Reviews of exegetical discussion are offered for the classic theological
traditions by Fritzhermann Keienburg, *Die Geschichte der Auslegung von
Römer 13:1-7* (Basel theological dissertation, Gelsenkirchen, 1956), and for
recent studies by Ernst Käsemann, "Römer 13:1-7 in unserer Generation,"
ZTK, 56 (1959), 316-376. A thorough verse-by-verse restatement, without
reaching out into wider theological interpretation, is that of Rolf Walker,
"Studie zu Römer 13:1-7," *ThEx,* 132 (1968). Even more for this present
chapter than for those which preceded, it must be said that no attempt is
made, or need be made for our purposes, to survey thoroughly the scholarly
consensus. The general outlines of our interpretation are not original; to
argue them in depth would interest a different readership than that for
which this text is prepared. The present view is much like those of Markus
Barth, *Acquittal by Resurrection,* pp. 34 and 159; of Herbert M. Gale,
"Paul's View of the State," *Interpretation,* 6 (1952), 409ff; and of Hans
Werner Bartsch, "Die Neutestamentliche Aussagen über den Staat," *EvT,* 19
(1959), 375ff. The first draft of this presentation arose from a "Peace
Witness Seminar" on "Evangelicals in Social Action" convened Nov. 30-Dec.
2, 1967, by Eastern Mennonite College, Harrisonburg, Virginia.

wise would seem to follow from Jesus' teaching or example. Every general affirmation we can make about this
text must therefore be pointed up by its central impact
upon that tradition.

> (1) *The New Testament speaks in many ways about*
> *the problem of the state: Romans 13 is not the*
> *center of this teaching.*

There is a very strong strand of Gospel teaching which
sees secular government as the province of the sovereignty of Satan. This position is perhaps most typically
expressed by the temptation story, in which Jesus did not
challenge the claim of Satan to be able to dispose of the
rule of all nations. If one makes this perspective central,
all the New Testament texts appear in another light.[2]

This position is offensive to the modern mind because
it stands in judgment on modern democratic humanism
and because it is held to in an extreme way by Jehovah's
Witnesses; but certainly no one can deny that it is a part
of the biblical material or that it remained a significant
thrust of the teaching of the early postapostolic church.
When it is seen from this perspective, we are reminded
that Romans 13 was written about pagan government.[3] It
constitutes at best acquiescence in that government's
dominion, not the establishing of a given state by God or
the installation of a particular sovereign by providential
disposition.

There is a strong strand of apostolic thought that sees
the state within the framework of the victory of Christ
over the principalities and powers. This position is stated
by Hendrik Berkhof and G. Caird.[4] Instead of a stable

2 One serious expression of this perspective is Archie Penner's *The New
Testament, the Christian, and the State* (Scottdale: Herald, 1959).

3 If, as a strong variant textual tradition suggests, we should read "*all*
authorities," the reference would probably be not to other governments
(than Rome) but rather to other kinds of authority.

4 Fuller interpretation and bibliography relating to the theme "victory
over the powers" is provided above, pp. 135ff, and by Markus Barth, *loc. cit.*

institution, dating from creation, the "state as such," we
are then told to think of a dynamic process related to and
reflecting the saving work of Christ, as this work reaches
even beyond the realm of the church. This wider perspective is especially significant because of the language of
"powers" present in the Romans text[5]—an observation
that should keep us from taking for granted that the text
can be interpreted standing alone, as is habitually done. It
is in this christological-cosmological context that Oscar
Cullmann finds the New Testament understanding of the
state to be expressed most clearly.

In the book of Revelation, most pointedly in chapter
13, we find an image of government largely comparable
to the one we referred to in the earliest portions of the
Gospels. The "Powers" are seen as persecuting the true
believers; the same is true in the assumed background of
Peter and James. We shall return later to the issue of the
relation between Revelation 13 and Romans 13; for now
it suffices to indicate that here again there is a statement
of the church's view of government which is strikingly
less simple and affirmative than the *traditional* interpretation of Romans 13. It is therefore in principle already
challengeable when Protestant political ethical thought is
dominated as much as it has been by this one text, as if it

___

[5] The term "powers" in Rom. 13:1 (*exousiae*) may have the specific
cosmological sense dealt with by Berkhof and Caird; this is the opinion of O.
Cullmann, following K. L. Schmidt. It is like the other passages of this kind
in that the word appears in the plural and (perhaps) with the adjective "all."
It differs from those other contexts in the absence of a string of synonyms
(rulers, thrones, angels, principalities . . .) and in the absence of express
reference to Christ. Thus it is also possible that it may have the simpler
functional sense of "authorities." Elsewhere in the New Testament the
cosmological sense predominates when the term appears in the plural; in the
singular both meanings are possible. Robert Morgenthaler, *op. cit.*, reinforces
by detailed comparison with Luke's usage the claim of Oscar Cullmann that
exousia has a political sense. The scholarly debate on this issue is very
significant as it relates to the "Powers" problem (cf. ch. 8) and the "Subjection" theme (ch. 9), but it is immaterial to the thesis of the present chapter.

were a kind of charter or constitution for the political realm.

> (2) *In the structure of the Epistle, chapters 12 and 13 in their entirety form one literary unit. Therefore the text 13:1-7 cannot be understood alone.*

Chapter 12 begins with a call to nonconformity, motivated by the memory of the mercies of God, and finds the expression of this transformed life first in a new quality of relationships within the Christian community and, with regard to enemies, in suffering. The concept of love then recurs in 13:8-10. Therefore any interpretation of 13:1-7 which is not also an expression of suffering and serving love must be a misunderstanding of the text in its context. There are no grounds of literary analysis, textual variation, or style to support the claim that we have here to do with a separate chunk of teaching which constitutes foreign matter in the flow of the text.[6]

The beginning of the unit of text (12:1) ties its thought firmly back to the "mercies of God" as the theme of the previous portion of the Epistle. These "mercies" included the unmerited calling of the Gentiles to the new life in God (chs. 1-5), the unmerited renewal of even the "body" through the Spirit (chs. 6-8), and the continuing unmerited redemptive concern of God for

---

[6] The foreignness of the passage to its context has been most sweepingly argued by James Kallas, "Romans 13:1-7; an Interpolation," in *NTS*, 11, 365-374. The argument is all based on Kallas' views as to the compatibility of the passage's teaching with other ideas held by Paul. Some scholars argue insertion by a later writer, others see Paul himself as quoting a tradition foreign to the rest of his thought. In order to be so convinced that the text does not fit the rest of Paul, most of these scholars must first assume for it a meaning that has been imposed on it by later readers, rather than the emphasis the present study finds in it. Those who challenge the authenticity of the passage first interpret it to mean something Paul probably would not have said. If the text were read with more openness to its wording and less acceptance of later tradition about its meaning, the argument would fall away.

ethnic Israel (chs. 9-11).[7] The continuation of our passage (13:11-14) looks forward in hope to a salvation so
concretely imminent and historical as to be "nearer than
when we first believed." It issues in a new quality of
concern for the "weak brother" (14:1-21) and in the
gathering of financial and spiritual resources to support
one another (14:26-29) and Paul (vv. 22-25, 30-33). The
entire text thus sees Christian nonconformity and suffering love as driven and drawn by a sense of God's triumphant movement from the merciful past into a triumphant future. Any interpretation of 13:1-7 that would
make it the expression of a static or conservative undergirding of the present social system would therefore represent a refusal to take seriously the context.[8] Any
interpretation in which God's mercies are not seen as
overcoming hostilities through the creation of community, reaching even to the nuts and bolts of financial
sharing and missionary support, has covered over the
meaning of each part of the text by not seeing it whole.

In addition to this kind of implication which follows
from the broader frame of the passage, there are specific
verbal cross-references which link the text with what
preceded and what follows. As we shall see later at
length, 13:8 begins with a verbal echo of verse 7. As
Oscar Cullmann and others have indicated, the submission
to the powers in 13:1 is motivated and exposited by the
hope in 13:11-14. Verse 10, by expositing verse 8, also

[7] Cf. below, pp. 224ff nn. 6, 7, and 12, the word of Bartsch and Minear
concerning the "political" aspect of all of Romans.

[8] A broader way to put the same question would be to apply the
traditional distinction between creation and redemption. The opening chapters of Romans may be seen as positing a duality between creation and
redemption. Then 13:1-7, describing the "Powers" as the order of creation
(cf. the phrase "creatures" in the parallel text of I Pet. 2:13), would be out
of place in a context of redemption. We do not pursue this question further
here, because the prior assumptions it makes about the distinct orders of
creation and redemption themselves need to be examined before they can be
assumed to throw light on the question.

gives a definition of the "good" in verse 3, whereby the
behavior of Christians under government is guided.

There is a most specific dialectical interplay around
the concepts of vengeance and wrath. Christians are told
(12:19) never to exercise vengeance but to leave it to
God and to wrath.[9] Then the authorities are recognized
(13:4) as executing the particular function which the
Christian was to leave to God. It is inconceivable that
these two verses, using such similar language, should be
meant to be read independently of one another. This
makes it clear that the function exercised by government
is not the function to be exercised by Christians. How
ever able an infinite God may be to work at the same
time through the sufferings of his believing disciples who
return good for evil and through the wrathful violence of
the authorities who punish evil with evil, such behavior is
for men not complementary but in disjunction. God can
in his own way, in his sovereign permissive providence,
"use" an idolatrous Assyria (Isa. 10) or Rome. This takes
place, however, without his declaring that such action
which he thus uses is morally good or that participation
in it is incumbent upon his covenant people. If the
statements of 12:19 and 13:4 were not in the same
passage, we might not necessarily cross-refer from one to
the other, so as to conclude that the prohibition of
vengeance in the one verse excludes the sharing of Christians in the outworking of vengeance as described in the
other. One could then say that the contexts are sufficiently different that the terms need not have exactly the
same meaning. But within the sustained reasoning of one
passage, with the same words being used in the midst of

---

[9] In general NT usage human wrath is a passion to be avoided (Eph. 4:31;
Col. 3:8; Matt. 5:22; I Tim. 2:8; Titus 1:7) or to be held in check (Eph.
4:26; James 1:19). Divine wrath is not to be understood in anthropomorphic
analogy to human passion (cf. Anthony T. Hanson, *The Wrath of the Lamb*
[London: S.P.C.K., 1957], esp. pp. 178ff) and is not served by human wrath
(James 1:20).

the same text, certainly it is a most likely interpretation that the "vengeance" or "wrath" that is recognized as being within providential control is the same as that which Christians are told not to exercise.

(3) *The subordination that is called for recognizes whatever power exists, accepts whatever structure of sovereignty happens to prevail. The text does not affirm, as the tradition has it, a divine act of institution or ordination of a particular government.*

One of the ways of understanding the "institution" of government by God is to claim that whatever government exists, it is by virtue of an act of institution, i.e. a specific providential action of God, that it came into being. Therefore this government exists by revelation. The events whereby it came to rule are themselves providential. If Germany finds itself under the control of Adolf Hitler, this very fact demonstrates that his government is "of God"; the events whereby this came to be thereby constitute a revelation given to the German people in the course of their history, by virtue of which they can know that they are to be subject to Hitler's authority and consider his cause to be divinely mandated. This concept of the givenness of a particular government as itself constituting its legitimacy we might call the "positivistic" view. It has tended in the past to be held in certain Lutheran circles. It certainly need not lead so far as to accredit Hitler; but it is significant and expressive of its theological structure that it could go that far without anything within the theological system necessarily needing to object. Whatever is, is the will of God. When we see what exists, we know thereby what God desires us to do. This position has evidently been discredited by the lengths to which it was taken by some in Hitler Germany; but it remains very much alive in popular piety and patriotism.

The weakness of the "positivistic" view is that the text of Romans makes no affirmative moral judgment on the existence of a particular government and says nothing particular about who happens to be Caesar or what his policies happen to be.

The other option, the alternative both logically and historically, is more at home in the Calvinistic tradition. We might call this the "normative" view. It runs from Huldrych Zwingli through Cromwell to Karl Barth and Emil Brunner. What is ordained is not a particular government but the concept of proper government, the principle of government as such. As long as a given government lives up to a certain minimum set of requirements, then that government may properly claim the sanction of divine institution. If, however, a government fails adequately to fulfill the functions divinely assigned to it, it loses its authority. It then becomes the duty of the preacher to teach that this has become an unjust government, worthy of rebellion. It can become the duty of Christian citizens to rise up against it, not because they are against the government but because they are in favor of *proper* government. The concept of just rebellion, in which the preacher himself does not become a revolutionary but does preach the moral obligation to rise up against unjust government in the name of proper government, finds its rootage in Huldrych Zwingli. In the second generation of the Reformed tradition, the generation of Calvin, it was already being worked out in some detail in its application to the position of the Huguenots in France. It continues through John Knox and Cromwell and through the American Revolution, and is currently being applied in a very consistent way by a particular current of ecumenical thought which would justify the rebellion of subject peoples in Latin America or Africa against white American and Western European cultural and economic imperialism.

The shortcoming of this view is partly internal. Who is

to judge how bad a government can be and still be good?
How much deviation from the norm is justifiable on the
grounds of human frailty? At what point is a government
disqualified? But a greater weakness is the simple fact
that nothing in the text of Romans 13 justifies the
concept of just rebellion. The conception of a "state
properly so called," in the name of which one would
reject and seek to overthrow the state which exists empirically, is totally absent in the passage. In the social
context of the Jewish Christians in Rome, the whole
point of the passage was to take out of their minds any
concept of rebellion against or even emotional rejection
of this corrupt pagan government. There is no definition
of the theoretical "proper state," by contrast with which
some other, "real" state would stand condemned to be
overthrown.[10]

One very frequent expression of the "legitimist" or
"normative" view is the balancing against one another of
Romans 13 (the good state) and Revelation 13 (the evil
state which glorifies itself religiously and must be re-
sisted). Christians are first to measure which kind of state
they have, and then to support it if it is the orderly state
of Romans and oppose it if it is the evil state of Revelation.[11] For this there is no ground in either text.

[10] In this section I have taken "rebellion" in the current sense of violent
overthrow. It is of course possible to redefine rebellion to cover any
disavowal of a government's legitimacy, even without violence and without
the creation of a counter-government. In this sense nonviolent noncoopera-
tion might be spoken of as a form of rebellion. If this usage were accepted
we would still need to challenge the integral distinction between good
governments, which Christians should bless, and bad ones against which they
should rebel. They should rather rebel against all and be subordinate to all;
for "subordination" is itself the Christian form of rebellion. It is the way we
share in God's patience with a system we basically reject. Cf. ch. 9 above.

[11] This posing of the alternatives is clearest in O. Cullmann, *The State in
the New Testament*, pp. 73ff, but is found very widely, from Karl Barth to
Eberhard Arnold. Cf. my *Christian Witness to the State*, p. 76.

The criticism of this "normative" approach has been made especially
strongly by a circle of German Protestant theologians around Ernst Wolf.

Neither text calls for active moral support or religious approval of the state; both texts call for subordination to whatever powers there be.

If both the "positivistic" and "normative" interpretations do violence to the text, what does the passage say? The Apostle is making a moral statement, not a metaphysical one. He is speaking to the present situation of the Roman Christians as representative of Christians throughout the Empire, and not to the nature of all political reality, nor does he prescribe an ideal social order.

God is not said to *create* or *institute* or *ordain* the powers that be, but only to *order* them, to put them in order, sovereignly to tell them where they belong, what is their place. It is not as if there was a time when there was no government and then God made government through a new creative intervention; there has been hierarchy and authority and power since human society existed. Its exercise has involved domination, disrespect for human dignity, and real or potential violence ever since sin has existed. Nor is it that in his ordering of it he specifically, morally approves of what government does. The sergeant does not produce the soldiers he drills, the librarian does not create nor approve of the book he catalogs and shelves. Likewise God does not take the responsibility for the existence of the rebellious "powers that be" or for their shape or identity; they already are. What the text says is that he orders them, brings them into line, that by his permissive government he lines them up with his purpose.

Their way of putting their point is their denial that the New Testament, or Rom. 13 in particular, contains a "doctrine of the state." By this is not meant that nothing is said about the state in the New Testament, nor that what is said on the subject is not clear, or not coherent. What is meant is that there is not one dogmatically authorized and unchanging statement of what the state must always be, which could then be used to accredit, but also to disqualify, particular states.

This is true of all governments. It is a statement both
de facto and *de jure*. It applies to the government of
dictators and tyrants as well as to constitutional democ-
racies. It would in fact apply just as well to the government of a bandit or a war lord, to the extent to which
such would exercise real sovereign control.[12]

That God orders and uses the powers does not reveal
anything new about what government should be or how
we should respond to government. A given government is
not mandated or saved or made a channel of the will of
God; it is simply lined up, used by God in his ordering of
the cosmos. It does not mean that what men in government do is good human behavior. As we noted, the
librarian does not approve of the content of a book he
shelves; God did not approve morally of the brutality
whereby Assyria chastised Israel (Isa. 10).

The immediate concrete meaning of this text for the
Christian Jews in Rome, in the face of official anti-
Semitism and the rising arbitrariness of the Imperial
regime, is to call them away from any notion of revolution or insubordination. The call is to a nonresistant
attitude toward a tyrannical government.[13] This is the

---

[12] The medieval and the classic Protestant idea of government as being
specifically instituted by an act of the divine will always assumes that if it
were not for this creative act "anarchy" would reign. But in real history
there is no such thing as anarchy. Where one power does not rule, another
does.

Having discerned the difference between "ordain" and "order" in this
way, we may now be able to state more clearly what would be needed if the
traditional view were to be right after all. To support the standard Protestant
concept of orders revealed in creation it would have to be affirmed by Paul
not only that the powers *exist*, but that there exists a standard, known to all
men by nature, to govern the functions of governments. Yet in the rare
places (e.g. Rom. 2) where Paul seems (according to some interpreters) to be
affirming that pagans possess some kind of moral insight, he never says the
standards for the social order are included in this natural knowledge.

[13] By "nonresistant" here, as in this entire study, is not meant com-
pliance or acquiescence in evil, but what Paul means in 12:7 and Jesus in
Matt. 5:39, the suffering renunciation of retaliation in kind. It does not
exclude other kinds of opposition to evil. Cf. above, n. 10.

immediate and concrete meaning of the text; how strange then to make it the classic proof for the duty of Christians to kill.

(4) *The instructions to the Romans are to be subject to a government in whose administration they had no voice. The text cannot mean that Christians are called to do military or police service.*

The functions Rome asked of its subject peoples did not include military or police service, which were considered either as hereditary professions or as citizens' privileges. There was no general military obligation. As slaves and as Jews, most early Christians would have been liable to no such obligation even if it had applied to Roman citizens. The functions the government did actually ask of its citizens did not include participation in bearing the sword of government. The functions described in verses 3-4 did not include any service that the Christian is asked to render. The "things due to the authority" listed in verses 6-7 do not include any kind of participation or service.

This observation is not simply about the substance of the text but also about the political situation at that time. It is therefore illegitimate to extend the meaning of the text as if it self-evidently applied as well to other kinds of services which other kinds of governments in other ages might ask of their citizens. Especially is it out of place for those who feel that simple literalism suffices to include unquestioning acceptance of the modern institution of conscription, as belonging under the heading of "being subject."

(5) *The function of bearing the sword to which Christians are called to be subject is the judicial and police function; it does not refer to the death penalty or to war.*

The sword (*machaira*) is the symbol of judicial authority. It was not the instrument of capital punishment, since the Romans crucified their criminals. It was not the instrument of war since it was but a long dagger. Like the pistol worn by a traffic policeman or the sword worn by a Swiss citizen-officer, it was more a symbol of authority than a weapon. This is not to say that the Roman government was mild or that this weapon was only symbolically present. But what it symbolizes is the way a given government exercises dominion over its subjects by appeal to violence, not the execution of capital offenders or the waging of hostilities against other nations.[14] At this time Rome was not carrying on major military hostilities against other nations. There were in fact no neighbor "nations" with whom Rome could very meaningfully wage war. The brush fire hostilities along the frontiers were more like police action than like war.

The distinction made here between police and war is not simply a matter of the degree to which the appeal to force goes, the number of persons killed or killing. It is a structural and a profound difference in the sociological meaning of the appeal to force. In the police function, the violence or threat thereof is applied only to the offending party. The use of violence by the agent of the police is subject to review by higher authorities. He applies his power within the limits of a state whose legislation even the criminal knows to be applicable to him. In any orderly police system there are serious safeguards to keep the violence of the police from being applied in a wholesale way against the innocent. The police power generally is great enough to overwhelm that of the individual offender so that any resistance on his part is pointless. In all of these respects, war is struc-

---

[14] On the other hand it is the normal weapon in hand-to-hand combat (Matt. 26:51f) and in insurrection (Luke 22:36ff). In non-Roman contexts it was used to put people to death (Heb. 11:37; Acts 12:2).

turally different. The doctrine of the "just war" is an
effort to extend into the realm of war the logic of the
limited violence of police authority—but not a very successful one. There is some logic to the "just war" pattern
of thought[15] but very little realism. At the very most the
only relevance of Romans 13 to war would be to a very
precise operation carried on within the very clear limitations of all the classic criteria that define the "justifiable
war." The more we would attempt honestly to define and
to respect such criteria, the more clearly we would see
that as far as any real or conceivable war is concerned, in
the name of any real or thinkable government, it is not
honestly possible to include that function under the
authorization given government by Romans 13.

(6) *The Christian who accepts his subjection to government retains his moral independence and judgment. The authority of government is not self-
justifying. Whatever government exists is ordered
by God; but the text does not say that whatever
the government does or asks of its citizens is good.*

(A) "The authorities are ministers of God, attending
to this very thing." What is the grammatical construction
of the participle "attending" (*proskarterountes*)? Most
translations consider it a simple further predication: "the
authorities are ministers of God *and* they busy themselves
with this very function (of meting out good to the good
and evil to the evil)." But this is from a grammatical
viewpoint not the most likely meaning of such a parti-
cipial construction. It is more likely that the participle
represents an adverbial modifier of the previous predica-

<hr />

[15] The use of the *term* "just war" has become unpopular in many circles
since Hiroshima; but the logic it refers to is still the only serious way of
dealing with the moral problem of war apart from pacifism. Even many who
call themselves pacifist are in fact still using "just war" reasoning. Cf. Ralph
Potter, *War and Moral Discourse* (Richmond: John Knox, 1969).

tion. We should then read "they are ministers of God *to the extent* to which they busy themselves" or "*when* they devote themselves" or "*in that* they devote themselves" to the assigned function. In the strictest sense we might take this adverbial modifier restrictively: "they are ministers of God *only to the extent to which* they carry out their function"; or we could take it more affirmatively: "they are ministers of God *by virtue of* their devoting themselves" to it. In any case, whichever of these meanings be Paul's intent, there are criteria whereby the functioning of government can be measured. According to the totality of the passage, we cannot measure whether we should revolt against the government, as if certain governments could fall short on the status of government, and therefore need to be revolted against. Nor can we measure by this yardstick whether a government has been permitted by God, because all government has been permitted by God. All the powers that be are subject to the ordering of God, and Christians are to be subject to them all. But we can judge and measure the extent to which a government is accomplishing its ministry, by asking namely whether it persistently (*present* participle) attends to the rewarding of good and evil according to their merits; to be "minister to you for good" is a criterion, not a description.

Thus far we have read verse 6 as if the rest of the traditional interpretation were correct. There are, however, two further difficulties of interpretation, each of which, if inspected carefully, would move us further away from the traditional affirmation.

The verb *proskartereo* normally does not take an accusative object. The verb may appear with no object or its object may be in the dative case. Its most current New Testament usage is in the phrase which the Authorized Version translates "continuing instant [in prayer]" (Acts 1:14; 6:4; Col. 4:2; Rom. 12:13). But that then means that the sentence cannot simply affirm concerning the authorities that "they do devote themselves to this very thing," since the accusative "to this very thing" cannot be the object of this verb. Therefore the translation would have to read "they are servants of God to this very end, devoting themselves persistently." In this construction it is even more likely that the participle has the adverbial sense and even less that it is a predication. This consideration then further supports the interpretive hypothesis already made above.

But a greater difficulty is that it is not immediately clear what is the antecedent of "they are." Interpreters in general assume that the *rulers* of verse 3 and the *powers* of verses 1 and 3 are somehow all merged together in one grammatical subject, which may be either feminine singular or masculine plural and always has the same meaning. This is, however, a most unusual way to disregard the keys to interpretation that gender and number provide. It is more appropriate to ask concretely what plural noun can be the subject of "they are" in verse 6. The most recent such plural noun referring to the realm of government was the "rulers" in verse 3, but that is rather far back to reach for an antecedent. Thus some serious scholars, including M. Dibelius, have argued that it is more likely that "ministers of God" should be itself the subject.[16] Then we would read: "the ministers of God are there for this very purpose (as they persist)." Then we must further choose between two meanings of the noun "ministers." In secular Greek usage of the time the term translated "ministers" (*leitourgoi*) referred to government functionaries, most currently to those who gathered tax money. Since the preceding sentence referred to the voluntary payment of taxes, it would be quite appropriate (with Dibelius) to move on to speak of government officials as ministering to God in this way; thus "tax

---

[16] Martin Dibelius, "Rom und die ersten Christen im Ersten Jahrhundert," in *Botschaft und Geschichte*, II (Tübingen: Mohr, 1956), 181 n. 9.

collection agencies exist for this very purpose when they are zealous." But the most current biblical usage of the word, like its near synonym *diakonos*, refers to the priest or the Christian who "serves" God in the sense of worship and sacrifice. There is thus nothing in the text to make sure that Paul does not intend "ministers of God" to refer to Christians. This would also fit quite smoothly in the context: The Christian is subject for the sake of conscience, it is for this reason that Christians pay taxes because Christians also, as ministers of God, devote themselves to the end that the good be approved and evil reprimanded.

All grammatical interpretations of the verse must be subject to the risks of probability; the main thrust of our present paragraph is not dependent upon any one of these hypotheses. This grammatical detour should, however, have permitted us at least to overcome the naive sense of self-evidence with which the reader of the English text has often heard it being said as a simple affirmation that, whatever government does, it is serving God and therefore what it is doing is a ministry which the Christian should always share.

Let it be noted that "good" and "evil" here cannot be understood in some wide historical sense such as to cover the preservation of democracy or the interests of the nation. The ministry for good is "to thee," i.e. it is to be measured by the welfare of each individual subject (not only of the full citizens).[17]

---

[17] Jean Lasserre points out ("Note complementaire sur Rom. 13,4," *CR* [Oct. 1968], pp. 39f) that thus to link the legitimacy of the exercise of governmental power to the welfare of the subject (not only to the formally defined rights of the full citizen) is a very substantial judgment upon the autonomy of the authorities (and, we might add, historically a very progressive one).

It might be recalled that according to the account of Acts, Paul's experiences with the authorities were that they had protected his missionary freedom against hostile Gentiles (19:35-41), and his life in the face of hostile Jews (23:12-24) and soldiers (27:42f).

(B) Whatever be the kind of criteria and discrimination to which *proskarterountes* points in verse 6, it is all the more clear in verse 7 that we are being instructed to discriminate. "Render to each his due" cannot normally be assumed to mean "render everything to government." Often this text is read as a sort of list of all the four kinds of things that are due to government; taxes, revenue, respect, and honor. Such an interpretation is quite common. It makes nonsense, however, of the prior invitation to be discriminating and to render to each just what is his due. It is therefore a much more serious reading of the entire passage to hear in this text, as do Cullmann and Cranfield, an implicit allusion to the words of Jesus. "Render to each what is due to him" means to render to Caesar what belongs to him and to God what belongs to him. Taxes and revenue, perhaps honor, are due to Caesar, but fear is due to God.[18]

Thus once again there are criteria that come into play in our attitude toward government. We are instructed to refuse to give government certain types of "honor" or "fear." The place of government in the providential designs of God is not such that our duty would be simply to do whatever it says. This discrimination commanded in verse 7 is further reinforced in verse 8. In English usage we do not note that the words "that which is due" in verse 7 and "owing" of verse 8 have the same root. (This similarity is incidentally a significant argument against those who claim that verses 1-7 constitute a foreign body within chapters 12-13.) Verse 7 says "render to each his

18 C. E. B. Cranfield, "Some Observations on Romans XIII; 1-7," *NTS,* 6 (1959-60), 241ff, argues convincingly (p. 248) that for Paul "fear" (*phobos*) is due only to God. Ethelbert Stauffer reports (*Christ and the Caesars,* p. 137) that the Carthaginian Christian martyr Donata, asked to swear "by the divine spirit of the Lord our Caesar," responded that she would "honor Caesar as Caesar but fear only God." This kind of discrimination was probably a settled usage. Cranfield, p. 247, agrees that Paul is here explicitly referring to Jesus' call to discrimination (Mark 12:7; Matt. 22:21; Luke 22:35); the verb "render" (*apodote*) is the same in both contexts.

due"; verse 8 says "nothing is *due* to anyone except love." Thus the claims of Caesar are to be measured by whether what he claims is due to him is part of the obligation of love. Love in turn is defined (v. 10) by the fact that it does no harm. In this context it therefore becomes impossible to maintain that the subjection referred to in verses 1-7 can include a moral obligation under certain circumstances to do harm to others at the behest of government.

It is not by accident that the imperative of 13:1 is not literally one of *obedience*. The Greek language has good words to denote obedience, in the sense of completely bending one's will and one's actions to the desires of another. What Paul calls for, however, is sub*ord*ination. This verb is based upon the same root as the *ordering* of the powers of God. Subordination is significantly different from obedience.[19] The conscientious objector who refuses to do what his government asks him to do, but still remains under the sovereignty of that government and accepts the penalties which it imposes, or the Christian who refuses to worship Caesar but still permits Caesar to put him to death, is being subordinate even though he is not obeying.

The imperative and the enablement of this subordination are found not in fear or in calculations of how best to survive, but as we saw "in the mercies of God" (12:1) or in "conscience" (13:5). But how does conscience motivate subordination? If the ground of our subordination is not God's having created the government, what is it? Further attention to the motif of subordination as it is urged upon the slave (I Pet. 2:13ff, 19ff), or upon wives and children (Eph. 5:21ff; Col. 3:18ff), shows the reason to be that Jesus Christ himself accepted subordination

---

[19] Cranfield, p. 242, underlines the difference between obedience and subordination.

and humiliation (Phil. 2:5ff).[20] The willingness to suffer is then not merely a test of our patience or a dead space of waiting; it is itself a participation in the character of God's victorious patience with the rebellious powers of his creation. We subject ourselves to government because it was in so doing that Jesus revealed and achieved God's victory.

A Conclusion

The purpose of this outline has not been to furnish a full or balanced exposition of the text in question,[21] but only to respond to the points at which the predominant traditions of interpretation seek to find support in this text for a view of government and of the Christian's obligation to it which can include the obligation to participate in war. In this mainstream tradition, which has prevailed in the churches since Constantine, Romans 13 and the other texts like it stand in tension with Matthew 5. This is said alike by Protestants and Catholics, by conservative and liberal theologies. They then conclude that in the tension between these two kinds of obligations or two kinds of statements, the duties of Romans 13 take precedence in the social realm and the duties of Matthew 5 in the personal one. Then it is easy to turn the interpretation back on one's interlocutor and to say that the pacifist is one who gives precedence to the personal realm over social obligation, preferring Jesus to Paul or eschatology to responsibility.

[20] Cf. ch. 9 above on the wider meaning of "subordination" in New Testament ethics. It bears repeating that the appeal at the outset of the passage Rom. 12-13 was not to God's working as creator or as providential governor over the state, but to the "mercies of God," and to the reconciling of Jew and Greek in one people.

[21] We have not intended to speak of every verse and every grammatical problem. We have, however, identified the central purpose of the Apostle's writing to the Romans (at the end of section 3 above, p. 204).

Some pacifists have accepted this analysis and gone on to argue that personal faithfulness is more important than social responsibility. This lets it be forgotten that the logic of the post-Constantinian position holds only under the assumption that the imperatives of Matthew 5 and Romans 13 are actually contradictory. If that were the case, there might well be some good reasons to stand with Jesus against Paul or with eschatology against responsibility; but the above exposition should have shown that the assumption itself does not hold. It is not the case that two imperatives are affirmed in the New Testament, obedience to government on one hand and loving the enemy on the other, between which we must choose when they contradict. Romans 12-13 and Matthew 5-7 are not in contradiction or in tension. They *both* instruct Christians to be nonresistant in all their relationships, including the social. They *both* call on the disciples of Jesus to renounce participation in the interplay of egoisms which this world calls "vengeance" or "justice." They *both* call Christians to respect and be subject to the historical process in which the sword continues to be wielded and to bring about a kind of order under fire, but not to perceive in the wielding of the sword their own reconciling ministry.

11

Justification by Grace
Through Faith

We have followed up our reading of the story of Jesus
with several sample soundings in the thought of the
apostolic church. We have observed the prevalence of the
language of discipleship, imitation, and participation, and
seen how this characterized not only the motivation but
also the shape of early Christian behavior. We have observed a parallel expression in the cosmology of the
Apostle where the "principalities and powers" language,
which might be called "mythological," nonetheless has a
very precise and fruitful burden of meaning with regard
to understanding the church's faithfulness within the
structured power relationships of society. We have observed that the willingness of the Apostle (sometimes
embarrassing for moderns) to live within the limits of a
society marked by slavery and radical social stratification,
also has a meaningful foundation in his understanding of
the work of Christ and the place of the church in the
continuation of that work.

It is thus not too much to claim that what we have
been describing are several significant strands of corrobo-
rative evidence for the survival of the social stance of
Jesus into the church of the Apostolic Age. But, the critic

215

may well say, this still leaves aside one fundamental observation. The Apostle may well have retained within his thought the vestiges of the Jesus kind of ethos; after all he did not claim to be uniquely pioneering on every subject. But was not his major *original* contribution to the life of the early church the position he took with regard to justification and the law? Is not the center of Pauline theology the argument, called forth by "Judaizers" and stated in different ways, especially in Romans and Galatians, that a man may be made righteous before God only on the grounds of faith, with no correlation to his keeping of the law?

Just as a guilty thief or murderer is still a thief or a murderer after a declaration of amnesty has freed him from his punishment, the argument runs, so a guilty sinner is still a sinner when God declares, on the ground of the work of Christ which no man could have accomplished for himself, that he shall henceforth be considered a new man, forgiven and restored to fellowship. But this "being considered" is, spiritually speaking, a legal fiction. It is valid only on the grounds of the sovereign authority of the judge who declared it to be so. The act of justification or the status of being just or righteous before God is therefore radically disconnected from any objective or empirical achievement of goodness by man.

This "disconnection" is only a part of the wider phenomenon of separation between body and soul, objective and subjective realities, outward and inward history, which are the key, are they not, to all the specific emphases of the Apostle Paul?

Was not the central message of the Apostle Paul his rejection of any objective dimension to the work of God which could be focused in piety, religious practices, or ethical behavior in such a way as to turn man's attention toward the human works instead of toward the gift of God? Does not the insistence that justification is by faith

alone and through grace alone, apart from any correlation
with works of any kind, undercut any radical ethical and
social concern by implication, even if Paul himself might ·
not have been rigorous enough to push that implication
all the way? If we truly join with classic Protestantism in
considering the proclamation of justification by grace
through faith to be the point at which the gospel stands
or falls, must we not then interpret the ethical tradition
which Paul took over from Jewish Christianity and shared
with his Gentile churches as a vestige of another system,
destined to fade away? Was it not, after all, at the cost of
forgetting Paul's emphasis upon grace that a later generation again made good works and a certain social stance
very important in the preaching of the church?

Paul and Modern Man's Question

This sweeping set of assumptions about what the
Apostle Paul must certainly have meant, when he spoke
about the righteousness of God becoming effective in
making men righteous, was so self-evident for centuries of
Protestant thought, and seemed so necessary as a corrective over against certain tendencies attributed to Catholic
piety, that it scarcely could occur to anyone to think that
it might be otherwise. It rhymed so well with the heritage
of Augustine and fit so neatly into Protestant preaching
patterns that there was no chink in the armor of self-
evidence through which a doubt could insinuate itself.

Or so it seemed, at least, until the advent of the
biblical scholarship of this century, which found more
freedom to distinguish between the initial cultural context of a biblical passage on one hand and the contribution it makes to contemporary thought on the other.[1] If
we may be freed by self-critical scholarly objectivity no

[1] Krister Stendahl, article "Biblical Theology," *Interpreter's Dictionary
of the Bible* (Nashville: Abingdon, 1962), I, 418ff.

longer to assume that the authority of the Bible resides in
its saying things that we agree with, we may be free as
well to hear more clearly what it really says instead of
giving it credit for saying what we already think.

Once the entering wedge of this capacity for critical
self-awareness had made possible a freer and less apologetic reading of the ancient documents, it became possible to call into question the far-reaching assumption
that the Apostle Paul was preoccupied with personal
acceptance. It is understandable that Martin Luther could
have found this preoccupation in the apostolic message
since it was his own question; Luther had been taught by
his monastic training to be personally in need of knowing
that he had found a God who would be gracious personally to him. Thus it was perfectly natural for Luther to
assume that this was also the preoccupation of the Apostle. It was also perfectly natural for a John Wesley, a
Kierkegaard, or today for an existentialist or a conservative evangelical reader to make the same assumption and
find the same message—for all of these are in their varie-
gated ways children of Luther, still asking the same
question of personal righteousness.

But let us once set aside the assumption that the
righteousness of God and the righteousness of man are
most fundamentally located on the individual level. Let
us make this, instead of an axiom, a hypothesis to be
tested. Let us posit as at least thinkable the alternate
hypothesis that for Paul righteousness, either in God or
in man, might more appropriately be conceived of as
having cosmic or social dimensions. Such larger dimensions would not negate the personal character of the
righteousness God imputes to those who believe;[2] but by

2 In view of the corrective intent of the present argument it should be
reiterated that our purpose is not to reverse a prior error by claiming that
justification is *only* social. We are objecting to a particular polemical application of the traditional doctrine, which used it to *exclude* the ethical and
social dimensions. By echoing scholars who have rediscovered the missing

englobing the personal salvation in a fuller reality they would negate the individualism with which we understand such reconciliation.

This axiom Krister Stendahl has set about to call into question in his article, "The Apostle Paul and the Introspective Conscience of the West."[3] Stendahl demonstrates one by one that all the constitutive elements of the classic "Luther-type experience" are missing in both the experience and the thought of the Apostle. Paul was not preoccupied with his guilt and seeking for the assurance of a gracious God; he was rather robust of conscience, and untroubled about whether God was gracious or not. He never pleads either with Jews or Gentiles to feel an anguished conscience and then receive release from that anguish in a message of forgiveness.

Second, Paul's understanding of the meaning of Hebrew law is not that its function was to make men know their guilt, to prepare men for the message of forgiveness by deepening their awareness of their sinfulness. The law was rather a gracious arrangement made by God for ordering the life of his people while they were awaiting the arrival of the Messiah. It is true that, once present, law makes its opposite, sin, more visible; but that is not its first purpose nor its primary effect for the believer.

Third, faith was for Paul not a particular spiritual exercise of moving from self-trust through despair to confidence in the paradoxical goodness of the judgment of God; faith is at its core the affirmation which separated Jewish Christians from other Jews, that in Jesus of Nazareth the Messiah had come. A Jew did not become a

dimensions we are not denying the personal. We are denying that it can most adequately be spoken about in abstraction from the rest, as certain recent Western traditions have assumed. This chapter is not expositing all of Paul's thought on justification; it is asking whether that thought supports the arguments against a "messianic ethic" as it has been held to do.

[3] *HTR*, 56 (July 1963), 199ff.

Christian by coming to see God as a righteous judge and a
gracious, forgiving protector. He believed that already,
being a Jew. What it took for him to become a Christian
was not some new idea about his sin or God's righteousness, but one about Jesus. The subjective meanings of
faith for the self-aware person, and its doctrinal meanings
for the believing intellect, build upon this prior messianist
affirmation. They cannot precede or replace it.

The heresy Paul was struggling against was not that
the Jewish Christians continued to be committed to keeping the law; Paul was quite tolerant of those who held to
such a conviction. He went out of his way to share their
ritual faithfulness when in Jerusalem. Nor was it their
thinking that by keeping the law they would be saved, for
the Jewish Christians did not believe that. The basic
heresy he exposed was the failure of those Jewish Christians to recognize that since the Messiah had come the
covenant of God had been broken open to include the
Gentiles. In sum: the fundamental issue was that of the
social form of the church. Was it to be a new and
inexplicable kind of community of both Jews and Gentiles, or was it going to be a confederation of a Jewish
Christian sect and a Gentile one? Or would all the Gentiles have first to become Jews according to the condi-
tions of pre-messianic proselytism?

Stendahl exemplifies this difference with one of the
classic texts, Galatians 3:24, which states that the law
was a "custodian" to order the life of the Jewish community until the Messiah should come. The point of
Paul's explanation is that now that the Messiah has come,
the Gentiles do not need to pass by way of the law, but
can be incorporated directly into the new community.
For Luther on the other hand "custodian" was interpreted as "schoolmaster," as representing a necessary step
which even now the Gentiles must go through. They do
not need to be educated by way of the details of the
Jewish legislation, but in order to be able to receive grace

one must first be broken under the yoke of some kind of law. All men must pass by the *usus elenchticus,* by the way of the judging impact of the righteousness of God.

What then was Paul's understanding of sin? When he does speak of himself as a serious sinner at all, this is not because of his existential anguish under the righteousness of God in general, but very specifically because, not having recognized that Messiah had come in Jesus, he had persecuted the church and fought the opening of God's covenant to the Gentiles. What is now set right in his life is not that he has overcome his inner resistances and has become able to trust in God for his right status before God; it is rather that through the inexplicable intervention of God on the Damascus Road and in later experiences, Paul has become the agent of the action of God on the right side, the privileged bearer of the cause of the ingathering of the Gentiles.

This was perfectly clear not only to Paul but also to his readers. What was at stake in the "proclamation of the righteousness of God to both Jew and Gentile" was precisely that it was to be proclaimed to both and that both were to become a part of the new believing community, some having come by way of the law and some not. It was only when in later generations the Jew-Gentile relationship was partly forgotten and partly distorted into a polemic one, that the Pauline language of justification could be reinterpreted, especially in the heritage of Augustine, and translated into the terms of Western man's self-examination and concern for his own authenticity. Since this transformation stated the justifying purpose of God in terms translatable for and accessible to every man, it could be considered somehow eternally or universally relevant, whereas the reconciling of Jew and Gentile can be understood and celebrated only particularly in the uniqueness of salvation history in given times and places.

Stendahl is quite tolerant. He does not reject outright

the possible claim that the new "Western" meaning might be, by certain criteria which we might consider useful, more "valid" or more "relevant" than the original one; the further "development of doctrine" may in some way be a good thing. But he nevertheless closes with the suggestion that *perhaps* the meaning enshrined in the salvation-history concern of the early church as a social reality might also be relevant for modern man, in addition to doing more justice to the biblical documents and the thought which they report.

The New Man

The most presumptuous and the clearest statement of the particular apostolic ministry of Paul is stated in the letter to the Ephesians.[4]

Here the Apostle makes claims to a knowledge and to a ministry that is not merely on the level of the other apostles but unique among the apostles. It is a particular grace which was given just to him to steward for the churches (Eph. 3:2), a "mystery" which was made known to him (3:3). "Mystery" is to be understood not as a spooky secret forever hidden from view, but rather as the strategic purpose of God which was not widely known until the point of its execution.[5]

The "plan of the mystery" was hidden for ages in God, but now it is known and in fact it is being made known beyond the church by the church, proclaimed even to the "principalities and powers in the heavenly places" (3:9f).

---

[4] We need not discuss here whether the present text of Ephesians is from the pen of Paul, or his amanuensis, or a later writer claiming to write in the same spirit. For a later writer to make these statements about Paul's ministry would be no less germane to our discussion.

[5] The usual context for this usage of "mystery" would seem to have been military. A battle plan is kept secret until the battle; but once the battle has begun it is public knowledge.

Just what is this divine purpose, hidden for a time and made known by revelation to Paul? It is precisely that Jew and Gentile are now reconciled in one community.

> *At one time you Gentiles in the flesh . . . were separated from Christ, alienated from the commonwealth of Israel and strangers to the covenant of promise . . . but now in Christ Jesus you who once were far off have been brought near in the blood of Christ. For he is our peace, who has made us both one, and has broken down the dividing wall of hostility, by abolishing in his flesh the law . . . that he might create in himself the one humanity instead of two, so making peace, and might reconcile us both to God in one body through the cross, thereby bringing the hostility to an end.*

The hostility brought to an end in Christ is first and foremost in this passage not the hostility between a righteous God and man who has trespassed against his rules, but the hostility between Jew and Greek. The overcoming of this hostility, the making of peace by eliminating the wall that had separated them, namely the Jewish law to which Jews were committed and which Gentiles ignored, is itself the creation of a new humanity. This is why the unique ministry of Paul as "prisoner for Jesus Christ on behalf of you Gentiles" (3:1) is inseparable from his own unique revealed insight into the "mystery" of God's purpose. The work of Christ is not only that he saves the soul of individuals and henceforth they can love each other better; the work of Christ, the making of peace, the breaking down of the wall, is itself the constituting of a new community made up of two kinds of people, those who had lived under the law and those who had not. The events the book of Acts narrates as the recent initiative of the Holy Spirit in opening up the churches, first at Jerusalem and then in Samaria, then in

Damascus and Antioch, to the fellowship of believing Jews and believing Gentiles, are here interpreted by Paul, a major actor in that drama and its accredited interpreter, as being the extended meaning of the cross and resurrection of Jesus.[6]

We have identified this message in the book of Ephesians, a relatively late document, where the word "justification" actually is not central, only in order to be able to perceive more readily its presence in the earlier writings where it is not equally developed. As elsewhere, we lean heavily upon a few contemporary scholars, testifying again to the fact that the thrust of the present book is not original except perhaps in the consistency with which it attempts to draw ethical conclusions from what more specialized scholars have already found.

The New Righteousness That Is Valid Before God

Markus Barth[7] plunges right to the heart of the classic discussion in Galatians (2:14ff):

[6] The recorded workings of the Holy Spirit in the book of Acts are always related to the opening up of the church to a wider view of her mission. The Holy Spirit is made known in those divine initiatives which drive the church to proclaim to a wider world. Cf. Harry Boer, *Pentecost and Missions* (Grand Rapids: Eerdmans, 1961). A current interpretation of Paul's understanding of the place in history of his own mission posits a temporal-causative relation between the evangelizing of the nations and the return of Christ; *when* the gospel has been proclaimed to all the nations, *then* the end will come (Matt. 24:14). This is the understanding especially of Oscar Cullmann and Johannes Munck (summarized in John Knox, "Romans 15:14-33 and Paul's Conception of His Apostolic Mission," *JBL,* 83 [Mar. 1964], 1ff). Krister Stendahl's understanding and that of Eph. 2-3 advocated here would turn it the other way round; because the end time is here, the Gentiles are now in the covenant. The ingathering of the Gentiles is not a means to an end or a precondition of the fulness of time; it is the end. The fulness of time is the precondition of the Gentile mission. Cf. as well Paul Minear, "Paul's Missionary Dynamic," in his *The Obedience of Faith; the Purposes of Paul in the Epistle to the Romans, SBT,* 2nd ser., 19 (1971), 91ff.

[7] Markus Barth, "Jews and Gentiles: the Social Character of Justification in Paul," *JES,* 5/2 (Spring 1968), 241ff. Cf. as well Barth's *Justification* (Grand Rapids: Eerdmans, 1971).

> *We have believed in Christ Jesus in order to be*
> *justified by faith in Christ and not by works of the*
> *law, because by works of the law no one shall be*
> *justified.*

What does "justified" mean here? Can it really mean,
as Protestant tradition assumes (Lutheranism most sweepingly, but the Anglican and Reformed liturgies give the
same testimony), that it refers only to the quasi-judicial
status of man's guilt before God, which is annulled or
amnestied by a declaration of the judge in response to the
act of faith?

Through very careful analysis of this classic passage,
Markus Barth clarifies that the particular issue at stake,
carried on unbroken from the earlier part of chapter 2,
was whether Jewish and Gentile Christians were to live
together acceptingly in one fellowship. To be justified is
to be set right in and for that relationship. "Justification"
is, in other words, in the language of Galatians the same
as "making peace" or "breaking down the wall" in the
language of Ephesians.

> *Sharing in the death and resurrection of Jesus*
> *Christ is the means of justification: only in Christ's*
> *death and resurrection is the new man created from*
> *at least two, a Jew and a Greek, a man and a*
> *woman, a slave and a free man, etc. . . . The new*
> *man is present in actuality where two previously*
> *alien and hostile men come together before God.*
> *Justification in Christ is thus not an individual mir-*
> *acle happening to this person or that person, which*
> *each may seek or possess for himself. Rather justifi-*
> *cation by grace is a joining together of this person*
> *and that person, of the near and far; . . . it is a social*
> *event.*[8]

Barth has thus confirmed, beginning his analysis from

[8] *Ibid.*, p. 259.

another direction and dealing with another text, what we
have already seen to have been demonstrated by Stendahl
and in Ephesians: that the relationship between divine
justification and the reconciliation of men to one another
is not a sequential relationship. It is not that "faith"
occurs first as an inner existential leap of the individual
past his concern for his finitude, and then God operates a
change in him which enables him to love his brethren.
Barth characterizes Albrecht Ritschl as having "considered forgiveness and justification as sort of psychic
release which enabled the individual member of the
church to participate in an ethical process," whereas for
Paul this relationship of prelude and sequence cannot
thus be distinguished.[9]

The "New Creature"

If there is any one biblical text that focuses for lay
understanding the individualism of the Pietist heritage it
is the statement of II Corinthians 5:17: "If anyone is in
Christ he is a new creature." It has seemed self-evident
that we were being promised here, overlapping with the
language of a new birth (John 3:5f), a metaphysical or
ontological transformation of the individual person. The
miracle of being made a new person has been promised in
evangelistic proclamation and has served in turn to illuminate traditional understandings of the rootage of Christian social concern. It is because only a transformed
individual will behave differently that some kinds of
social activism are fruitless; it is because a transformed
individual will definitely behave differently that the
preaching of the gospel to individuals is the surest way to
change society.

It is not the concern of the present study to deny that
such a thrust has had a wholesome corrective impact in

---

[9] In general the New Testament word *pistis* would better not be translated "faith," with the concentration that word has for modern man upon
either a belief *content* or the *act* of believing; "faithfulness" would generally
be a more accurate rendering of its meaning.

certain contexts in the history of Protestant thought and Protestant church life. Like Stendahl, we may concede a certain usefulness to nonbiblical thought patterns. Nor are we setting aside the "new birth" imagery of John 3 or parallel themes elsewhere. Our question is only whether this is what *Paul* is saying in *this* text. This becomes extremely doubtful when we look more carefully at the text itself.

As the italics in the AV indicate, the words "he is" are not in the original text. Now it can regularly be necessary to add the English "is" in order to make clear a predication which in the Greek requires no copulative verb. But the addition of "he," thereby identifying an antecedent in the previous clause, is quite another matter. It is grammatically not impossible to reach back to the "anyone" earlier in the verse as the understood subject of this predication; but that is not the only interpretation, and others should be tried first.

A second shortcoming of this traditional interpretation of "the new creature" as the transformed individual personality is that the word *ktisis,* here translated "creature" or "creation," is not used elsewhere in the New Testament to designate the individual person. It in fact most often is used to designate not the object of creation but rather the act of creating (e.g. Rom. 1:20), "from the creation of the world." Secondarily it may mean the entire universe (Mark 16:15; Col. 1:15, 24; Rom. 8:19-22; Heb. 9:11). The single reference to "human creation" refers to social institutions (I Pet. 2:13). In the one other place where the phrase "new creation" is used, it is quite parallel to the "new humanity" of Ephesians 2:15, not a renewed individual but a new social reality, marked by the overcoming of the Jew/Greek barrier; "neither circumcision nor uncircumcision but a new creation" (Gal. 6:15).[10]

---

[10] Even the verb *ktizo* tends to be used in the sense of the "new humanity": "created in Christ for good works" (Eph. 2:10); cf. 2:15; 4:24; Col. 3:10.

Putting together these strictly linguistic observations it becomes enormously more probable that we should lean to the kind of translation favored by the more recent translators: literally, "if anyone is in Christ, new is creation," or more smoothly, "there is a whole new world" (NEB). The accent lies not on transforming the ontology of the person (to say nothing of transforming his psychological or neurological equipment) but on transforming the perspective of one who has accepted Christ as his context.

This is certainly the point of the rest of the passage in question. Paul is explaining why he no longer regards anyone from the human point of view;[11] why he does not regard Jew as Jew or Greek as Greek, but rather looks at every man in the light of the new world which begins in Christ. "The old has passed away, behold the new has come," is a social or historical statement, not an introspective or emotional one.

To the Jew First but Also to the Greek

A quite different segment of Paul's writings is the framework of introduction and conclusion around his letter to the Christians at Rome. Hans Werner Bartsch points out[12] that Paul never calls the total Roman com-

[11] One standard interpretation of this passage has Paul defending his apostolate against those who argue that he had not known the earthly Jesus as the other apostles had. This meaning is excluded by Paul's going on to deny that he "knows" anyone else in this way. Cf. J. B. Souček, "Wir kennen Christus nicht mehr nach dem Fleisch," *EvT,* 19/7 (July 1959), 300ff. I Cor. 3:3f also uses "after the flesh" to describe the practice of placing men in categories, with the effect of dividing the church. "After the flesh" can simply mean "by biological descent" (Rom. 1:3; 4:3; 9:3-5; I Cor. 10:18; 11:18; Gal. 4:23).

[12] Hans Werner Bartsch, "Die Historische Situation des Römerbriefes, *Communio Viatorum,* 8/4 (Winter 1965), 199ff. Cf. also Étienne Trocmé, "L'Église Romaine et la méthode missionnaire de l'Apotre Paul," *NTS,* 7/1 (Oct. 1960), 148ff. Paul Minear (*op. cit.*), working quite independently of Bartsch, Barth, and Trocmé, comes to the same conclusion.

munity a "church"[13] and that the issue of the polarity of Jew and Gentile is present at major turning points throughout the argument of the book, as well as in the introduction and conclusion. The foreground meaning of the issue of the place of the law was not systematic theological speculation about how men are to be made acceptable to God, but rather the very concrete Roman situation in which Jew and Greek, legalistic Christian and pagan Christian needed to accept one another. "Law" is written about neither as a means of soul salvation, nor as a hindrance thereto, but as the historically concrete identity of the Jewish separateness which made the problem that justification resolves.

We could in fact most properly say that the word "justification" (like the word "creation" examined above) should be thought of in its root meaning, as a verbal noun, an action, "setting things right," rather than as an abstract noun defining a person's quasi-legal status as a result of a judge's decree. To proclaim divine righteousness means to proclaim that God sets things right; that it is of his nature and the nature of his covenant that he is a right-setting kind of God.

Bartsch supports this interpretation of the concern of Romans with a wealth of detailed textual observations. That the Christians in Rome are not referred to as a "church," in view of Paul's usage elsewhere, is presumed to indicate that the unity of that group constitutes a problem to them and to him. Bartsch emphasizes the recurrence of reference to Jew and Greek at all the turning points of the document, to say nothing of the special significance of chapters 9-11, whose entire concern is the place of Jewish identity in view of God's having created the church. From the obedience of faith

[13] In ch. 16 Paul greets twenty-four individuals by name, plus two families (or house fellowships? vv. 10, 11) and another group of saints (v. 15); but only for the group in the house of Aquila does he use the name "church."

(1:5) through the "accepting one another" (14:1; 15:7)
to Paul's concern for collecting funds for Jerusalem
(15:28), his desire is that there should come into being in
Rome this kind of new community where the brokenness
of mankind is set right and where men who were not
born under the law obey it from the heart.[14]

If the reader can grant that in the company of Stendahl, Barth, Bartsch, and Minear we may properly understand Paul's concept of justification as a social phenomenon centering in the reconciliation of different kinds of
people, what has that to do with the problem with which
our study began, namely the ethic of revolutionary nonviolence which Jesus offers to his disciples?

Perhaps most evident is a kind of double negative
impact upon the state of the debate in theological ethics.
This debate has been dominated by a negation, which
appealed in its support to what was supposed to be
unique about the message of Paul. Because Paul is different from Jesus or because justification is different from
social ethics, therefore the way of Jesus, it was classically
held, has lost its bindingness for our age. It is this negation which a more open reading of the apostles in turn
negates. The negation of this negation is all the more
significant because the scholars I have been quoting were
simply going about their erudite business, with no predis-
position to support my reading of Jesus' or of Paul's
ethics.[15]

---

[14] The difference between the function of the law in Paul and that in
Luther is not merely that the Gentiles do not pass by way of the law to
come to the gospel; it is also that the law continues to have a validity for all
believers. Thus the law is not done away with but rather restored in its
life-giving, nondivisive intent.

[15] This outline has thus leaned on the lessons offered by contemporary
New Testament scholars, who themselves did not intend to support my
thesis. This should defend against any suspicion of special pleading. But it
should not be thought that this view of Romans first arose in the 1960s.

The argument that the message of Paul is more social, less "existential"
than it has been made by Protestant tradition, has been present in the

But the proclamation that God reconciles classes of men is in itself far more than a double negative. To proclaim it as Paul did in his writings years and even decades after Pentecost is to confirm that such reconciliation is a real experience and therefore a real invitation. Paul is saying, somewhere toward the *end* of the evolution of apostolic Christianity, what Jesus had said somewhere near the beginning. That he can still say it now is proof that, at least to some modest degree, experience had confirmed it. He says that the triumph of God's love in his own sustaining of his creation is that he blesses equally insider and outsider, friend and enemy, in such manner that the genuineness (Jesus said, "perfection") [16] of our love is also made real at the point of its application to the enemy, the Gentile, the sinner. There is a sense in which the ethics of marriage and the prohibition of adultery, or the ethics of work and the regulation of attitudes toward slavery, or the opening up of communication and the prohibition of falsehood are all part of the promise of a new humanity enabled and created by God, and already being received by men of faith. But it is *par excellence* with reference to enmity between peoples, the extension of neighbor-love to the enemy, and the renunciation of violence even in the most righteous cause, that this promise takes on flesh in the most original, the most authentic, the most frightening and scandalous, and therefore in the most evangelical way. It is the Good News that my enemy and I are united, through no merit

academic underground for a century, especially in Johann Christoph Blumhardt, and the "religious socialism" of European Protestantism *ca.* 1910-25. The movement broke up on the rocks of personal and theological conflict between its two strongest spokesmen, Leonhard Ragaz and Karl Barth, both of whom had made this point about Paul.

16 The "perfection" to which Jesus calls his hearers in the Sermon on the Mount (Matt. 5:48; cf. Luke 6:35f) is not flawlessness nor impeccability, but precisely the refusal to discriminate between friend and enemy, the in and the out, the good and the evil. It is revealed to men in the indiscriminateness in which God loves the good and the evil alike (cf. above, p. 119).

or work of our own, in a new humanity that forbids henceforth my ever taking his life in my hands.

Perhaps a retrospective word should extend to all our section on the thought of Paul what was said with regard to "justification." Our presentation, in order to correct for the one-sided social ethic which has been dominant in the past, emphasizes what was denied before: Jesus as teacher and example,[17] not only as sacrifice; God as the shaker of the foundations, not only as guarantor of the orders of creation; faith as discipleship, not only as subjectivity. The element of debate in the presentation may make it seem that the "other" or "traditional" element in each case—Jesus as sacrifice, God as creator, faith as subjectivity—is being rejected. It should therefore be restated that—as perusal of the structure of our presentation will confirm—such a disjunction is not intended. We are rather defending the New Testament against the exclusion of the "messianic" element. The disjunction must be laid to the account of the traditional view, not of ours. It is those other views that say that because Jesus is seen as sacrifice he may not be seen as King, or because he is seen as Word made flesh he cannot be seen as normative man.

[17] The theme of obedience and imitation in response to Jesus as teacher and example has not been absent from scholarship or piety (cf. above, p. 131 n. 32); but it has seldom entered into formal ethical discourse, and its relevance has been more to motivation than to substance. "Be like Jesus, this my song . . . " refers to unselfish purpose, not to distinctive behavior.

12

The War of the Lamb

Jesus and Paul have been the foci of our exposition. They must represent the centers of any New Testament theological synthesis, due both to their originality and to the amount of the material that makes them knowable to us. But there are other figures, other minds at work. A thorough treatment would demand that we test there as well the reading we have taken already. There would be the thought of the author of Matthew or of the writer to the Hebrews; there would be the mind of Peter, of John, of Jude, or of the seer of the Apocalypse. There is reason to trust that the reading there would confirm the orientation already sketched. Here, however, we must renounce the further cross-referencing and leap ahead to a summary, rooted nonetheless especially in the last-named Apocalypse. We shall seek briefly to characterize the stance of that book, as it might by contrast throw some light on our contemporary agenda and at the same time draw together the argument of the entire book.

One way to characterize thinking about social ethics in our time is to say that Christians in our age are obsessed with the meaning and direction of history. Social ethical concern is moved by a deep desire to make things move in the right direction. Whether a given action is right or not seems to be inseparable from the question of what effects it will cause. Thus part if not all of social concern has to do with looking for the right "handle" by which one can "get a hold on" the course of history and move it in the right direction. For the movement called Moral Rearmament, ideology is this handle; "ideas have legs," so that if we get a contagious new thought moving, it will make its own way. For others, it is the process of education that ultimately determines the character and course of the civilization; he who rules the teachers' colleges rules the world.

Rambunctious students believe that the office of the dean or the president is the center of the university and therefore they occupy that office. Che Guevara believed the peasant to be the backbone of the coming Latin American revolution, so he went to the hills of Bolivia. The Black Economic Development Conference directs its Manifesto to the administrators of denominations because it believes that is the point of decision-making for white racist American society. Conservative evangelicalism focuses its call for change upon the will of the individual because it believes that when the individual heart is turned in another direction the rest is sure to follow. For still others it is the proletariat or geopolitics that explains everything.

Whichever the favored "handle" may be, the structure of this approach is logically the same. One seeks to lift up one focal point in the midst of the course of human relations, one thread of meaning and causality which is more important than individual persons, their lives and well-being, because it in itself determines wherein their well-being consists. Therefore it is justified to sacrifice to this one "cause" other subordinate values, including the life and welfare of one's self, one's neighbor, and (of course!) of the enemy. We pull this one strategic thread in order to save the whole fabric. This kind of reasoning can be seen with Constantine saving the Roman Empire, with Luther saving the Reformation by making an alliance with the princes, or we can see it in Khrushchev and his successors saving Marxism by making it somewhat more capitalistic, or the United States saving democracy by alliances with military dictatorships and by the threatened use of the bomb.

If we look more analytically at this way of deriving social and political ethics from an overview of the course of history and the choice of the thread within history that is thought to be the most powerful, we find that it involves at least three distinguishable assumptions.

1. It is assumed that the relationship of cause and effect is visible, understandable, and manageable, so that if we make our choices on the basis of how we hope society will be moved, it will be moved in that direction.

2. It is assumed that we are adequately informed to be able to set for ourselves and for all society the goal toward which we seek to move it.

3. Interlocked with these two assumptions and dependent upon them for its applicability is the further postulate that effectiveness in moving toward these goals which have been set is itself a moral yardstick.

If we look critically at these assumptions they are by no means as self-evident as they seem to be at first. There is for one thing the phenomenon Reinhold Niebuhr has called "irony": that when men try to manage history, it almost always turns out to have taken another direction than that in which they thought they were guiding it. This may mean that man is not morally qualified to set the goals toward which he would move history; it at least means that he is not capable of discerning and managing its course when there are in the same theater of operation a host of other free agents, each of them in his own way also acting under the same assumptions as to his capacity to move history in his direction. Thus even apart from the other more spiritual considerations, the strategic calculus is subject to a very serious internal question. It has yet to be demonstrated that history can be moved in the direction in which one claims the duty to cause it to go.

The other question we must raise at the outset about

the logic of the "strategic" attitude toward ethical decisions is its acceptance of effectiveness itself as a goal.
Even if we know how effectiveness is to be measured—i.e.
even if we could get a clear definition of the goal we are
trying to reach and how to ascertain whether we had
reached it—is there not in Christ's teaching on meekness,
or in the attitude of Jesus toward power and servanthood, a deeper question being raised about whether it is
our business at all to guide our action by the course we
wish history to take?

It is, however, not the concern of our present study to
deal logically or systematically with this kind of question
within the traditional or contemporary idioms of theological debate. In recent centuries debate around the question of the meaning of history, and the place of Christian
decision within that meaningfulness, has generally been a
conversation of the deaf, with some so committed to
preenlightenment understandings of the stability of the
proper social order that any sense of movement is only a
threat, and others committed with an equally unquestioning irrationality to the progressivist assumptions of postenlightenment Western thought, according to which the
discernible movement of history is self-explicating and
generally works for good, and therefore is the only ter-
rain of significance from which ethics should self-evidently be derived. From neither direction has there been any
expectation that light might be thrown upon the question
from the NT. What medieval Christendom, with its vision
of the divine stability of all the members of the *corpus
christianum*, has in common with postenlightenment pro-
gressivism is precisely the assumption that history has
moved us past the time of primitive Christianity and
therefore out from under the relevance of the apostolic
witness on this question.

The earlier portions of this book have sought to spell
out in considerable detail the elements of a vision of the
Christian's place in the world that can claim rootage in

the thought of Jesus and Paul. It remains, we have said, to test the concordance of this approach in the remaining sections of the canonical literature. This literature (the General Epistles and the Apocalypse) is less unified, less easy to understand, and there is also less of it; so we cannot ask for the fulness of delineation toward which we have pointed in the earlier sections of the study. We can, however, ask whether that which it is possible to discern in these writings is concordant with the other strands of apostolic witness we have been pursuing; and it is fitting to center this question upon the concern for history's meaning.

For a sense of the apostolic perception of the meaning and course of history and especially of the interplay of trust and coerciveness within history, we shall find that the most immediate resource comes from that segment of the biblical literature from which we are least accustomed to learn, namely from the liturgical literature which is embedded in the NT at certain scattered points, but which especially dominates in the book of the Revelation of John.

In his first vision (Rev. 1 5) the seer of Patmos is presented with the image of a sealed scroll in the hand of the "one that was seated upon the throne" (a circumlocution for God himself, who cannot be looked at directly, but whose presence is known as Light).

The question laid before John by his vision of the scroll sealed with seven seals is precisely the question of the meaningfulness of history. This is a question that, the vision says dramatically, cannot be answered by the normal resources of human insight. Yet it is by no means a meaningless question or one unworthy of concern. It is worth weeping, as the seer does, if we do not know the meaning of human life and suffering.

Speaking more generally let us affirm, as numerous historians of philosophy are arguing, that to be concerned about history, to assume that history is meaningful, is

itself a Judeo-Christian idea. The concern to know where
history is going is not an idle philosophical curiosity. It is
a necessary expression of the conviction that God has
worked in past history and has promised to continue thus
to be active among men. If God is the kind of God-
active-in-history of whom the Bible speaks, then concern
for the course of history is itself not an illegitimate or an
irrelevant concern. No mystical or existentialistic or spiri-
tualistic depreciation of preoccupation with the course of
events is justified for the Christian.

But the answer given to the question by the series of
visions and their hymns is not the standard answer. "The
lamb that was slain is worthy to receive power!" John is
here saying, not as an inscrutable paradox but as a meaningful affirmation, that the cross and not the sword,
suffering and not brute power determines the meaning of
history. The key to the obedience of God's people is not
their effectiveness but their patience (13:10). The triumph of the right is assured not by the might that comes
to the aid of the right, which is of course the justification
of the use of violence and other kinds of power in every
human conflict; the triumph of the right, although it is
assured, is sure because of the power of the resurrection
and not because of any calculation of causes and effects,
nor because of the inherently greater strength of the good
guys. The relationship between the obedience of God's
people and the triumph of God's cause is not a relationship of cause and effect but one of cross and resurrection.

We have observed this biblical "philosophy in history"
first of all in the worship life of the late New Testament
church, since it is here that we find the most desperate
encounter of the church's weakness (John was in exile,
Paul in prison) with the power of the evil rulers of the
present age. But this position is nothing more than a
logical unfolding of the meaning of the work of Jesus
Christ himself, whose choice of suffering servanthood

rather than violent lordship, of love to the point of death
rather than righteousness backed by power, was itself the
fundamental direction of his life. Jesus was so faithful to
the enemy-love of God that it cost him all his effectiveness; he gave up every handle on history.

Not only does the New Testament church affirm his
knowledge about the meaning of history or the meaning
of meekness in history; it relates this very specifically to
the coming and the ministry of the man Jesus. If we had
only the book of Revelation we would not necessarily
know what is meant by this Lamb in whom all sovereignty is said to reside. What therefore matters ultimately is
how this Lamb relates to the rest of the human history of
the people who praise him. The answer lies of course in
the person of Jesus himself, of whom this same early
church said in another context that "the Word became
flesh and dwelt among us."

Thus early Christian confession means two things for
our present concern. Speaking negatively, it means that
the business of ethical thinking has been taken away from
the speculation of independent minds each meditating on
the meaning of things and has been pegged to a particular
set of answers given in a particular time and place. Ethics
as well as "theology" (in the sense in which in the past
they have been distinguished) must, if it is to be our
business as Christians to think about them, be rooted in
revelation, not alone in speculation, nor in a self-inter-
preting "situation."

But still more important is the other side, the positive
side of this confession. This will of God is affirmatively,
concretely knowable in the person and ministry of Jesus.
Jesus is not to be looked at merely as the last and greatest
in the long line of rabbis teaching pious people how to
behave; he is to be looked at as a mover of history and as
the standard by which Christians must learn how they are
to look at the moving of history.

The War of the Lamb

Thus the most appropriate example of the difficult choice between effectiveness and obedience, and the most illuminating example, is that of Jesus himself. What it means for the Lamb to be slain, of whom then we sing that he is "worthy to receive power," is inseparable from what it meant for Jesus to be executed under the superscription, "King of the Jews."

The name "Christ," i.e. the one anointed to rule, will have to suffice for present purposes to express symbolically that his ministry among men was inseparable from the political concerns then related most intimately to fulfilling the hopes of his people in their oppression. The possibility that he might have guaranteed politically efficacy and what some call "relevance" by undertaking a political alliance with the forces of the Zealots or with some other power group in Palestinian society was according to the most careful Bible study a genuine option. The choice that he made in rejecting the crown and accepting the cross was the commitment to such a degree of faithfulness to the character of divine love that he was willing for its sake to sacrifice "effectiveness." Usually it can be argued that from some other perspective or in some long view this renunciation of effectiveness was in fact a very effective thing to do. "If a man will lose his . . . life he shall find it." But this paradoxical possibility does not change the initially solid fact that Jesus thereby excluded any normative concern for any capacity to make sure that things would turn out right.

This renunciation is most profoundly stated in the hymn of the early church, which we already noted: "He counted equality with God not a thing to be seized hold of."

In other ages, we observed, theology understood these words as having to do with the divine nature of the eternal Son of God and his condescending to take on human nature. This was the best way to say it when men could think most meaningfully in terms of "essences" and "substances." But it is equally relevant—and much closer to the substance of the text of this hymn as we shall see in a moment—to see in "equality with God" also the element of providential control of events, the alternative being the acceptance of impotence. Christ renounced the claim to govern history.

The universal testimony of Scripture is that Christians are those who follow Christ at just this point. The text we were just reading, Philippians 2, was cited by the Apostle as part of his plea to the Christians at Philippi to live together more unselfishly. The visions of the book of Revelation go on from the heavenly throne room, where the Lamb is praised, to a vision of triumph (ch. 12) where the multitude of "our brethren" has defeated the dragon "by the blood of the lamb and by the word of their testimony, for they loved not their lives even unto death." Elsewhere, Paul can describe the entire apostolic ministry with its inner and outer sufferings as a matter of "carrying about in our bodies the putting to death of Jesus, so that in our bodies the life of Jesus also may be made manifest." This is what Jesus himself meant by recognizing as a disciple only him who is ready to take up a cross and follow him.

The reason Paul drew upon the hymn to the servant Lord was that he sought to move the Christians in Philippi to a more unselfish attitude to one another, in the interests of more brotherly relationships within the congregation. It was in this connection that we referred to the hymn, since it is one more example of the call to the Christian to imitate his Master.

But the original meaning of the hymn was far more than we perceive if we note only the point at which a Christian can be invited to respect the example of Christ. The initial confession of the hymn to the servant Lord was the dramatic juxtaposition of his condescension to

the point of death with his victory. The renunciation of
equality with God (v. 6) has been understood in later
Christian doctrinal development as referring to the metaphysical meaning of deity and incarnation, but probably
the first meaning in the hymn was the more concrete
Godlikeness promised by the serpent to Adam in the
garden, which would have consisted in unchecked dominion over creation. Or perhaps it refers as well to the
kind of Godlikeness claimed by Caesar. What Jesus renounced was thus not simply the metaphysical status of
sonship but rather the untrammelled sovereign exercise of
power in the affairs of that humanity amidst which he
came to dwell. His emptying of himself, his accepting the
form of servanthood and obedience unto death is precisely his renunciation of lordship, his apparent abandonment of any obligation to be effective in making history
move down the right track.

But the judgment of God upon this renunciation and
acceptance of defeat is the declaration that this is victory.
"Therefore God has greatly exalted him and given him
the title, which every creature will have to confess, *the
Lord*." "Lord" in the earliest Christian confessions was
not (as it is in so much modern piety) a label to state a
believer's humility or affection or devotion; it is an affirmation of his victorious relation to the powers of the
cosmos. That ancient hymn, which since it could be
incorporated as a block in the apostolic writings is one of
the earliest extended snatches of Christian worship on
record, is thus affirming that the dominion of God over
history has made use of the apparent historical failure of
Jesus as a mover of men.

We said before that this text affirms a philosophy of
history in which renunciation and suffering are meaningful. After the further ground our thoughts have covered
we can affirm still more roundly that for the Apostle this
renunciation must have been seen as profoundly linked to
the human career of Jesus, who did concretely renounce

the power offered to him by the tempter and by the
Zealots. This hymn is then not as some would make it
simply a Hellenistic mystery-religion text about a mythical Christ figure, coming down from heaven and returning
thither; it is at the same time the account of the human
Jesus whose death was the very political death on the
cross. The renunciation of the claim to govern history
was not made only by the second person of the Trinity
taking upon himself the demand of an eternal divine
decree; it was also made by a poor, tired rabbi when he
came from Galilee to Jerusalem to be rejected.

This Gospel concept of the cross of the Christian does
not mean that suffering is thought of as in itself redemptive or that martyrdom is a value to be sought after. Nor
does it refer uniquely to being persecuted for "religious"
reasons by an outspokenly pagan government. What Jesus
refers to in his call to cross-bearing is rather the seeming
defeat of that strategy of obedience which is no strategy,
the inevitable suffering of those whose only goal is to be
faithful to that love which puts one at the mercy of one's
neighbor, which abandons claims to justice for oneself
and for one's own in an overriding concern for the
reconciling of the adversary and the estranged. I Peter 2
thus draws direct social consequences from the fact that
Christ "when he suffered did not threaten but trusted
him who judges justly."

This is significantly different from that kind of "pacifism" which would say that it is wrong to kill but that
with proper nonviolent techniques you can obtain without killing everything you really want or have a right to
ask for. In this context it seems that sometimes the
rejection of violence is offered only because it is a cheap-
er or less dangerous or more shrewd way to impose one's
will upon someone else, a kind of coercion which is
harder to resist. Certainly any renunciation of violence is
preferable to its acceptance; but what Jesus renounced is
not first of all violence, but rather the compulsiveness of

purpose that leads men to violate the dignity of others. The point is not that one can attain all of one's legitimate ends without using violent means. It is rather that our readiness to renounce our legitimate ends whenever they cannot be attained by legitimate means itself constitutes our participation in the triumphant suffering of the Lamb.

This conception of participation in the character of God's struggle with a rebellious world, which early Quakerism referred to as "the war of the lamb," has the peculiar disadvantage—or advantage, depending upon one's point of view—of being meaningful only if Christ be he who Christians claim him to be, the Master. Almost every other kind of ethical approach espoused by Christians, pacifist or otherwise, will continue to make sense to the non-Christian as well. Whether Jesus be the Christ or not, whether Jesus Christ be Lord or not, whether this kind of religious language be meaningful or not, most types of ethical approach will keep on functioning just the same. For their true foundation is in some reading of the human situation or some ethical insight which is claimed to be generally accessible to men of good will. The same is not true for this vision of "completing in our bodies that which was lacking in the suffering of Christ." If Jesus Christ was not who historic Christianity confesses he was, the revelation in man of the character of God himself, then this one argument for pacifism collapses.

Accepting Powerlessness

We thus do not adequately understand what the church was praising in the work of Christ, and what Paul was asking his readers to be guided by, if we think of the cross as a peculiarly efficacious technique (probably effective only in certain circumstances) for getting one's way. The key to the ultimate relevance and to the triumph of the good is not any calculation at all, paradoxical or otherwise, of efficacy, but rather simple obedience. Obedience means not keeping verbally enshrined rules but reflecting the character of the love of God. The cross is not a recipe for resurrection. Suffering is not a tool to make people come around, nor a good in itself. But the kind of faithfulness that is willing to accept evident defeat rather than complicity with evil is, by virtue of its conformity with what happens to God when he works among men, aligned with the ultimate triumph of the Lamb.

This vision of ultimate good being determined by faithfulness and not by results is the point where we modern men get off. We confuse the kind of "triumph of the good," whose sole guarantee is the resurrection and the promise of the eternal glory of the Lamb, with an immediately accessible triumph which can be manipulated, just past the next social action campaign, by getting hold of society as a whole at the top. What in the Middle Ages was done by Roman Christianity or Islam is now being attempted by Marxism and by democratic nationalism. In spite of all the difference in language, and in the detailed vision of just what a good society would look like (and as a matter of fact even the visions are not that different), the real uniqueness of each of these positions is only that it identifies differently the particular moral elite which it holds to be worthy of guiding its society from the top. We may well prefer a democratically controlled oligarchy to some other kind. We may well have a choice between Marxist and Islamic and other statements of the vision of the good society. But what modern man finds himself practically incapable of challenging is that the social problem can be solved by determining which aristocrats are morally justified, by virtue of their better ideology, to use the power of society from the top so as to lead all men in their direction.

Once a desirable course of history has been labeled, once we know what the right cause is, then it is further assumed that we should be willing to sacrifice for it; sacrifice not only our own values but also those of the neighbor and especially the enemy. In other words, the achievement of the good cause, the implementation in history of the changes we have determined to be desirable, creates a new autonomous ethical value, "relevance," itself a good in the name of which evil may be done.

In the past, Christians and especially pacifists have debated the theoretical issue of whether evil may be done for the sake of good. But really the deeper question is the axiom that underlies the question, namely that it is a high good to make history move in the right direction. For only if that assumption is made does the further "opportunistic" justification of evil follow.

If what we have said about the honor due the Lamb makes any sense, then what is usually called "Christian pacifism" is most adequately understood not on the level of means alone, as if the pacifist were making the claim that he can achieve what war promises to achieve, but do it just as well or even better without violence. This is one kind of pacifism, which in some contexts may be clearly able to prove its point, but not necessarily always. That Christian pacifism which has a theological basis in the character of God and the work of Jesus Christ is one in which the calculating link between our obedience and ultimate efficacy has been broken, since the triumph of God comes through resurrection and not through effective sovereignty or assured survival.

This clarification, however, places before us a new question, one that would not have to be looked at if we were content to consider pacifism simply as rejection of violent means. Does it make sense to ask the public authorities in civil society to enforce standards of fraternity and equity which Christians can seek after in the church on the basis of the free assent of those who claim to be committed to Christian obedience? Does it make sense, first of all as an expression of moral consistency, since any appeal to public enforcement involves a clear calculation of efficacy and use of pressure toward that end? Does it make sense, secondly, in the sense of radical appropriateness? Assuming that we have some factual and perhaps prophetic insight into the nature of the abuses under which our society suffers and some vision of possible solutions, is it more appropriate to appeal, in order that these solutions might have some chance of being accepted and implemented, to the convincing power of truth? Or may we honestly and more fervently appeal to lesser motives, to public opinion, resentment, isolationism, fear of the bomb, or to the unrealistic hope that the enemy may be a good guy after all?

What does it mean to raise this question? Does it mean that pessimism about the appropriateness or the possibility of a Christian witness to the social order should lead us to return to the self-centeredness and lack of social concern that have characterized so many churches so much of the time? I suggest that it would rather lead us to see judgment beginning at the house of God. We should then recognize that the distortions and the misunderstandings of truth and goodness which lead to war, have their origins within the Christian camp. The roots of the crusading mentality are not "secular" in the modern sense, nor are they rooted in the mores of pagan religions. They constitute a deformation of biblical faith. Because the church bears this responsibility for having contributed to the mentality in which men make war, the polemic of a valid Christian pacifist witness must be theological and first of all be directed to the church.

Even if the roots of this witness against the crusade and in favor of the cross were not characteristically christological as I have been claiming, this would still be the context to which we should first speak. Whatever help we may receive from a growing modern understanding of social techniques, what really needs to be debated is a Christian view of the nature of man and the direction of history. The audience to whom it needs to be directed is the circle of those who have affirmed knowledge of and commitment to an overarching divine purposefulness active in history.

Perhaps Christians in our age are being made ready for a new awareness of the continuing relevance of the message of the Apocalypse. There is a widespread recognition that Western society is moving toward the collapse of the mentality that has been identified with Christendom. Christians must recognize that they are a minority not only on the globe but also at home in the midst of the followers of non-Christian and post-Christian faiths. Perhaps this will prepare us to see how inappropriate and preposterous was the prevailing assumption, from the time of Constantine until yesterday, that the fundamental responsibility of the church for society is to manage it.

And might it be, if we could be freed from the compulsiveness of the vision of ourselves as the guardians of history, that we could receive again the gift of being able to see ourselves as participants in the loving nature of God as revealed in Christ? Perhaps the songs of the earliest church might restore this to us if the apostolic argument cannot. A church once freed from compulsiveness and from the urge to manage the world might then find ways and words to suggest as well to men outside her bounds the invitation to a servant stance in society.

In Sum:

The secularistic and the Marxist criticism of the vision of marching to Zion claims that the promise of pie in the sky bye and bye cuts the nerve of action today. The expectation of "fairer worlds on high" is supposed to detach the present from that which is promised.

This may well have been the case when in recent centuries the beneficiaries of the social system appealed to a future world to encourage their subjects to remain docile. But our interest is not in asking whether the eighteenth-century religion could be the opiate of the people, but rather understanding the function of the apocalyptic vision in the first-century church, whose seers were not on any drug.

In the world view of that time the gap between the present and the promise was not fundamental. What we are now doing is what leads to where we are going. Since the "this-worldly" and the "other-worldly" were not perceived in radical dichotomy, to be "marching through Emmanuel's ground" today is to be on the way to Zion. Terms like "hereafter" are in that kind of context affirmations not negations. They do not say that that to which we look forward is in a radically different kind of world from the world in which we now live, but rather that it lies farther in the same direction in which we are being led. The unforeseeable future is farther along in the same direction as the foreseeable future for which we are responsible.

The modern critic who has no lively sense either of heaven or of Zion begins listening to a hymn like the classic gospel processional "Marching to Zion" under the shadow of the negative assumption that there is no connection between the here and the hereafter. Therefore he must attribute to those who speak of "a world beyond" spiritualizing intentions dominated by the chasm between this world and the other world. This interpretation can go so far (as for instance in Rudolf Bultmann) as to claim that mythical language (i.e. language according to which *here* and *hereafter* are in the same universe) is intentionally used with the purpose of affirming the division between the two; so that if the meaning of the myth is demythologized, what it really wants to affirm is only that religion is not of this world.

But if on the other hand one does not begin by assuming the unbridgeable gap between here and there, then this proclamation of a meaningful future cannot possibly have the sense of turning away from the present. They are statements of the same promising future, throwing light back upon the present imperative, for which precisely recent "secular theology" has been looking.

The future that the seer of Patmos sees ahead is a universe—i.e. a single system—in which God acts and we act, with our respective actions relating to each other. The spiritual and providential laws which we expect to see at work in this system are as solid for the believer as are the laws of dialetical materialism for the Marxist.

The beginning assumption of the irrelevance of apocalyptic, which has so often made it hard to see social meaning in the book of the Apocalypse, even though its entire message has to do with kingdoms and empires, is in its ultimate impact another aspect of the relativizing of present obedience with which we have been debating through the entire book. "Whatever the early Christians meant by a fulfillment of history, it must not have been within history that they thought of it," runs the argument. Yet the closer we look at this "demythologizing" line of thought the clearer it is that the conclusion was dictated by the beginning definitions.

We are left with no choice but to affirm that the General Epistles in which the popular thought pattern of the earliest church has undergone least reflective analysis, and the liturgical elements imbedded in NT writings which testify to the coming age, are restatements in another key of the same kind of attitude toward history that we found first in the more organized writings of the Gospels, and of Paul. A social style characterized by the creation of a new community and the rejection of violence of any kind is the theme of New Testament proclamation from beginning to end, from right to left. The cross of Christ is the model of Christian social efficacy, the power of God for those who believe.

> *Vicit agnus noster, eum sequamur.*
> Our Lamb has conquered; him let us follow.

Index of Proper
Nouns and Concepts

251

Index of Authors

Index of Scripture References